Teaching about Europe

Margaret Shennan

CASSELL

Cassell Educational Limited
Villiers House   387 Park Avenue South
41/47 Strand   New York
London WC2N 5JE   NY 10016–8810
England   USA

First published 1991

British Library Cataloguing in Publication Data
Shennan, Margaret
  Teaching about Europe.
  I. Title
  940.071241
ISBN 0–304–32292–X
    0–304–32288–1 (pbk)

Library of Congress Cataloging-in-Publication Data
Shennan, Margaret
    Teaching about Europe / Margaret Shennan.
      p.   cm.—(Cassell Council of Europe series)
    Includes bibliographical references and index.
    ISBN 0–304–32292–X (hb); ISBN 0–304–32288–1 (pbk.)
      1. Europe—Study and teaching (Secondary) I. Title II. Series.
    D16.2.S47   1991
    940'.071'.2—dc20   91–20967
                                                                      CIP

The views expressed in this book are those of the author and do not necessarily reflect those of
the Council for Cultural Cooperation of the Council of Europe or its Secretariat.

Phototypeset by Fakenham Photosetting Limited, Fakenham, Norfolk
Printed and bound in Great Britain by Dotesios Ltd, Trowbridge, Wiltshire.

TEACHING ABOUT EUROPE

Cassell Council of Europe series
This series is the result of a collaboration between the Council of Europe and Cassell. It comprises books on a wide range of educational material, drawn largely from seminars and research which have been initiated and sponsored by the Council of Europe.

Contents

For Joe

Figures and Tables

Acknowledgements

In writing this book I was greatly assisted by a number of individuals and organizations and to all of these I should like to record my gratitude.

First, I am indebted to the Council of Europe for sponsoring this work and, in particular, to Mr Maitland Stobart, Deputy Director of Education, Culture and Sport, for inviting me to undertake this study and for making available to me all the relevant material published by the Council for Cultural Co-operation and by other European bodies.

Certain organizations provided me with useful printed material and advice, in particular: The Association for Teacher Education in Europe; The Centre for Information and Language Teaching and Research; The Central Bureau for Educational Visits and Exchanges, London; the Europe at School Coordinating Unit, Bonn; The European Association of Teachers; The European Centre of Cultural Classes, St Jean d'Angély; The UK Centre for European Education; Lancaster University Library.

Among those individuals to whom I am also indebted are:

Sir Christopher Audland, who kindly gave me the benefit of his enormous knowledge and insight into post-war Europe, particularly with regard to the roles of the Council of Europe and the European Community;

Professor A. M. Ross, Emeritus Professor of Educational Research and formerly the Director of the School of Education at Lancaster University, for kindly reading the completed manuscript and offering me useful comments on secondary education in the UK;

Dr John Trim, Academic Director of the Cambridge Centre for Languages; Mrs Elspeth Cardy, Head of the Schools Unit, Central Bureau, London; Dr Peter Knight, Lecturer in the Department of Educational Research at Lancaster University; and Dr Chris Hill of the Department of International Relations at the London School of Economics and Political Science, for kindly reading sections of the manuscript and giving me their expert opinion;

Mr J. Frank Fitz-Gibbon, Deputy Head of Ruffwood School, Kirkby,

Liverpool, and a former colleague at St Martin's College, Lancaster, whose conceptual understanding of curricular issues and practical skills in the classroom and lecture room I have long admired. Our discussions on the secondary curriculum and on school management were crucial in the early stages of preparation of the manuscript;

Professor Terence Keefe of the Department of Modern Languages at Lancaster University; Professor John Slater, formerly Senior Inspector for History in Her Majesty's Inspectorate, and more recently the National Coordinator of the UK European Awareness Pilot Project; Dr Ian Bliss of St Martin's College; Mr L. Hardy; and the late Mrs Glenys Checkland, all of whom drew my attention to valuable information relevant to this study;

Mrs Olive Ashworth and Mrs Janina Quinn of Heysham High School, Lancashire, who very kindly shared with me their expertise on the needs of secondary pupils and allowed me to draw on the fruits of their curriculum development work in the area of personal and social education;

Mr Roy Wake, formerly of Her Majesty's Inspectorate, whose stimulating thoughts on 'the concept of Europe' and on its implications for education were conveyed freely and generously to me over a period of fifteen years;

Mr William Pearson, Town Clerk of Lancaster, and his staff; Mrs Jacqueline Hampson and Ms Marie Wood of York; and Mr Howard Dickenson, Director of Development, York, who advised me initially on contacts with local organizations sponsoring ongoing European initiatives in these two cities;

the staff of Lancaster University Library for their many kindnesses;

and finally, my husband, Professor J. H. Shennan, Professor of European History and Pro-Vice Chancellor of Lancaster University, who gave patient counsel and generous support throughout the production of the manuscript, and with whom I share a warm commitment to European culture and a sturdy faith in the unifying concept of Europe.

Margaret Shennan

Foreword

This is a book which has long been awaited. There has been a genuine need for it.

How to introduce a European dimension into the school should not be a matter of controversy. It is of paramount importance that during the different stages of school education pupils should learn about our European context and opportunities as well as about our rich and unique national heritage. The two kinds of study are complementary, not competitive, for Europe as a continent is a unique place of historical diversity. The rest of the world, particularly the United States and the Third World, should not be forgotten, but in looking at these parts of the world also there are European dimensions.

The text of the book covers many aspects of the subject and should stimulate discussion as well as provide information. It is exactly the right kind of book to introduce 1992 in proper perspective.

Asa Briggs, Worcester College, Oxford   14 March 1991

Preface

The European dimension of education is not a new subject, and the Council of Europe and other organizations have worked on it, in one way or another, for some forty years. However, for a long time, it was seen as a simple 'education for reconciliation and better understanding', and it concerned a few idealists and teachers.

Recently, there has been a sea-change, if not a revolution, in thinking about the European dimension of education. It has evolved into a broader and much more dynamic concept which has wide-ranging implications for: the content of the school curriculum; school organization; school-leaving examinations; guidance and counselling; and extra-curricular activities.

The European dimension of education is, of course, not confined to schools, and ambitious initiatives are under way to:

* promote the equivalence of academic diplomas and mobility;
* help university students to spend periods of study in other European countries;
* foster co-operation among European universities and postgraduate institutions;
* set up a European open university based on co-operation among distance teaching universities in European countries;
* pool the results of educational research in Europe.

In other words, the European dimension is becoming an increasingly important factor in educational planning and practice.

The main reasons for this sea-change are the dramatic events in Central and Eastern Europe and the approach of 1993.

The changes in Central and Eastern Europe have spelt the end of the division of our continent after a generation of suspicion, tension and Cold War. As was stressed in the Charter of Paris for a New Europe, which was adopted last November by the Heads of Government of the thirty-four countries of the Conference on Security and Co-operation in Europe, 'ours is a time for fulfilling the hopes and expectations that our peoples have cherished for decades: steadfast commitment to democracy based on human rights and fundamental freedoms; prosperity through economic liberty and social justice; and equal security for all countries.'

The countries in Central and Eastern Europe need assistance in their constitutional, legislative, administrative and educational reforms, and they are very interested in the Council of Europe's know-how and experience in their transition to pluralist democracy. As this book goes to press, the Council of Europe has become the widest intergovernmental and interparliamentary forum in Europe, and twenty-nine states – including Czechoslovakia, Hungary, Yugoslavia, Poland and the Soviet Union – take part in our programmes on education, culture, sport and youth.

Nineteen ninety-three is, of course, an important, even a magic date, because it is compelling Europeans and their governments to reflect on the future of their continent, even when their country is not a member of the European Communities. This can be seen from the current negotiations between the European Free Trade Association and the European Communities to establish a European Economic Area covering the eighteen member countries of the two organizations. On the other hand, 1993 is not an isolated event – a date plucked out of the sky. It is an integral part of the process of European co-operation and integration that has been under way in Western Europe since the late 1940s.

This development of co-operation among governments in Europe has been accompanied by a parallel expansion of co-operation among professional associations and private citizens. For example, there is now an impressive number of European educational associations and networks like the European Association of Teachers, the Association for Teacher Education in Europe, the European Association for Special Education, the European Curriculum Network, the European Association of Secondary Heads, the European Standing Conference of Geography Teachers' Associations, the European Bureau of Adult Education, the European Rectors' Conference, the European Parents' Association and the Organising Bureau of European School Students' Unions.

The political importance of the European dimension is demonstrated by the fact that the Council of Europe's Standing Conference of the European Ministers of Education chose it as the main theme for its session in October 1991 in Vienna. The theme was chosen in order for Ministers to review the consequences, for the education of all young people, of the momentous changes under way in Europe, and to indicate what should be the balance between national and European priorities in education.

At grassroots level, there has been a radical change of scale in the interest shown in the European dimension of education by teachers and other educators all over Europe. There has been a veritable explosion in the number of international, national and local conferences and workshops on the subject of the European dimension, and the Council of Europe and the other European organizations are flooded with requests from teachers who are looking for basic information, teaching resources, training and partners.

Margaret Shennan's book is one of the Council of Europe's responses to these requests. Our organization has always recognized the vital role of education in bringing the peoples of our continent closer together and creating a sense of 'being at home in Europe'. Margaret Shennan analyses the Council of Europe's extensive work on history, geography and modern languages, as well as on such areas of multidisciplinary study as human rights education, intercultural education and media education. She also reviews the knowledge, attitudes and skills that young Europeans will need for life in an interdependent world characterized by diversity and constant and rapid change. The Council of Europe is very grateful to Margaret Shennan for undertaking this immense task.

Over the next three years, the Council of Europe will carry out an ambitious new project on the European dimension of secondary education. Its aim is to provide policy-makers and educators with practical advice and examples of good practice.

As the European dimension of education is a dynamic, evolving concept, it is difficult to encapsulate it in one tidy little definition. This task is further complicated by the fact that the term covers three distinct notions: education in Europe; education about Europe; and education for Europe. The Council of Europe argues that the term 'Europe' should extend to the whole of the continent and that it is in no way synonymous with the membership of any single European organization.

The European dimension does not involve the introduction of a new subject into the school curriculum. In teaching about Europe, we are, of course, not starting from scratch. Europe is already present in such subjects as history, geography, civics, economics, modern languages, literature, music, the visual arts and environmental education. On the other hand, teaching about Europe often lacks coherence because of insufficient cross-referencing or co-ordination among subjects.

Furthermore, the European dimension does not imply the uniformity of education systems from North Cape to Cyprus or Malta, from Reykjavik to Berlin to Vladivostok. There must be respect both for diversity and for local, regional and national specificities.

Programmes to promote the European dimension must not, in turn, promote Eurocentric or selfish attitudes, and the Council of Europe recommends that educational systems should encourage all young Europeans to see themselves 'not only as citizens of their own region and countries' but also as 'citizens of Europe and of the wider world'.

Extra-curricular activities can reinforce, in a significant way, formal teaching about other countries and cultures, and teachers and pupils in Europe are seeking opportunities for direct contacts with their contemporaries in other countries through correspondence by letter, audio-cassette or video. The new communications technologies are now being used to extend the traditional range of school correspondence and exchanges and to open windows on the world with the help of electronic mail, teleconferencing and satellite relays.

Schools can also encourage their pupils to take part in other extra-curricular activities with an international dimension, such as the annual European Schools' Day Competition, which is a joint activity of the Council of Europe, the European Communities and the European Cultural Foundation. About 600,000 pupils from nineteen countries take part in the competition every year.

In other words, curriculum planners and teachers interested in the European dimension should think in terms of an extended curriculum, which makes full use of extra-curricular activities, draws on the rich resources that exist in the local and wider community and takes account of the exciting possibilities offered by the mass media.

As Margaret Shennan shows, the opportunities and challenges facing European educators are considerable, and they will make heavy demands on their vision and commitment. However, as President Havel said in his speech to the Council of Europe's Parliamentary Assembly, 'we must not be afraid of dreaming the seemingly impossible if we want the seemingly impossible to become a reality. Without dreaming of a better Europe, we shall never build a better Europe.'

Maitland Stobart
Deputy Director of Education, Culture and Sport
Council of Europe

Note. Although the phrase 'the European Communities' is correct legal usage, the author has generally followed the accepted practice of referring to 'the European Community' in the singular form.

The Europe of the Twenty-Four

The Council of Europe, with a membership of twenty-four European parliamentary democracies, is the largest of the European political institutions. It represents a total population of some 425 million citizens across the breadth and depth of Europe – from Iceland to Turkey, from Portugal to Norway.

Founded in 1949, the Council of Europe was the first European political organization set up after the Second World War. It stemmed from an idea expressed by Winston Churchill in 1943 that, in addition to the proposed United Nations, regional councils would be required to deal with the problems facing the world after the war. The idea took root and was developed by the leading political figures of the post-war period.

On 5 May 1949 the Statute of the Council of Europe was signed by the ten founding states: Belgium, France, Denmark, Ireland, Italy, Luxembourg, the Netherlands, Norway, Sweden, the United Kingdom. It was unanimously agreed that, to symbolize post-war reconciliation, the headquarters of the organization should be in the French frontier city of Strasbourg, the capital of Alsace.

The aims of the Council are:

- to work for greater European unity;
- to uphold the principles of parliamentary democracy and human rights; and
- to improve living conditions and promote human values.

It also seeks to develop the common features shared by all the peoples of Europe: the 'European dimension' to their lives. Thus although the Council's work is largely carried out through intergovernmental co-operation, the interests of the individual remain its prime concern.

The Council of Europe's Statute declares that each member state must recognize the principle of the rule of law and guarantee its citizens the enjoyment of human rights and fundamental freedoms. Any European state that accepts these democratic principles can apply to become a member. Since 1949 the membership has grown from ten to twenty-four countries, with the accession of Austria, Cyprus, Finland, Germany, Greece, Hungary, Iceland, Liechtenstein, Malta, Portugal, San Marino, Spain, Switzerland and Turkey.

The Council of Europe works in close co-operation with other international organizations such as the United Nations, the European Community and the Organisation for Economic Co-operation and Development. However, the organization's particular role in international co-operation results from three characteristics which distinguish it from these:

- in *structure*, the Council is more than just a purely intergovernmental body: in addition to a Committee of Ministers it has an Assembly composed of members of national parliaments and it involves local authorities and non-governmental organizations in its deliberations;
- in *scope*, the Council covers practically all aspects of European affairs, with the exception of defence;
- in *membership*, the Council includes all the European Community states, a number of 'neutral' and 'non-aligned' countries and other European democracies who share its ideals. It also opens many of its activities to non-member states, thus extending co-operation beyond the 'twenty-four'.★

It is this combination of wide membership, general competence and a flexible structure that give the Council of Europe its unique character. Indeed, as a regional organization it has served as a model for other regional groups of countries in Africa, Asia and Latin America.

★Twenty-nine states take part in the Council's work on education and culture – the twenty-four plus Czechoslovakia, the Holy See, Yugoslavia, Poland and the Soviet Union.

PART 1

A FRAMEWORK FOR EUROPE IN THE SECONDARY SCHOOL

CHAPTER 1

Change: The Context for the 1990s

During his celebrated visit to West Germany in June 1963, President John F. Kennedy addressed the citizens of Frankfurt. 'Change', he said, 'is the law of life. And those who look only to the past or the present are certain to miss the future.' At a time of instability, these words touched the sensibilities of Europe's young generation, but the armed equilibrium centring on Europe was to last another quarter of a century before the Soviet president, Mikhail Gorbachev, echoed the words of his US predecessor. Inheriting a state whose claim to superpower status rested substantially on its military might, President Gorbachev asserted that only if a country understands its past and present can it map its future. Despite their disparate perspectives, both men perceived change to be the great contemporary challenge of the twentieth century. Certainly, the revolutions of 1989 prove how swiftly events can overtake intransigent elder statesmen who fail to appreciate the progress made in electronic communications or the volatility of human kind in the passage of time.

The presidential pronouncements have a message for everyone concerned with education. Since the broad aim of education is to provide a preparation for life, the learning process ought rationally to include the study of what President Kennedy called 'the law of life' in its natural framework of the past, present and future. To neglect any of these contexts, or to concentrate excessively on one at the expense of the others, is to see life with warped vision. For example, to reject all that the past can tell us is to go through life without sight and memory, and to understand the evidence of change, of cause and consequence, and the impact and fluctuating tempo of change – processes to which we apply words like evolution, revolution, transformation, decline, revival, innovation – is to gain significant insight into the human condition. Conversely, those who bury themselves in the past are unlikely to fulfil their potential; and those who are ill-informed about the contemporary world will also struggle to cope with the future. Indeed, some experts argue that, with the technology available in our information society, the study of the present and the future could figure more prominently in the curriculum, without falling into the trap of technological determinism.

To illustrate these points we only need to ponder the last eighty years. Change, spectacular and seemingly irreversible, has been the hallmark of the twentieth century. Traditional empires have been eclipsed; ancient, once invincible dynasties, the Manchu Ch'ing of China and in Europe the Romanovs and the Habsburgs, eliminated in one momentous decade from 1911. Then a generation later the grand finale of western imperialism was played to the discordant accompaniment of the Second World War. During the post-war era, the British, French, Dutch, Belgians and Portuguese surrendered their colonial territories in India, Africa and the Far East, conceding independence voluntarily or in the face of determined nationalist revolt, before handing over their global roles to the USA and the USSR. Now, after forty years of policing the world, the two superpowers have been forced to balance the political gains with the economic cost. A new alignment may be perceived: the USA drawn by economic reality into an uneasy partnership with Japan and the rising states of the Pacific Rim, while Russia returns by force of circumstance to its 'common European home'.

Meanwhile, in the course of this century boundaries, cities, nationalities, peoples and total environments have been shifted, obliterated or bulldozed for reasons of state. Subsequently, some have been forgotten, others reformed or rebuilt, as and when political circumstance allowed. New ideologies have produced new nations. New power relationships have emerged, both on an international plane and affecting ethnic and class structures. From outer space new visions of the universe have been transmitted to human kind, demonstrating the triumphs of modern scientific and technological progress. And if the history of the century thus far has been shaped by revolutionary change, the events of 1989–90 suggest that we can confidently expect the final decade to maintain that momentum.

POLITICAL CHANGE IN EUROPE

In the unfolding drama of the modern world, the transformation of Europe has once again taken centre stage. After 1914, change was synonymous with decline for most European states. The questions were why, and how deep-rooted was Europe's loss of power and prestige. A generation later the Second World War left Europe materially and spiritually impoverished, and in the post-war period the political balance came to rest, not on a renewed system of nation-states, but on two armed camps and a partitioned Germany. 'Europe' had no discrete identity in 1945: such was the price of peace. Although recovery proceeded in the 1950s and 1960s, Europe was divided by an Iron Curtain: on one side a Soviet-dominated Communist bloc and on the other an arc of Western nations hostile to Communism, broadly committed to democratic values and bound to defend them, if necessary, with US nuclear assistance. Faced in the 1970s with a landmass divided by two ideologies, the Czech exile,

Milan Kundera, wrote that 'The idea of Europe is dying. It is the end of Europe.' If the Helsinki Conference of 1975 on security and co-operation marked the first stage in an uncertain process of détente, as late as 1989 the possibility of a single European order seemed to many people no more than a mischievous illusion.

However, during the 1980s a sea-change was at work. The dramatic metamorphosis within the Soviet Union, associated with the rise to power of Mikhail Gorbachev and the revolutionary upsurge in Central and Eastern Europe, together with the impressive growth of the European Community in Western Europe, have profoundly altered both global strategy and Europe's self-image. Whatever the ultimate outcome of the president's reforming policies and the upheavals triggered by them, the permafrost of the Cold War has thawed, whilst at a more simplistic level the events of the late 1980s added two new words to the vocabulary of the average European-in-the-street, *glasnost* and *perestroika*. 1989 was the year in which the unthinkable happened, not once but repeatedly, when the West watched incredulously as people power clutched at the chinks in Communism's state armour and (with the exception of China) successfully tore it down. In the aftermath, the bipolar structure of Europe was demolished and the way prepared for different models of Europe in the 1990s. Ethnic groups may reassert themselves in atavistic solidarity and from this may come new nations or states. A united Germany has already arrived faster and more dramatically than even close observers had predicted. Alternatively, a single European entity, a broad union of states and peoples may emerge, linked by cultural roots and integrated through multiform mechanisms. The idea of a community in Europe will then take on a new meaning.

The idea of political renewal through unity was mooted in the 1940s at a time when rehabilitation and security were still the main priorities. Speaking in Zürich in 1946, Winston Churchill gave his remedy for Europe's post-war ills. 'It is to re-create the European Family . . . and provide it with a structure under which it can dwell in peace, in safety and in freedom. We must build a kind of United States of Europe.' In broad terms there was much sympathy among the political leaders of the West for a form of union. Men like Jean Monnet, Robert Schuman, Paul-Henri Spaak, Alcide de Gaspari and Konrad Adenauer belonged to the first generation of committed pro-Europeans (just as Jacques Delors, François Mitterrand and Helmut Kohl belong to the second), believing that European federation was essential to guarantee civilized existence in the advanced industrial world.

However, opinions at large varied on the matter of unity. To the people of Central and Eastern Europe, unity perforce came exclusively from allegiance to the Soviet Union and to Communist ideology. In the West many Europeans were too war-weary in the 1940s to contemplate radical change. Others were sceptical of any form of European union. Yet the idea of European unity is centuries old. It was expounded by Renaissance humanists, conscious of the decline of Roman Christendom as a unifying force and wary of the potential power of secular states to wage wars or enforce their own peace. In that

)n, the best answer seemed to be some form of confederation. The Grand Design of 1610, attributed to the French king, Henry IV, was one such solution. In the next hundred years other utopian schemes were aired. The Moravian educational reformer, Comenius, wrote a *Brief Proposal* suggesting that the young should learn about the common culture of Europe. He shared a belief in universal peaceful co-existence with the English Quakers William Penn and John Bellers. The Abbé de Saint-Pierre, a courtier and diplomat in the service of Louis XIV, promoted the idea of the 'European Republic'. His *Project for Everlasting Peace* (1713) affirmed the sentiments of Bellers' *Reasons for an European State* (1710). Indeed, the eighteenth century, the Age of Enlightenment, produced the most sophisticated appeals to international law and order, and ideas for the rational resolution of problems and the brotherhood of man. After 1800 lone Romantic voices continued to speak out for co-operation, but the reality was more discouraging. Metternich's Concert of Europe proved to be a club of self-seeking superpowers, and the ideal of European unity was largely submerged for a hundred years, while strident nationalism became the order of the day.

The climax of European xenophobia occurred in the two world wars. But the last forty years have seen remarkable progress towards permanent international co-operation within Europe. The first landmark came in 1949 with the establishment of the Council of Europe. The original signatories – Belgium, Denmark, France, Ireland, Italy, Luxembourg, the Netherlands, Norway, Sweden and the United Kingdom – pledged their determination not only to work for greater European unity but also to defend the principles of parliamentary democracy and human rights, and to develop the 'European dimension' which was the heritage of Europe's citizens. In a spirit of reconciliation, Strasbourg, the capital of Alsace, was chosen as the site for the permanent headquarters of the main organs of the Council of Europe, the Parliamentary Assembly and the Committee of Ministers representing the governments of member states, served by an international secretariat. By 1990, the membership of the Council of Europe had risen to twenty-four states, representing over 400 million European citizens. However, the statistics will soon have to be revised. The Council has already built up a network of political, legal and cultural contacts with Central and Eastern Europe, involving its educational and cultural offshoot, the Council for Cultural Co-operation (CDCC). Poland, Yugoslavia and the USSR have guest status in the Assembly, and Czechoslovakia, Bulgaria and Romania have applied. It is reasonable to assume that in due course these countries will be admitted to full member status.

Many of the Council of Europe's achievements will emerge in the course of this study. One of the most significant is the European Convention of Human Rights, drawn up in 1950 to safeguard the basic rights and freedoms of citizens against the power of the state. On the other hand, matters of defence, the issue on which fledgling organizations such as the European Defence Community and the European Political Community were to founder in 1954, were excluded. However, from slow beginnings the pace of change towards

European integration accelerated in the 1950s, helped by the separation of the defence issue from that of economic integration. If the creation of the Council of Europe was a major advance, the signing of the Treaty of Paris in 1951 and of the two Treaties of Rome in 1957 was to prove even more far-reaching. 'The greatest voluntary and organized transformation in the history of Europe' was the verdict of the Belgian Foreign Minister, Paul-Henri Spaak. Since the setting up of the European Economic Community on 1 January 1958 its membership has doubled, and it is set to increase further in the years ahead as and when other European countries apply for membership.

Monnet and Spaak were perhaps the two most impressive of the founding fathers of European unity: both had a wider vision than most statesmen of their generation. But the concept of unity has always been open to conflicting interpretation and defenders of national autonomy or regional diversity are still highly vocal. It has sometimes proved difficult (though not impossible) to reconcile entrenched national interests, notably on issues such as sovereignty, inflation and the environment, with collective European problems like the modernization of agriculture or the definition of basic social rights. And yet the system is such that once Community decisions are taken, they are likely to endure. So the EC has been, paradoxically, both a dynamic and a conservative force in European politics. The Single European Act of 1986 extended the Treaty system of qualified majority voting: much more important, it became the catalyst which led member states to treat such voting as normal and routine. Thus, the Community has confronted the issue of sovereignty head-on, preparing the way for the establishment of a fully integrated market by 1992, which, in the words of Jacques Delors (the President of the Commission) will 'act as a motive force for European union'. The setting up of an exchange rate mechanism (ERM) is the first stage in this process but the completed European monetary system (EMS) would require the establishment of a single currency and a European central bank.

If, in the fullness of time, federal union on a European scale is achieved, the Helsinki Conference of 1975 will be seen as a preliminary step, for it was the Helsinki Final Act that first set out agreements on security and disarmament. However, the dramatic events of 1989 will also be seen as a necessary precursor to unity. Viewed from the standpoint of the 1990s, certain political trends in Eastern Europe are clear. First, change was already stirring in the USSR by the mid-1980s, due to the Soviet Union's crushing military burdens and its mounting economic crisis. The pre-condition of economic renewal was political reform. The moral authority of the Communist party, first dented by Khrushchev's attack on Stalin at the Twentieth Party Congress, had degenerated by the seventieth anniversary of the Bolshevik Revolution. The elections of March/May 1989 for the Congress of People's Deputies, publicized in the full glare of Western television, underlined policy changes signalled earlier by the freeing of political prisoners, the withdrawal of Soviet forces from Afghanistan and Mongolia, and the accommodation of Soviet negotiators at Vienna on the issue of international arms reduction. Despite daunting economic and political difficulties and entrenched Stalinist structures, what President Gorbachev undertook in 1989–90 was a new Russian Revolution. In political terms it seemed he was attempting a controlled reorganization of the federal structure of the USSR, the substitution of traditional authoritarianism by the rule of law and some form of parliamentary democracy.

However, the rejection of the doctrines of Stalin and Brezhnev could not be contained within the frontiers of the USSR. During 1989 the spirit of *glasnost* spilled over the whole of Eastern Europe. One by one, from Kadar to Ceausescu, the old guard were toppled and old heroes (such as the late Imre Nagy, the resilient Alexander Dubcek, and Lech Walesa with the other leaders of Solidarity) were rehabilitated or acclaimed. Hungary and Poland led the way in the bewildering task of dismantling Communist state machines and establishing democratic procedures in their stead. Their example was impatiently taken up by the citizens of the DDR, Bulgaria, Czechoslovakia and Romania in a sequence of government debacles and mass demonstrations throughout the autumn of 1989, which were a remarkable exposition of the domino theory. The status quo of forty years crumbled within a few months. Political systems which appeared firmly in place at the start of 1989 were suddenly defunct; attitudes and practices tolerated for forty years were jettisoned and consigned to history. Lack of political experience on the part of untried leaders could still expose the fragility of the new regimes but the peoples of Central and Eastern Europe have made clear their preference for democracy as they face the 1990s.

Furthermore, the centrifugal forces unleashed in 1989 have rebounded on the USSR. As the Soviet Union's external empire subsided under the pressure for independence, so its internal empire has been cracking under calls for autonomy. The 'nationalities' issue' is a historic problem for this giant multinational state. But since the resurgence of nationalism in the spring of 1989 – first in the Baltic republics of Latvia, Estonia and Lithuania, then in Transcaucasia and Central Asia (where ethnic divisions are so bitter that civil war has erupted) and less stridently in Georgia, Moldavia and the Ukraine – the long-term future of the present structure of the USSR must be open to question. 'The end of Empire is a fact', a Soviet spokesman, Sergei Plekhanov, admitted in January 1990 when the subject of secession was raised. What remains unclear is whether the Union will be transformed by force or through orderly reform under *perestroika* by a new generation of leaders such as Boris Yeltsin.

Finally, looking outside the USSR, the ending of the Cold War equilibrium has – ironically – pitched European relations into a volatile state. Nothing illustrates this better than the issue of German re-unification. Initially many Western observers contemplated the undercurrents of *glasnost* and *perestroika* with detachment, confident that they would have no direct bearing on the West's progress towards unity and integration. In the second half of 1989, however, the implications became steadily clearer. A new vision of Europe is required for the 1990s, implying interdependence rather than rivalry. President Gorbachev drew attention to this priority when he addressed the Parliamentary Assembly of the Council of Europe in July 1989:

The idea of European unification should be collectively thought over once again in the process of the co-creation of all nations – large, medium and small ... In today's interdependent world the geopolitical notions brought forth by a different epoch turn out to be just as helpless in real politics as the laws of classical mechanics in the quantum theory ... It is time for the present generation of the leaders of the European countries, USA and Canada, to discuss ... how they contemplate future stages of progress toward a European community of the 21st century.

Subsequently, the representatives of the participating states at the 1990 Conference on Security and Co-operation in Europe (CSCE) proclaimed that 'the era of confrontation and division of Europe has ended'. The Charter of Paris for a New Europe (1990) confirmed Europe's threefold commitment to democracy based on human rights and freedom, to prosperity through economic liberty and social justice, and to equal security for all states. Guidelines for the future implementation of CSCE principles were also agreed.

Clearly Western leaders had to react positively to the new political situation with offers of assistance to the nascent democracies. While the British Foreign Secretary called for 'an imaginative response to the extraordinary effort being made by the peoples of Eastern Europe', Chancellor Kohl moved towards German monetary union as a prelude to a unified Germany, all the more assured in view of Soviet acquiescence. Invitations to the Central and East European states to join the Council of Europe added another dimension to European co-operation in view of the Council's proven contribution to the promotion of democracy, human rights and the rule of law. Meanwhile, a timetable is being drawn up for political unity alongside the economic integration of the European Community by 1993, and it takes little imagination to anticipate further developments. The Council of Europe and the Community of the Twelve face an unequalled opportunity: to bring about the ultimate integration of Europe through the creation of an all-European Community before the year 2000, a plan that would go further than the 'lofty dreams' which (as Gorbachev reminded his Strasbourg audience) are part of the European experience.

ECONOMIC CHANGE IN EUROPE

Economic forces mirrored political change in Europe after 1945. It is difficult for the young today to comprehend the extent to which Europe was devastated by a world war which left some 40 million of its citizens dead; or to appreciate the magnitude of the tasks facing politicians and international organizations in 1945. The stark contrast between the underdeveloped area Paul-Henri Spaak observed in 1947 and the affluent society of the 1980s is a measure of Europe's economic recovery.

That process began in 1947–8 with the setting up of the Organisation for

European Economic Co-operation (OEEC) to implement the massive American aid programme for Europe known as the Marshall Plan. In the event, this remarkable injection of material aid, which by 1952 had totalled over 13 billion dollars, was poured into the countries of Western Europe because in 1947 the USSR, claiming to speak for its East European satellites as well as itself, rejected the Marshall Plan for fear of inviting US political and economic interference inside the Soviet Eastern bloc. Consequently, from that time economic policies ran parallel with political developments. The Cold War hardened the lines of demarcation between East and West and the Cominform was set up by the Soviet Union in 1947 to co-ordinate the actions of the East European Communist parties. The next year the Council for Mutual Economic Aid (COMECON) was established to ensure economic co-operation, and in 1955 the signing of the Warsaw Pact guaranteed collaboration between the Communist states on issues of defence and security.

Meanwhile, after 1949 the North Atlantic Treaty Organization (NATO) provided a corresponding defensive system for the Western powers. As for economic policy, in the light of hindsight there is a logical progression to the changes which culminated in the formation of the European Economic Community in 1957. The starting point was the creation of the Benelux Customs Union between Belgium, the Netherlands and Luxembourg in 1947, followed in 1948 by the setting up of the OEEC with responsibility for trade and investment, and one month later by the recommendation of Western ministers meeting at The Hague that there should be both political and economic union in Europe.

The division of attitudes over economic union demonstrates the element of paradox which seems a permanent feature of Europe. Jean Monnet's proposal to merge the economies of the two former wartime allies, France and Great Britain, was rejected by the British Labour government in 1949, just as Britain's entry into the Common Market was twice vetoed by France. Yet Robert Schuman's bold plan to unite the heavy industries of two former enemies, France and West Germany, in the European Coal and Steel Community (ECSC) transformed the prospects for economic co-operation, especially after Belgium, Italy, the Netherlands and Luxembourg agreed to join with them as founder members in 1951. But again, paradoxically, the economic boom which followed in the 1950s led to the formation of two rival economic groups, not one. The first, in 1958, was the European Economic Community – the EEC – linking the six ECSC countries: they simultaneously constituted the European Atomic Energy Community (EURATOM). The second, a year later, was EFTA, the European Free Trade Association, smaller in terms of population and trade volume but a coalition of Europe's 'outer seven states', Austria, Denmark, Great Britain, Norway, Portugal, Sweden and Switzerland. Subsequently some partners changed places. Between 1973 and 1986 the European Community (EC) expanded from the Six to the Twelve (with Denmark, Ireland, Great Britain, Spain, Portugal and Greece) to include some 340 million consumers. However, economic co-operation between

EFTA and the EC has steadily developed, notably since the 1984 Luxembourg Declaration expounded a new concept of the European Economic Space (EES).

Until the mid-1970s the mood of Western Europe was optimistic and expansionist, buoyed by growing material prosperity. A change came about when world-wide inflation and recession followed in the wake of the dramatic rise in oil prices after 1973. The worst affected areas were those regions with traditional heavy industries, where restructuring in the face of technological progress was already under way. In 1988 there were still 21 million unemployed people in the Council of Europe's member states, 16 million of them within the European Community. In response, governments became more pragmatic in their economic solutions, emphasizing individual responsibility and initiative: in short, forcing people to come to terms with the enterprise culture. The grassroots response, a proliferation of new small businesses, liberated some of Europe's potential for economic growth. There were, however, certain side-effects. In the restructuring of Europe's industrial base, labour has been transferred to the tertiary or service sector on a large scale. And a further significant tendency has been the increasing level of interdependence between countries and a new international division of labour introduced by managers of multinational corporations. The policy of industrial decentralization, which they have implemented on a large scale, shows how these multinational companies are now among the principal vehicles of fundamental world-wide change.

By 1992 the European Community's 'frontier-free Europe' will be complete. Integration will involve a considerable range of economic activities, striking a balance between entrepreneurial freedom and international control. It is the apparent success of the West's free-market economics which has won the envy and admiration of many people in Central and Eastern Europe in the last decade. In those areas disillusionment over the centralized directives of the trade organization COMECON (now effectively moribund) and the failure of state-controlled systems to raise living standards and satisfy demand have fuelled political disenchantment. It should not be forgotten that it was the economic crisis that produced the policy of *perestroika* in the USSR, a crisis that has shown little sign of diminishing despite the new economic mechanism established by the 1987 law on state enterprises and the 1988 law on co-operatives, which permits private enterprise. The costly nuclear disaster at Chernobyl and the earthquake in Armenia were widely publicized but the massive pollution problems of the Soviet Union and its neighbours are only now being assessed; and the absence of an entrepreneurial, capitalist tradition in the USSR exacerbates Gorbachev's task of creating a more market-oriented economy.

What reasonable expectations – in economic terms – can Europe have in the foreseeable future, assuming that there is no dramatic political reversal? In the West there are many precedents for scientific and industrial collaboration; joint research and development schemes produced Concorde, the Airbus and projects such as EUREKA and ESPRIT. The European Organization for Nuclear Research (CERN) and the European Space Agency spearheaded scientific and technological co-operation. The ongoing co-operation between EFTA and the EC is likely to produce the more structured partnership proposed in 1989 by Jacques Delors, the President of the EC Commission. In a symbolic joint declaration of June 1988, the European Community and the Council for Mutual Economic Assistance (CMEA) formerly recognized each other, thereby paving the way for substantive trade and economic co-operation between the Soviet Union, Central and Eastern Europe and the European Community. In his speech to the Parliamentary Assembly of the Council of Europe in July 1989, President Gorbachev pointed to the 'intensive inter-state dialogue, both bilateral and multi-lateral . . . For the first time contacts have been established between NATO and WTO [the Warsaw Treaty Organization], between EC and CMEA.' Since then the free movement of people and services has become a reality. President Mitterrand's proposal for a development bank was approved by Community leaders at the end of 1989, and the European Bank of Reconstruction and Development (EBRD) began work in the spring of 1991. Emergency relief for Romania, Bulgaria and Czechoslovakia and an extensive aid programme for Poland and Hungary, already in hand, will be followed by co-operation agreements, offering easier access to the EC market for East European goods, and joint ventures such as the giant Fiat project to boost car production in the USSR. In the longer term, if we accept the opinion of the futurologists, East Germany and the Danube Basin (taking in Austria, Galicia, Hungary, Slovakia and Slovenia) is the area with the greatest growth potential, which could overtake the current megalopolis stretching from the Midlands of England to Milan and the Po valley. However, membership of the European Community is certainly likely to expand and draw in new members from among the neutral and non-EC democracies of EFTA and Central Europe; a new status of associate membership may be accorded to other European countries from the Baltic states to Turkey.

Such developments are feasible in the favourable climate of arms detente. The cost of defence may cease to drain the economic resources of individual European countries, since defence systems will depend increasingly on multilateral programmes of space technology. Meanwhile, the Soviet Foreign Minister's visit to NATO headquarters in late 1989, the discussions between Warsaw Pact and NATO commanders in Vienna early in 1990, and the signing of the Treaty of Conventional Armed Forces in Europe by twenty-two participating states (1990) were a prelude to the promise of economic benefits from peaceful co-existence within Europe.

SOCIAL CHANGE IN EUROPE

Changes in society are not easy to encapsulate in a few paragraphs but the view that the European nations are once again at a turning point in their history is frequently expressed. The social stresses and transformations of the late twentieth century are related to economic change. Europe's old industrial and commercial society was a casualty of the world wars. From the 1950s a degree of recovery in Western Europe was assisted by the migration of workers from the Mediterranean seaboard and by immigrants from former overseas colonies. Thus in the last forty years the composition and structure of Europe's population has changed to the point that the total of foreign-born citizens exceeds twenty million. Governments have had to deal with a range of problems arising from a multicultural society. In addition, since 1965 there has been a decline in the fertility rate of Europeans, leading to a fall in the birth rate and coinciding with lengthening life expectancy and an ageing population. This imbalance is expected to continue for the rest of the century, and according to forecasts from the Organisation for Economic Co-operation and Development (OECD), the demographic advantage will then shift southwards from Western Europe to the Mediterranean and Africa, bringing about new migrations and social tensions.

The acceptance of equal rights between the sexes, including women's economic autonomy enshrined in their right to work, has altered the composition of Europe's workforce since the 1970s. For example, the contribution of married women to the increase of the workforce during the years 1975–80 was about 100 per cent in Switzerland, 70 per cent in Denmark and 60 per cent in Norway.

The diminishing stability of the family is another feature of late twentieth-century society. The breakdown of marriages and the disintegration of families, assessed in terms of human and financial cost, are now recognized as a significant burden on modern society. In some urban areas of Europe over 20 per cent of children come from one-parent families.

In the 1980s a new phenomenon was added to the diversity of living standards in the regions and between social groups, the so-called new poverty of the homeless and those driven to the margins of society by drug abuse or AIDS, the disadvantaged who experience the flip-side of Europe's affluent consumer society. To these we might add the hapless victims of industrial pollution. Until the mid-1970s people pinned their faith on the infinite capacity of science and technology to improve their quality of life. Opportunities for mobility and leisure, standards of health and life expectancy were noticeably improved. A steady and sustained growth in the economy, guaranteeing full employment and ever-rising living standards, was considered a reasonable goal by the industrialized nations. Greater pluralism seemed a reasonable price to pay for a successful consumer society.

The shock to that society when economic expansion ground to a halt was profound. Existing problems were exacerbated and the social devastation of mass unemployment took its toll. It was not simply the young who turned their backs on traditional supports – family, church, school, laws – in favour of the cults of hedonism, vandalism and violence. In time came the harsh realization that economic growth was not a perpetual force like gravity; nor could it sustain indefinite social progress. So unemployment dogged the 1980s, and two-fifths of those out of work in the European Community in 1981 were under 25 years of age. Western governments tried to respond to social dysfunction by generating a new kind of dynamism. This entailed tapping diverse sources of wealth, encouraging the tertiary sector and harnessing the language and attitudes of the entrepreneur to all social issues. At the same time people reacted to the social cost of industrialization and materialism. The Green movement to protect the environment caught the imaginations of millions of Europeans, creating a tension between enterprise and responsibility. Undoubtedly a radically different social climate emerged in a number of countries, though it is too early to assess its long-term effects or to say whether it will be sustained throughout the 1990s.

The uncertainty arises from the complicating factor of the information-based economies in the West. During the 1980s Western Europe developed into a post-industrial, information society, a society in which the creation, processing and transmission of information is a central activity. Already the new information and communications technology (NICT), such as television, satellite communications, compact disc technology, interactive videos, telecommuting or artificial intelligence, has profoundly altered our cultural environment. But as the speed of change accelerates and new technology comes forward – as the optical computer takes over from its electronic precursor – the full social effects are difficult to grasp. For example, it is still unclear whether computer illiteracy will cause massive unemployment, personal alienation and gender inequality or whether the revolution in work and leisure patterns will be largely beneficial. All we know is that 'for the first time in the history of society, the economy is based on a key resource which is not only renewable by man at will but capable of generating itself.'[1] Certainly, the social consequences of NICT could prove a daunting challenge to educators, a fear which led the Carnegie Commission on Education to conclude that the greatest priority is 'technology literacy'; in other words, that people should not only understand but should *question* how and when and why their society is being reshaped by new technological hardware.

With the launching of Sputnik in 1957 the USSR not only embarked on the conquest of space but initiated global satellite communication. In Central and Eastern Europe, however, high technology was the preserve of the armed forces and the state machine. For thirty more years there was social stagnation for the mass of the people, except for isolated episodes such as the Hungarian rising of 1956 and the Prague Spring of 1968. In the era of *glasnost* it is clear that the pressures facing Soviet society far exceed tensions in the West. For instance, the standard of living of the Soviet people has been estimated at somewhere between fiftieth and sixtieth in the world; one seventh of the population, that is some 40 million people, live below the poverty line. The Soviet abortion rate is the highest in the world. Infant mortality is double that of the advanced nations, considerably worse in parts of Soviet Central Asia. Alcohol remains a dire social disease; violent crime is booming; for too long, enterprise has been stifled by a bureaucracy 18 million strong. The effects on the average Soviet citizen of a lifetime of economic deprivation, censorship of free expression and a remorseless propaganda machine are incalculable. The arrival of *glasnost* brought matters into the open but could not eradicate social strains, which are currently channelling themselves into explosive forms of nationalism.

Social and economic backwardness also extend to the Soviet Union's neighbours, although in terms of living standards there are distinctions to be made between the mainly peasant population of a country like Romania and the skilled workers of Czechoslovakia. As a capitalist–consumer society is established during the 1990s, the process is likely to develop in Central Europe. However, even in Western Europe social disparities are considerable. It is only through the co-ordinating policies of international organizations like the European Community or the Council of Europe that Europe's disadvantaged can be helped and greater social equality be achieved whilst living standards are simultaneously raised. The EC Commission's proposed Social Charter for the protection of workers' rights is the cornerstone of the Community's programme for social justice. There are, of course, precedents in the Council of Europe's European Social Charter and the European Code of Social Security. The Scandinavian nations, too, have enjoyed more social cohesion since 1952 through the work of the Nordic Council. There have also been singular examples of mutual support between the people of Eastern and Western Europe, such as the campaign known as Operation Romanian Villages, launched by a group of young Belgians in 1989 to stir international outrage against Ceausescu's systematization policy.

In the long run, however, social harmonization and international understanding can only develop through education and a grass-roots willingness to co-operate. Again, there are well-established precedents in European-wide bodies such as the European Trades Union Confederation and the Standing Conference of Local and Regional Authorities of Europe. In the area of education, there are a number of professional bodies and EC programmes such as ERASMUS, providing for exchanges in the university sector; COMETT, an action programme for education and training in technology; YES, which is devoted to assisting youth; EURYDICE, the Community's Education Information Network, the Council of Europe's European Documentation and Information System for Education (EUDISED); and the European Centres, which aim to create a truly European spirit among their members. These ventures and organizations are concrete evidence of existing collaboration. As the Council of Europe has stated, 'Whatever form it takes, European co-operation is part of the daily lives of governments, business people, trade unionists, professional groups and private citizens.' Education, too, is an important element in this trend: indeed, education about Europe and education for life within an interdependent Europe are a major social priority for the 1990s.

EDUCATION: A REFLECTION OF SOCIAL CHANGE

Since 1945, education in the West has been subject to sweeping innovation consonant with social change. It transpires that democracy gave Europe two conflicting legacies: on the one hand the ideal of equality, and on the other the notion of personal rights and liberties. Egalitarianism places high value on universal education as the means of developing all human potential, and after the Second World War attempts were made to extend educational opportunities and heal pre-war social divisions. There was popular support for a range of developments, including pre-school education, the improvement of compulsory basic schooling, the raising of the school-leaving age, the expansion of higher education and training and the general broadening of the curriculum to take account of all pupil abilities. Yet the concepts of personal freedom and choice embodied in democracy present obstacles to a levelling uniformity. In Western Europe, old inequalities and anomalies die hard, while diversity remains in evidence with the dichotomy between secular and religious institutions or between highly centralized and largely decentralized systems.

In Central and Eastern Europe, egalitarianism has operated differently. Sexual discrimination has been less pronounced – much of the hard physical labour undertaken by Western men is regarded as suitable for women there – and the principle of social equality has not prevented the Party elite from enjoying considerable privilege. However, until the revolution of 1989 diversity and change were less in evidence because they implied deviance from orthodoxy and the decisions of central planners. In contrast, education in democratic societies can never be static because people have the right to expect their changing needs to be met by legislators and educators. Indeed, as I have suggested, there is a symbiosis between social change and education. Thus the rise of a mass consumer society coincided with the development of child-centred education and growing demands for parental choice. Concern about sex stereotyping in schools indicates society's increasing insistence on equality of opportunity. The enterprise culture of the 1980s, now applicable in both East and West Europe, requires education both to be cost-effective and to match the requirements of a technological society. As interdependence becomes the watchword of international relations, the role of the school and its teachers has developed into one of partnership with parents and family, the peer group, the community and the media. Currently, the impact of high technology has started to revolutionize education and lifestyles in our information society. Education is already seen as a rolling, lifelong process, in which individuals can expect greater opportunities to develop their potential and adapt to a changing environment, while schools are seen as partners rather than sole agents of education.

In the educational continuum, early childhood and the primary school years are regarded as essential in providing a firm foundation for later learning. At this stage children acquire basic cognitive and social skills, like literacy, numeracy and the ability to communicate. Attitudes are shaped, so caring, tolerant, creative and democratic impulses can be fostered. Last but not least, a framework of knowledge has to be established that will be receptive to development at secondary school and in adulthood. This is the time, for instance, when the basis of foreign language learning can be effortlessly laid and when empathy towards 'the common European home' can take hold of young imaginations.

Several priorities face those in charge of European education in the 1990s. In the first instance, there is a need for imagination and vision in planning and financing dynamic systems of in-service education that will give higher status to the teaching profession and encourage flexibility and innovation on the part of teachers, while involving them in the successful exploitation of the new information technology. And in addition, the decision-makers should remember the adage that education has a dual role: to preserve the good roots of the culture while planting new seeds that have the capacity to bear rich fruit in a rapidly changing society. In the context of Europe in the 1990s this involves cultivating a sense of Europeanness and bringing an explicit European dimension to the whole of education. It also entails providing the young with a range of skills for life and work in European society. However, if Europe is to prosper its peoples must rekindle their intrinsic dynamism, not in an atavistic sense, but by encouraging the next generation to approach the challenges of an interdependent world with global empathy and a commitment to European values.

The process of infusing education with a European dimension is at present the responsibility of national governments. In offering advice, experts in the Council of Europe and the European Community respect the extent of national diversity. Yet while the final onus rests on government ministers advised by their officials, it must be recognized that the success of implementing programmes rests on the commitment and capacities of individual teachers and on the leadership of head teachers. They and they alone face the task of putting Europe into the secondary curriculum.

This study aims to examine the issues involved in that process. In a survey of the whole curriculum, it charts the areas of progress, points to unresolved problems and promising developments, and outlines the challenge facing the educational services of Europe as they prepare for 1993 and beyond.

NOTE

1 Balle, Francis (1991), 'The information society, schools and the media' (Report for the 16th session of the Standing Conference of European Ministers of Education, Istanbul, October 1989), reprinted in Eraut, M. (ed.), *Education and the Information Society*, London: Cassell, p. 88.

CHAPTER 2

Putting Europe into the Curriculum

WHY TEACH ABOUT EUROPE?

For the young in Europe today a 'European' education is a political, social and economic necessity and an affirmation of their cultural birthright. There is scarcely need to go beyond this statement to justify introducing a coherent European dimension into the secondary curriculum. It represents a growing body of informed opinion and the view of most European professional bodies in education. It also underpins the policies of leading international organizations, such as UNESCO, the United Nations Educational, Scientific and Cultural Organization, and the Council for Cultural Co-operation, representing the educational interests of the Council of Europe.

The importance of teaching and learning about Europe can no longer be ignored by those with the authority to influence the shape of European curricula. The argument that the young need to understand and appreciate Europe's common heritage has been widely repeated since 1949, when the Council of Europe committed itself to achieving European unity and the safeguarding of those ideals and principles bequeathed by past generations of Europeans. Five years later the European Cultural Convention bound contracting governments to foster the study of the language, history and civilization of Europe, and from that time the ground was laid for an explicit European emphasis in education. However, history shows that ideas sown by one generation require time to germinate and flourish. In educational terms, there is likely to be a period when new ideas are discussed, tried out in the classroom and then evaluated. In some European countries studies about Europe underwent this process from the late 1960s.

It is generally accepted in democratic societies that education is to do with increasing people's, and especially children's, knowledge and awareness of themselves and of others, broadening their experience and hence their understanding of the world about them. The secondary school stage is important because that is when childhood impressions are reinforced and extended, while adult attitudes and patterns of behaviour towards the external world are certainly determined by adolescent experience. Experts often resort to analogy to show how children's learning benefits from the sequential structuring of knowledge and progression in pupil activities. A child's conceptualization of the external world is sometimes portrayed as a cluster of concentric circles. The innermost ring comprises the familiar streets and sights of the town, suburb or village in which the child's home stands. Outside this neighbourhood environment, children are surrounded by other 'circles' or communities to which they equally belong. And so among the early lessons of school is the development of a wider sense of belonging, to the historic district, county or province, the geographical area or region; and at a greater distance, but binding its citizens with a special sense of identity and loyalty, the community of the nation-state. Finally, every child should be fully aware that there is an international community. All citizens are part of a family of nations related by their affiliation to a common civilization; and ultimately, there is a global community uniting all peoples.

If the first lesson, then, is about awareness, the second is about relationships. Young Europeans have to realize that the family of nations to which they belong is increasingly bound in mutual dependence and responsibility. The kinds of issue which once governed international relations, such as geographical proximity, religion or dynastic ambition, are less relevant today. Global economics have given rise to a new realism, demanding pragmatism, agreement and concerted action. So the need for co-operation is the third lesson that we should encourage the young to learn.

And lastly, we are moving towards a society where there will be greater harmonization, where there is already greater shared experience and uniformity. Now more than ever before, our family of nations – Europe – exercises influence over the daily lives of individuals, adults and children. Whether we like it or not, a significant part of Europe already has the institutional framework of judicial courts, laws, parliamentary bodies, ministers, commissions and civil servants to go on shaping the lives of millions of citizens for the indefinite future. For this reason – a simple but profoundly important one – European children are entitled to be prepared for life within European society. So, as the twenty-first century approaches, teaching and learning about Europe must be treated as an educational priority.

These educational arguments are supported by international developments. The decision in 1976 by the Council of Ministers of Education of the European Community to adopt an action programme 'to give a European dimension to the experience of pupils and teachers in primary and secondary schools' was an important milestone in changing perceptions of European education, as was the 1983 Recommendation of the Committee of Ministers of the Council of Europe that member states should promote European awareness in their secondary schools. When social and political circumstances coincide with shifts in educational thought, those in positions of power and influence should have the courage to act. As Shakespeare's Julius Caesar observed, 'There is a tide in the affairs of men, / Which, taken at the flood, leads on to fortune.'

Three crucial trends, as we have observed already, are now coalescing to produce a change of tempo in European development. The first is the prospect of social and economic integration after 1992 and the probability of an enlarged Community and political unification, perhaps as early as 1993. The second trend is the development of new technology which opens up radical opportunities for links between Europeans; and the third, the revolutions in Central and Eastern Europe during 1989–90 which have expanded our vision of Europe. The plea made by President Gorbachev in July 1989 before the Parliamentary Assembly of the Council of Europe, that European nations should co-operate 'to make peace together', anticipated the free movement of people, services and ideas between the two halves of Europe, and mutual assistance in matters of common concern. Overarching these developments is the probability of a Europe united by democratic systems in the 1990s. It is obvious that educational policy needs to respond with an accelerated programme to promote a sense of European identity and prepare the young to take a full part in the multiplex community of the future.

EUROPE IN THE CURRICULUM: THE NATURE OF THE TASK

It would be a great mistake if new teachers were led to believe that they were entering totally uncharted waters, where Europe floated like flotsam in the school curriculum. The progress of the last twenty years deserves to be mentioned briefly, not only as testimony to those teachers who helped to draw the parameters of Europe in the curriculum, but as proof that 'European education' is no flash-in-the-pan response to the current political situation. Since the 1950s many organizations have made European education a priority. A prominent consortium, the International Federation of Europe Houses (FIME) now includes sixty-four institutions in sixteen states, and under its aegis the Institute for European Teacher Education in the European Academy, Berlin, has become a centre for international seminars on teaching about Europe. Another institution responsible for a network of curricular research is the Centrum voor europese vorming in het Nederlandse onderwijs (CEVNO). In the UK, secondary schools took on the responsibility for themselves of developing a new subject called European Studies. However, the main initiatives came from the Council for Cultural Co-operation and the European Community after 1976. Their partnership in education was one of the significant developments of the 1980s, while their collaboration in special celebrations such as European Music Year, European Road Safety Year and International Youth Year helped to increase European awareness.

In September 1989 the Parliamentary Assembly of the Council of Europe affirmed the 1983 recommendation on European awareness. The Assembly also recommended further strategies relating to the European dimension and urged the Committee of Ministers to work closely with the EC, UNESCO and, where possible, the governments of Eastern Europe. Meanwhile, by a resolution of 24 May 1988, the Council of Ministers of Education of the Community launched a series of measures for the period 1988–92 to develop the European dimension in all sectors, including secondary schools. Member states were charged with the dual task of devising national measures to re-inforce the European dimension and reporting on their proposals by 30 June 1991. There is now an unequivocal obligation on those in charge of education in the states of Europe to implement European awareness programmes, an obligation which the Federal Republic of Germany, for example, has taken seriously since 1978.

Already in this exposition it may be noted that certain expressions recur: 'European awareness', 'the European dimension', 'Europe in the curriculum', 'European education'. These terms are used both in informal discussion and in official documentation. They refer to two aspects of the curriculum, the sub-stance of learning and the process of teaching. What precisely is involved? *Prima facie*, the matter of process signifies improving the quality and breadth of pupil knowledge by making Europe a new focal point of normal school experi-ence. It also involves taking a fresh look at those school subjects which custo-marily deal with European topics – History, Geography, Modern Languages, the Creative Arts – to review their important contributions. At the same time, newer subject areas with a bearing on contemporary Europe – Economics, Environmental Education, the Social and Political Sciences – should be inte-grated into the curriculum, so that pupils receive a more rounded perspective. To implement this policy, a number of questions have to be asked. For example, is there a definitive body of knowledge about Europe that we should expect pupils to acquire before they leave school? How can the essential know-ledge be defined and selected from the amorphous mass of information avail-able? What kinds of knowledge are appropriate at different stages of pupil development? Should allowance be made for regional or national priorities? How should knowledge about Europe be organized within the curriculum and how can it be best presented to pupils to ensure effective learning takes place? These sample questions indicate the complexity of the problem.

Knowledge, it must be said, is only one aspect of learning, and teaching is much more than conveying information to pupils. Knowledge must be a springboard for other processes, such as encouraging positive responses and attitudes in pupils, and Europe is a prolific medium for the values area of the curriculum. In the 1990s Europe will also be a pluralist, increasingly partici-patory society. The experiential aspects of education are already a priority as preparation for life is seen to be a matter of adaptability, mobility, sociability, technical mastery and fluency in communication; so a premium has been placed on the capacity to mobilize and exercise skills. In addition to learning *about* and *through* Europe, pupils need to learn how to cope with living and working *within* Europe, how to fulfil their potential and exercise their democratic rights.

21

The 'European dimension' in the school curriculum has to meet these diverse functions. However, if European curricula are to be at all homogeneous, teachers need to proceed from a set of common assumptions. Before looking at the curricular implications, we need to clarify what people understand by the word 'Europe'.

WHAT IS EUROPE? PROBLEMS OF DEFINITION

To the uninitiated, 'What is Europe?' may sound a simple question to which there must be a simple answer. However, experience shows that the subject provokes contrary views or a blurred distinction between the ideal and the reality. In fact, it is a question that invites varied replies, depending on the situation. Evasion is a common reaction and has prompted all manner of facetious response, such as 'It is difficult to define an elephant, but I know one when I see one!'[1] The problem is that the subject can be interpreted at more than one intellectual level.

Over the last century Europe has provoked a lively academic debate among professional geographers, historians and philosophers concerned to establish scholarly accuracy. But during the last half century the more pertinent factor in shaping perceptions has been the Iron Curtain. Lack of information on both sides created a sense that 'the other Europe' was largely irrelevant. The Council of Europe's surveys conducted during the 1950s and 1960s revealed the obstacles in the way of giving Western secondary pupils a balanced, informed, comprehensive view of Europe. The deficiencies were reinforced in the 1970s by the educational tendency to focus on familiar aspects or regions of Western Europe, such as the countries of the EEC. There was also insufficient com- munication between teachers at school and higher education levels, so that available knowledge was not always effectively pooled and disseminated. The perception of a fractured region was endorsed by politicians and statesmen; Charles de Gaulle, for one, spoke of a Europe of the nation-states, and more recently, the state premiers of the Federal German *Länder* have spoken out in favour of a Europe of Regions. The changes of 1985–90, however, force us to rethink what Europe means and is likely to mean by the end of the century. The optimist would say that the changes demonstrate Europe's inherent dynamism, the pessimist that we are entering a period of destabilization in which there can be no rational certainty. In the opinion of some, only a polymath could be competent to define Europe. The practical solution for schools is to treat the reappraisal of Europe as a multidisciplinary task, because there is not one question to be answered but several: not simply 'what?' but 'where?', 'how?', 'why?', 'when?' and even 'who?'.

If we begin with the first question, most people in practice think of Europe in spatial terms. They use the word as a geographical expression to describe a sizeable landmass. Indeed, they go further and speak of 'the continent of

Europe'. But purists have refuted this definition on the grounds that it is too static, the landmass too varied and fragmented. Jean Gottmann, the Russian-born Professor of Geography at Oxford, put forward the notion of a 'tidal Europe', ebbing and flowing according to political and demographic change. An earlier theory (1904) of the eminent Halford J. Mackinder identified the Russian Empire as the 'heartland' or 'pivot area' of Eurasia, the land to the west (which we call 'Europe') being a mere appendage or subcontinent. Since then the definition of Europe has been under constant review.[2]

The responsibility for classifying Europe as a continent is usually attributed to the ancient Greeks. They were the first people to coin the word 'Europa', but for them it denoted the mainland of Greece and the limited region to the north and west which they had colonized before the sixth century BC. The Hebrew tradition, embodied in the Book of Genesis, and the Ptolemaic world-view of the second century AD, confirmed Europe as the third continent of the globe. So from the classical period the issue which absorbed astronomers, cartographers and others was Europe's eastern limit: where does Europe end and Asia begin? One answer, provided in 1683 by Louis Moreri in his *Grand Dictionnaire Historique*, was that 'if one draws a line from the river Don or Tanais to the river Ob and then to the Arctic Ocean to the north, all that lies to the left belongs to Europe and all to the right to Asia.'[3] For all that, nineteenth-century geographers placed the 'natural' boundary variously at each of the major Russian rivers from the Dniester to the Yenisei, the majority settling in the end for a combined river–mountain barrier, the Urals. But the matter was not allowed to rest there.

In his seminal *Study of History* (1954), the philosopher Arnold Toynbee criticized the geographical profession for turning the Ural Mountains into a household word, on the grounds that they were no more significant as a topographical feature than the Chiltern Hills of southern England. In fact the philosopher was making a historical point, that the Russian people had main-tained an irresistible drive eastwards since Yermak the Cossack's crossing of the Urals in the late sixteenth century, from which time Siberia fell perma-nently under Russian influence. His thesis ran contrary to the opinion of nine-teenth-century physical geographers and climatologists who had pronounced the topography and climate of Siberia to be non-European. The issue of whether Siberia is or is not within the European orbit may be settled in the future if its eastern seaboard secedes to join the Pacific Rim powers or if the Central Asian provinces revert to their ancestral sphere of influence. Mean-while, the geographer Gordon East added a sceptical voice to the argument by questioning the significance of the Urals as the eastern boundary of Europe, but the matter of Russia and Europe has remained one of the most heated political controversies until the present day.[4]

If Halford Mackinder stood the question of whether Russia is a part of Europe, on its head by his heartland theory, Mikhail Gorbachev thrust it into the public arena with his famous assertion that 'Europe is our common home'. The Soviet President was concerned to remind Westerners that after six decades of isolation the Russian people were still Europeans at heart. Notable scholars had thought otherwise; in addition to Toynbee, the Russian Klyuchevsky and the Polish historian Halecki went along with the view of Reynold, a Swiss scholar, that 'Russia does not belong to Europe ... Russia is the geographical antithesis of Europe.'[5]

On purely geographical criteria, there have been two schools, the exclusionists and the pragmatists, the latter being those who accepted some division of the USSR and believed that the historic political–cultural centres of Russia – Kiev, Novgorod, Moscow and Leningrad – being in the western belt, were in something called 'European Russia'. This notion had historic origins predating the academic debate. The idea that 'Muscovy' was outside the European family of nations was strongly felt in the West during the sixteenth and seventeenth centuries – the Duc de Sully, for example, regarded Russia as an Asiatic misfit – and by common consent this alienation was the result of the thirteenth-century Mongol invasions. Thereafter Russia had been cut off from the cultural and economic influences of Western Europe and developed in political, social and spiritual isolation. On the other hand, medieval scholarship points to Russia's Slav origins and legacy, to the tradition of Moscow the Third Rome and the symbiotic relationship between Roman and Byzantine Christianity; and modern history underlines the European connection, as first the Russian Empire and then the USSR were involved in the maelstrom of European politics. Arguably, in the fullness of time the seventy years of isolation will be judged a temporary deviation from the European path.

The Soviet position also affects the way relations between the West and the rest of Eastern Europe are perceived. Addressing the people of Poland in 1979, Pope John Paul II passed judgement: 'Is it not what the Holy Spirit disposes, that the Polish Pope, this Slav Pope, should at this precise moment manifest the spiritual unity of Christian Europe?' And shortly after, the historian James Joll, musing on the possibility of the Iron Curtain being torn down, anticipated what now seems self-evident, that Eastern Europe and Russia share a common tradition with the West and that once again Europe will include Cracow, Wroclaw, Budapest and Goethe's Weimar.

Translated into educational terms – in terms of syllabuses, books, resources, teacher expertise and training – the new reality poses enormous problems for teachers. For half a century or more, our pupils have been taught about a Europe of the Western nations, while a Europe from the Atlantic to the Urals was virtually *sub judice*. The revolution in telecommunications may have done something to counter chauvinism, but teachers alone can judge the scale of the problem. It would be interesting to ask what Italian or Greek children know of Scandinavia or what children in Portugal learn about the geography of Poland. What do students in Belgium know about the history of the Baltic states? What do pupils in England and Wales understand about conditions in Bulgaria or Romania? And so on. The richness and diversity of European experience has been masked by our bipolar vision of the recent past. President Gorbachev has asked questions which must make every teacher think afresh about Europe.

What can they do to give their pupils a sense of 'being at home' there? What sort of 'European house' should be their model? And continuing Gorbachev's metaphor, 'what will be the architecture of our "common home"? how should it be built . . . and how should it be furnished?'[6]

However, important though it is, the Russian question is apt to distract the mind from other issues. For by far the majority of Europeans neither the existence of Europe nor their belonging to it is in any doubt. The 'continental tradition' has been a political and cultural reality for centuries (as those who live on the periphery have perceived). For the most part it is a common bond for those regions which were once part of the Roman and Carolingian Empires in the West or embraced Christian civilization in the early Middle Ages; and mainland countries, largely or totally landlocked, can be expected for good reason to develop a 'territorial' mentality. However, Europe's indented coast-line – some 80,000 kilometres long, or twice round the Equator – is complemented by offshore islands such as the British Isles, and massive peninsulas such as Scandinavia, which have experienced influences not shared by mainstream Europe. British insularity, for instance, is still a powerful force and there is a popular tendency to speak of 'going *to* Europe' or of linking 'Britain *and* Europe'. Iceland, Malta and Cyprus are considered European, though the first shares little, in terms of climate, experience of a common past, with the other two. And what of Greenland, the largest island in the world, an autonomous region of the Danish kingdom yet situated off the North American continent, and within the Arctic Circle rather than the temperate zone? Or the Azores, the most westerly offshore archipelago, belonging since the fifteenth century to Portugal? Are they European? As for Turkey, history recalls that it was known as Asia Minor and its Ottoman sultans were the scourge of Christendom and Habsburg Europe during four centuries of occupation of the Balkans. Yet 130 years later, modern Turkey is perceived to have respectable European credentials. It is a member state of NATO and of the Council of Europe. Clearly, there is no simple answer to these questions.

If there are anomalies, they illustrate the limitations of a rigid geographical definition. That was the point of Jean Gottmann's 'tidal Europe' and behind the observation of Hans Freyer, the philosopher, that Europe was a continent not by nature but by history. The same view was expressed by the historian Geoffrey Barraclough: 'The term "Europe" does not stand for a fixed quantity, but is, on the contrary, "an historical idea".' Certainly history has evidence on its side, for during the heyday of the Roman Empire and the Middle Ages alternative concepts prevailed. *Pax Romana* and *Respublica Christiana* or *Civitas Mundi* were phrases denoting the realities of a millennium of European history when the term 'Europe' was rarely, if ever, used. Barraclough argued that 'Europe' was a product of the historian's imagination struggling to make sense of the expanding world of the Renaissance, the period when the changeover from 'Christendom' to 'Europe' occurred. As another English historian, R. A. Wake, observed, 'It is in this rapidly changing society [of the late fifteenth–sixteenth centuries] that the word Christendom is used less and the word

Europe more: it described a disunited, tense, eager and aggressive expanding Christendom.'[7]

Those adjectives are meant to imply the quality of dynamism which emerged in modern times. To quote Barraclough again: 'Europeans have always reached for the stars', and the Swiss scholar, Denis de Rougemont, echoed his proposition: 'European man is he who always goes farther, beyond the limits set by nature, beyond traditions fixed by his ancestors, even beyond himself – on to adventure.' Neither goes so far as to say that European dynamism is unique, but Richard Hoggart picked out the same quality when he described Europe as 'the restless continent'.[8] The proof is not simply with the Portuguese navigators who charted the maritime route via the Cape of Good Hope to the Far East in search of spices and the legendary Prester John, nor with the Dutch merchants who explored the East Indies and Australasia for profit, the *conquistadores* who imposed themselves on the New World, the British who reconnoitred and settled the seaboard of North America before diversifying into trade and colonization in most parts of the globe, nor even with the Cossacks who exploited Siberia's waterways, criss-crossing that inhospitable environment to reach the frontiers of China, the Arctic and the North Pacific. It is demonstrated, too, by the 34 million who emigrated between 1870 and the outbreak of the First World War and in the vast numbers, equivalent to one quarter of all peoples of European stock, who were living outside the bounds of Europe prior to 1939.

These remarks are a comment on European civilization, a culture which has influenced the rest of the world, just as it has been touched by other influences. The word 'culture' is not used here in the sense of artistic achievement but to describe a community of peoples bound by common beliefs, values and ways of life. In other words, part of the distinctiveness of Europe lies in the character of its people. Many of their values are deeply rooted in the past and have been transformed over time. The people have proved inventive and adaptable in the face of economic forces which produced urbanism and industrialism. In fact, R. A. Wake defined Europe as 'a set of ideas and attitudes, backed for a long time by technological development far in advance of that of any other area in the world', and he did not emphasize this aspect in order to suggest superiority to other civilizations but to exemplify distinctiveness and difference.[9] Its diversity, complexity and creative pragmatism gave Europe the reputation for being a 'contradictory' and 'fragile' continent.[10]

A CONCEPT FOR TEACHING

This discussion has tried to shed light on the problems of reconciling varying interpretations within competing areas of knowledge. Does it make the task of definition easier? European teachers do not speak with one voice but almost certainly they would vote against an esoteric formula because it would be open to misinterpretation and muddle: so to describe Europe as, for example, the outcome of a set of relationships, or as a place where certain values are the norm, is neither helpful nor suitable for curriculum planning. Since there is no such thing as a uniform European system of education, most teachers want a realistic definition which they can interpret to suit their particular school situation. They also want to be certain of the academic validity of the curriculum which they teach.

'Europe' is not a simple notion; it is a complex concept with three dimensions. I have chosen here to illustrate the conceptual process and substance in the diagrammatic form of interlocking rings (Figure 1). At the heart is Europe,

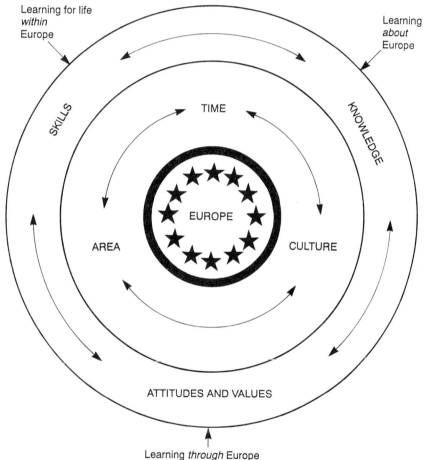

Figure 1 The European dimension: process and substance

encapsulated in its substantive dimensions of time, area and culture. Though these are distinct aspects of knowledge, they are also multifaceted. 'Culture', as I hinted above, denotes the particular features of a society as well as the creative legacy of a civilization; 'time' refers to the present and the future as well as the past. Furthermore, the three components constantly interact with one another:

so, for instance, Europe's artistic achievements and its multicultural legacy are products of time, and the European environment reflects the diversity of life-styles and social priorities of its regions. Teachers may feel that this binds them to an encyclopaedic interpretation, but they should be reassured that 'Europe as time, area and culture' (TAC) is merely a guiding concept and that a degree of interpretative discretion can be used. None the less, it is important to proceed with a shared vision, which does justice to Europe's spatial, temporal, human and qualitative characteristics. That point was confirmed in the recommendations of a symposium of Council of Europe experts a decade ago. In a precise formula, they proposed that

> For the purposes of secondary education, Europe can be defined as the past, the present and the future of the peoples living in the geographical area which stretches from the North Cape to the Mediterranean, from Iceland and Cape Roca to the Urals. It should not be seen as being synonymous with the membership of any particular European organisation.[11]

Some teachers have found this statement a little over-prescriptive but they accept that it presents an unequivocal three-dimensional definition.

CURRICULAR IMPLICATIONS

Goals and approaches to knowledge and concepts

We start with the matter of knowledge because that is something all European teachers understand. The primary purpose of knowledge – that is to say, of factual content – is to *inform* pupils, so that they can make reasoned judgements and sensible and humane responses. However, there is no finite body of knowledge about Europe, just as there is no single methodology for teaching about Europe. The transmission of knowledge requires teachers to exercise strict discrimination because pupils cannot be expected to digest a large amount of amorphous information. So what criteria should determine the selection of content about Europe?

In the *Guidelines on European Awareness* (1983), the Council of Europe made three fundamental recommendations with regard to the selection of content: first, the secondary curriculum should build on the work of the primary years; secondly, teaching should guarantee coherence of learning, and thirdly, knowledge should reflect what is intrinsically *distinctive of or even unique to* Europe. To these I would add a fourth, namely, that content should be practical and empirical, to take account of the *dynamic* nature of the European dimension. These criteria, which are the bedrock of sound curricular planning, confirm that content-selection is a complex task.

At present the European content in most school curricula is the responsibility of specialist graduates teaching traditional disciplines: subjects like History,

Modern Languages and Geography. In addition, as we suggested earlier, there is a role for other Human Sciences, the Creative Arts and even the Natural Sciences. So in effect, Europe is spread over several disciplinary bases. This is a healthy situation because it confronts us with the fact that teaching about Europe is not the sole prerogative of one subject, nor should it be. If Europe is a multifaceted concept, then the study of Europe is a multidisciplinary exercise drawing on many methodologies. Even where there is pressure to increase the level of cross-curricular suffusion there may be sound organizational reasons for leaving the direction of the European dimension to specialist teachers, and the traditional subject-based approach is an option that Council of Europe experts have frequently endorsed.[12]

However, in a system of separate subject departments, it is difficult to guarantee continuity and coherence of learning. The Council of Europe recognized this problem and recommended that schools should make special provision for cross-disciplinary linkages. Congruity can be achieved in a variety of ways: by extra-curricular activities involving teachers from several disciplines or departments, by regular consultation between subject teachers over common goals, and by linking the European dimension with normal assessment and attainment procedures. Another, more radical option is to adopt a different teaching system. If the rationale for selecting what is taught about Europe were based on cross-curricular goals rather than on existing discipline structures, the new goals could take account of subjects without being determined by them. Content would then be selected on the basis of goals. The Council of Europe *Guidelines* accept that 'It is possible to teach about Europe in secondary schools through separate subjects, or *through interdisciplinary courses*' (emphasis added). Yet, as expectations grow for effective cross-curricular implementation of the European dimension, schools may have to reappraise their teaching structures and make significant changes in organization.

Ultimately, there are three ways of approaching the teaching of European studies: by means of single subjects, by a multidisciplinary or by an interdisciplinary approach. In the second, a team of teachers co-operate in teaching a course in which the contributory disciplines complement and overlap each other and the interrelationship of ideas is explored as far as possible. This method is used in Scottish Modern Studies courses and in the German *Gemeinschaftskunde*. It is similar to but not identical with the third way, the interdisciplinary approach. Here the individual teacher teaches a synthesis of European subject matter compositely across subject boundaries.[13] Interdisciplinarity is associated with the practice of interpreting knowledge in terms of 'concepts'. It is a well-established procedure, used for example in the pioneering work carried out at the European Academy in Berlin under the direction of Gunter Renner. Teachers in the UK may also recall the English Schools Council National Humanities project, History, Geography and Social Science (Time, Place and Society) for 8–13 year olds. Key concepts also underpinned many of the schemes of European Studies for pupils of 11–16 years which appeared in the UK from the mid-1960s onwards. These were based on various interdisciplinary (or so-called 'integrated') models, usually combining History, Geography and Social Studies with a Modern Language component. Their weaknesses (and the reason that, despite more stringent examination syllabuses, they remain a minority subject in the UK) were less the fault of the concept-approach they sprang from than a failure to preserve the discrete methodologies of the contributing subjects or to apply them with rigour. A more recent and specific concept-based initiative was the project on European Integration, promoted jointly in 1986 by the Commission of the European Community and the Association of Socialist Teachers and formulated at the European Academy in Berlin. This venture is in a long line of attempts since 1978 to explore ways to teach about the concept of European integration, and the methodology of teaching about co-operation remains under active discussion.

The advantages of the concept-approach for our purposes are that it blends with the flexible teaching styles used in many primary schools and therefore helps to provide continuity of method. Secondly, it lends itself to co-ordinated planning and monitoring of the kind increasingly practised in schools in the West. And last but by no means least, concepts should enable teachers to focus economically on the distinctive and essential aspects of Europe. In the light of those advantages, it may be helpful for teachers to consider the list of twenty goals for teaching about Europe (pages 36–7), which are couched in terms of the kinds of concepts, skills, attitudes and values which should illuminate pupil understanding of European issues. These goals were compiled with specialist teachers in mind but they should also assist cross-curricular programmes on European awareness.

Advice on the questions raised by the introduction of interdisciplinary courses was also given by three senior European Inspectors in a CDCC publication, *Innovation in Secondary Education in Europe*.[14] In offering guidance on social and political content, they made it clear that interdisciplinary teaching was far from easy, and their study was subtitled '*A Minefield for the Unwary*'. Teachers must be convinced that in pooling their expertise, their teaching fulfils a range of goals more effectively than could be achieved by traditional methods. They must be willing to surrender a part of their autonomy and to devote considerable time to co-ordinated planning.

Perhaps another cautionary word might be added. Concepts are blunt instruments of course planning unless they are carefully honed. For instance, there is a distinction between key concepts, those general ideas which serve as diagnostic tools for organizing content, and procedural concepts, concerned with the methodological process of learning. There is also a difference between these two categories and the concepts associated with the more blurred area of attributes, competences and values, known as value concepts (referred to by some experts as 'procedural values': Table 1). This is not a semantic quibble. Despite relationships of meaning, these types of concept have a different function. Key concepts are umbrella terms which provide an external framework for the curriculum. To select content we proceed from the general to the

Table 1 Some examples of concepts relevant to the European dimension

Key concepts	Value concepts	Procedural concepts
		Methodology
		Enquiry
		Evidence
Unity	*Equality*/Universalism, *Integration*/Internationalism, *Co-operation*/Union/Federation	Holism/Induction, Generalization, Correlation/Co-ordination
Diversity	Variety/Multiplicity, Inequality/Abundance	Paradox/Contrast, Deduction
Change	Revolution/Reformation, Rise/Decline, Progress	Process, Cause/Effect, Evaluation
Continuity	Tradition/Customs/Institutions, Evolution	Continuum, Coherence
Interdependence	Interrelatedness/Collaboration, *Pluralism*, Affiliation/*Communication, Tolerance*	Interaction, Active Co-operation, Relationships, *Open-mindedness*
Conflict	*Power*, War/Dispute, Nationalism/Xenophobia	Antithesis, Dialectic, Dissonance
Liberty	*Human Rights and Freedoms, Justice/Individuality, Democracy/*Self-determination, Radicalism/Rebellion/Subversion/Anarchy	Respect, Originality, Participation, Non-conformity
Security	Socialism, Collectivism/Centralization, Totalitarianism, Peace/Order/Non-violence	Commitment, Authority, Decision, Understanding
Rationality	Legalism, Responsibility/Moderation/Reason	Analysis/Criticism, Experience/Objectivity, Judgement/Interpretation
Emotionality	Creative Expression, *Culture*, Sensitivity/Humanity	Appreciation/Awareness, *Empathy*, Subjectivity
Materialism	Capitalism/Wealth, Urbanism/Industrialism/Pollution, Obsolescence/Redistribution	Enterprise/Choice, Repetition/Practicality, Leisure/Retraining
Spirituality	*Values/Ideals*, Ethics/Morals, *Heritage*	Toleration, Imagination, Stewardship
Naturalism	Preservation/Moderation, Environmentalism/Conservation, Health	Equilibrium, Intuition, Exercise
Systematization	Organization/Production, Constitutions/*Society*/Classification, *Technology*	Systems/Pattern/Method, Categorization, Numeracy/Technical Skills
Similarity	*Community*/Communalism, Homogeneity/Uniformity	Comparison, Analogy/Model
Difference	Minority, Hierarchy, Deviance	Idiosyncrasy, Selectivity/Discrimination, Division/*Distinctiveness*

particular, reducing concepts to broad themes in the first instance, and thence to topics or case-studies. During this process, value concepts are often helpful as discriminating tools by which cross-curricular themes and later the smaller units of study – the topics and case-studies – can be determined. They also point to the methods of implementation, that is to say, they indicate the appropriate procedural concepts. At this stage the individual preconditions of each school also come into play, but whatever the particular circumstances, it is vital that the choice of content should accurately reflect the concepts specified and that all themes, topics and case-studies should be demonstrably coherent and valid. These criteria can be verified by using checklists. In the course of detailed planning, thought has also to be given to the skills which will be involved. Finally, a progression of strategies and attainment levels, according to the age and ability range of the pupils, should be ascertained as a basis for pupil assessment and for regular evaluation.

Goals, skills, attitudes, values and attributes

There is an alternative concept-approach, much favoured by teachers of the social sciences. This alternative model replaces knowledge concepts as the determinant of curriculum planning by values and value concepts. It has to be said that the Council of Europe Guidelines give prominence to value concepts such as democracy, human rights, freedom, tolerance and pluralism, and much of the work on Social Education and Human Rights Education by the Council of Europe hinges on value centrality. Initially, value-centred planning suffered from one of two faults: either there was a lack of clear and achievable goals or there were too many high-sounding declarations of intent and too little organized content. On the merit side, the *a priori* justifications for teaching the humanities and the human sciences are usually expressed in terms of values, so it could be argued that there is a rational case for organizing the learning process around value concepts.

In particular, the principal aims underlying the whole move to give education a European dimension can be summarized in the language of values and attitudes, a point that emerges clearly from Goals 15 20 of the table of twenty goals (pages 36–7). These emphasize the importance of helping pupils to develop positive attributes: awareness, empathy, respect and tolerance towards other people and their values, a sense of responsibility and a co-operative disposition. A prior necessity, however, is self-understanding and the development of consciousness of identity, which is a matter of family, then of regional, ethnic and national affiliation. Of these competing loyalties, there is no doubt that for some 150–200 years identity with the nation-state has been the most powerful determinant of affiliation in Europe. However, there is no necessary contradiction between attachment to the homeland and European identity. Speaking from their experience, a group of European primary teachers judged that:

A Europe-oriented mentality is possible only if the individual has first become 'localised' in his home country. Children must regard themselves as native before they can evolve a European consciousness ... Later on national feelings will play a smaller role, the emphasis being increasingly laid on attachment to a wider regional grouping, whence it will be easier to impress the notion of a common loyalty to Europe ... The primary teacher's most urgent task will be to awaken in the pupils an emotional approach to Europe: they must become capable of understanding and respecting each other and of living together ... They should at the same time retain patriotic pride and a love of their homeland, while becoming European in mentality.[15]

What are the implications for secondary school students? Can a powerful sense of European awareness – or European consciousness, to use another phrase – be developed by means of a European dimension in the curriculum? There is a rider to this second question. The term 'European consciousness' should not, of course, be confused with Eurocentrism, any more than the term 'national consciousness' should be equated with xenophobia. The answers to these crucial questions are implicit in the 'European' programmes of the CDCC: they suggest that if young people are better informed about Europe and their perceptions become attuned to European values, they will develop 'a real European consciousness'. The Ministers of Education of the *Länder* of the Federal Republic of Germany have also resolved that European awareness should be treated as a pedagogical assignment of every school.[16] So the learning process is partly a matter of knowledge (as elaborated in later chapters), but it is far more a matter of developing the 'right' attitudes and perceptions. Indeed, one academic expert sees the whole values area of the curriculum as the nub of the problem of encouraging the young to think of themselves as members of a greater European community (with a small 'c') and the key to the transformation of ingrained patriotism, pride and national consciousness into an innate European consciousness.[17]

Research suggests that the young are more receptive to the notion of Europe than the public at large, and they are more natural affiliators than the old. Open-mindedness is the key to affiliation with other people and other nationalities. A receptive attitude of mind is compounded of curiosity, knowledge, empathy and a positive desire for peace (rather than a negative desire to avoid disputes and conflict). An Austrian head teacher explained from his experience that the teacher's task was to encourage pupils to be

- more critical of the media;
- more attentive to press information about other countries;
- more open and, for example, more willing to listen to foreign songs;
- more wide awake to the local surroundings, to matters such as frontiers, local languages and dialects, ethnic customs, and more aware of the neighbourhood;
- more curious about historic sites and legends;

- more prepared for contacts with relatives (and others) abroad;
- more understanding of the features peculiar to foreign countries;
- quicker to recognize the cultural, scientific or sporting achievements of others.[18]

There are indications that people of smaller states, like Denmark or Ireland, find it easier to achieve a receptive state of mind than citizens of large, influential states. Curricular models to induce European consciousness are still in the developmental stage (Figure 2). Yet a number of practical strategies are being pursued. First, there is evidence that an open school structure and a communal ethos provide an environment conducive to tolerance, open-mindedness and empathy; so if the young are given opportunities to participate actively in decision-making, they adapt to affiliation more naturally. Secondly, regular, personal contact between the young remains the most effective way of stimulating a sense of community and mutual respect, a feeling of 'being European'. Thirdly, the new information technology represents the most effective means of providing young Europeans with vicarious experience of co-operation and communality. Networks of school links and special communications projects should assume a high educational priority in the 1990s.

European consciousness straddles the areas of values, attitudes and skills. The word 'skills' covers many different kinds of ability and competence. In recent years there has been a growing emphasis on those active and participatory skills needed to exercise civic responsibilities. Lately, too, the whole field of creativity, imagination and audiovisual perception has been the subject of attention. Changing social priorities also put greater stress on activity-based experience and recreation for which physical skills are vital. In the past there was a tendency to concentrate on the higher-order cognitive skills at secondary school, if only to prepare students for examinations and entry into a highly competitive world. Cognitive skills remain immensely important as the basis for clusters of abilities which constitute high-level numeracy, literacy and technology-literacy. The European dimension provides fertile ground for reinforcing all these areas of competence. However, there is one area of special relevance to European consciousness, namely language and communication. In the past decade great strides have been made in improving communicative competence, and this momentum must be maintained at a time when Europe's horizons are expanding. Modern languages hold the key to understanding between Europeans, to mobility, employment and culture within the European community. Language and communication are, *par excellence*, the *enabling* skills for life in an extended, democratic Europe.

This outline stakes out the ground for the rest of the study. In the following two sections, attention will focus on the European dimension within the formal curriculum. Consideration will be given to the teaching and learning of the traditional disciplines and the newer subject areas, in which Europe raises a multiplicity of issues.

1 Governing principle

European consciousness and identity

Definition

Organizers

Discriminators

C
h
e
c
k
l
i
s
t

Goals

Enablers

2 Europe?	
3 Key concepts	
4 Value concepts	
6 Cross-curricular themes	
5 Knowledge	
8 Topics, case-studies	
7 Skills	
9 Procedural concepts	
10 Teaching strategies	
11 Pupil outcomes	
12 Assessment and evaluation	

Figure 2 Steps towards a cross–curricular/concept–based European dimension

TWENTY GOALS FOR TEACHING ABOUT EUROPE

Knowledge

1 To provide pupils with some understanding of the European landscape and the principal differences and similarities of the physical environment and lifestyles.

2 To enable pupils to understand the variety of pattern and process in human settlement and forms of production.

3 To examine political and economic trends and policies for their present and future effects upon European society.

4 To convey awareness and understanding of the environmental interaction between people and nature and its implications for the present and future.

5 To ensure that pupils understand the degree of continuity and the concept of change over time as it has operated in Europe, and to comprehend the nature, causes and effects of change.

6 To foster an understanding of the significance, use and variety of evidence as the basis for subsequent judgement.

7 To foster a knowledge, where possible through direct experience, of the rich diversity of Europe's cultural heritage.

8 To ensure that pupils are properly informed and understand the implications of Europe's pluralism and diversity and of those organizations, institutions and ideas that make for greater unity and co-operation to counter conflict and division.

9 To help pupils understand the social structures, mores, institutions, issues and problems of contemporary society.

10 To foster knowledge and understanding of those international trends, modes of thought and patterns of behaviour which are changing European society and are likely to affect the future of pupils in adulthood.

Skills

11 To enable pupils to speak at least one European language other than their mother tongue at a level that ensures effective communication.

12 To develop social skills in support of linguistic skills as a means of effective communication.

13 To reinforce basic learning skills and advanced cognitive skills.

14 To develop audiovisual and imaginative skills in order to induce aesthetic awareness and appreciation of a range of cultural forms.

15 To provide opportunities for pupils to practise a range of political skills as a preparation for active citizenship.

Attitudes and values

16 To make pupils aware of and help them to respect the rich cultural heritage they share with other young Europeans.

17 To encourage in pupils appreciation of European values in general and in particular democratic values such as tolerance and equality.

18 To develop in pupils greater empathy and awareness of the value of living in a multicultural, pluralist society, while drawing strength from those movements, organizations and aspirations promoting unity within Europe.

19 To stimulate the development of empathy in order to generate greater understanding between people in Europe and a greater disposition to active co-operation.

20 To enable pupils to accept their responsibilities as citizens of Europe and to develop constructive attitudes towards pressing issues such as peace and human rights throughout the world.

NOTES

1 Cited in Otto Ernst Schüddekopf, in collaboration with Edouard Bruley, E. H. Dance and Haakon Vigander (1967), *History Teaching and History Textbook Revision*, Strasbourg: CDCC. For an historiographical explanation of the term 'Europe', combined with an analysis of its geographical use, see Sattler, R. J. (1971), *Europa: Geschichte und Aktualität des Begriffes*, Braunschweig: International Schoolbook Institute.

2 A pithy discussion of the debate is to be found in Parker, W. H. (1968), *An Historical Geography of Russia*, London: London University Press, pp. 27–9. It was also raised at a recent geographical symposium: see Graves, Norman (forthcoming), *Report of the Symposium on Geographical Information and Documentation on European Countries, Utrecht, September 1989*, Strasbourg: Council of Europe.

3 Cited in Shennan, Margaret (1976), *The European Dynamic*, London: A. & C. Black, p. 28.

4 East, Gordon (1967), 'Europe and its regions', in *Geography Teaching and the Revision of Geography Textbooks and Atlases*, Strasbourg: CDCC. Russia's exclusion from Europe is the underlying theme of Schoepflin, George, and Wood, Nancy (eds) (1989), *The Search for Central Europe*, Oxford: Polity Press, a collection of seventeen essays.

5 Cited in Parker, *Historical Geography*, p. 27.

6 Speech of President Mikhail Gorbachev to the Parliamentary Assembly of the Council of Europe, July 1989.

7 Wake, R. A. (1980), 'The Idea of Europe', unpublished paper, p. 6; see also

Shennan, *The European Dynamic*, pp. 11–25. The difficulties of defining Central Europe were pinpointed by the journalist Neal Ascherson when he asked 'Is the place to be found in the old Habsburg lands of the baroque, or does it comprise everything between Denmark and Bulgaria? Was it once-upon-a-time or is it all about us now, or can we only reach it by wading across time to the beach of tomorrow?' (*The Observer*, 13 August 1989).

8 Hoggart, Richard, and Johnson, Douglas (1987), *An Idea of Europe*, London: Channel 4 Publications, pp. 10–11.

9 Wake, 'The Idea of Europe', p. 9.

10 Hoggart and Johnson, *An Idea of Europe*, pp. 9, 11.

11 Peacock, D. (1982), *Report of the CDCC Symposium on Europe in Secondary School Curricula: Aims, Approaches and Problems, Neusiedl-am-See, Austria, April 1981*, Strasbourg: Council of Europe. p. 31. This definition effectively restated the recommendation of the World Confederation of Organizations of the Teaching Profession agreed at Stavanger, October 1980:

> For the purposes of European Studies, Europe is not just the 9 member countries of the EEC nor even the 23 countries of the Council of Europe's Council for Cultural Co-operation. It may be defined geographically as the continental landmass extending to the Ural Mountains in the East and including the British Isles and Iceland. Europe's common heritage connotes what it owes to the intermingling of diverse cultures and peoples over a period of more than 2000 years. ((1981), *Selection of Texts on Education for International Understanding and Teaching about Europe, produced for the Symposium on Europe in Secondary School Curricula: Aims, Approaches and Problems, at Neusiedl-am-See, Austria, April 1981*, Strasbourg: Council of Europe), p. 35.

12 Resolution of the Council and the Ministers of Education on the European dimension in education, 24 May 1988 (88/C 177/02).

13 For instance, Peacock, *Report on Europe in Secondary School Curricula*; Committee of Ministers, Council of Europe: Recommendation No. R (83) 4 on the promotion of an awareness of Europe in secondary schools.

14 Wake, R. A., Marbeau, V., and Petersen, A. D. C. (1979), *Innovation in Secondary Education in Europe*, Strasbourg: CDCC.

15 Trybus, K. (1986), *Report of the 30th European Teachers' Seminar on Europe in Primary Schools, Donaueschingen, November 1985*, Strasbourg: Council of Europe, pp. 32–3.

16 Recommendation 1111 (1989) (1) of the Parliamentary Assembly of the Council of Europe on the European dimension in education; Resolution of the Standing Conference of the Ministers of Education and Cultural Affairs of the *Länder* in the Federal Republic of Germany, 7 December 1990 – see Chapter 7, Table 8.

17 Jacobsen, Bo, 'How to develop a European consciousness in pupils' minds: some research perspectives', in *Report of the European Teachers' Seminar on Teaching about European Co-operation and Integration in Upper Secondary Schools, Ebeltoft, Denmark*, Strasbourg: Council of Europe, pp. 9–11.

18 Halbritter, Hermann (1985), 'Europe in the Primary School', in *Report on Europe in Primary Schools*, pp. 15–16.

PART 2

LEARNING ABOUT EUROPE THROUGH THE FORMAL CURRICULUM

CHAPTER 3

Europe and the Time Dimension

HISTORY: PURPOSE AND METHODOLOGY

The conventional subjects of the curriculum are a natural starting point because their contribution to European consciousness can be judged the most directly. By tradition, teaching and learning about Europe has depended on the contribution of the Human Sciences, History being most commonly singled out for its focal importance.[1] Yet in many European countries *national* history forms the backbone of the curriculum, while in others there has been a deliberate move towards a *global* approach. This brings us face to face with an anomaly, which at the very least means we should clarify the place of Europe in the History curriculum. As 1992 draws near, some teachers may still be inclined to question whether a syllabus centred on the history of European civilization is suitable for pupils brought up in a multicultural, multilingual society. Where there is dissent, it is over *what* History should be taught and what are the likely outcomes, rather than *how* the subject should be taught. So if Europe is to be effectively harnessed to the History curriculum, there must be appreciable benefits to the pupils in terms of constructive changes of attitude, a widening of mental horizons and opportunities: in other words, evidence of greater European awareness and enriched understanding.

History should be a prime facilitator of the European dimension for three reasons. Quite simply, Europe is the product of history and history is about time. Yet it is not exclusively about the past. As a study of the whole field of human behaviour, events, thoughts and emotions, it helps to explain the actions of people in Europe today and the values of contemporary society. Could history be about Europe's future too? The assertion that history repeats itself has only become a cliché because it contains an element of truth. Assimilating the processes by which human kind has reached the present goes some way towards anticipating the problems of the future. A second consideration, complementing the first without replicating it, is that history enables us to make sense of Europe's qualitative dimension. European culture is not a product of the here-and-now; it is the legacy of two millennia of history. And lastly, the discipline of History is an indigenous product of European scholarship and, particularly, of the European Enlightenment. As a symposium of experts testified, 'History is a unique discipline, concerned with a special kind of training of the mind and the imagination.'[2]

Within the mainstream liberal tradition of scholarship prevailing in the Western world, historians feel obliged to eschew all forms of dogma, ideology and determinist bias as the basis for their explanations of the past.[3] Their professional obligation is to uncover the truth, however unpalatable, by a process of disinterested investigation. In reality, however, Western scholarship, like liberal democratic politics, favours the middle ground. Relying on two contrasting procedures, it subsumes contradiction. First, it assumes the freedom to interpret evidence without preconceptions and to apply imagination and intuitive judgement without intellectual constraints. This is no simple task because history is fraught with emotive issues which have to be interpreted, and interpretation is itself an ambivalent process. The second *modus operandi* is the search for a consensus as to what is appropriate and reasonable, a consensus that rejects extreme or irrational interpretations, inimical to humane values.

So, historical methodology does not have the precision of law, though just as democracy allows individual freedom subject to the law so Western historians enjoy freedom of interpretation, subject to the rules of scholarship. Their professional integrity prevents them from deliberate distortion of the truth or from indulging in personal prejudice and anachronism. They have an obligation to pay empathetic regard to people and events, to sift evidence carefully and to apply reason and common sense to its interpretation. But their conclusions are merely interpretations, so despite claims to objectivity, historians exercise a good deal of subjective judgement and choice. That is why they can and do disagree with one another and why their disagreements turn on shades of opinion. That is also why controversy spills over into the History curriculum and into teaching.[4]

By implication, History teaching is much more than recalling and regurgitating what is dead and gone. As skilful teachers know from experience, History is an opportunity for looking with pupils at the legacy of human creativity, assessing the impact of people on society, on the landscape and ideas; for considering the consequences and the factors which caused or conditioned human action. Teaching History helps the learner to develop empathy, an informed curiosity which leads to an appreciation of heritage. This awareness and propensity to identify with others is an important learning outcome. Affective skills, however, are complementary to cognitive skills. While reinforcing basic study skills, History directs the young towards evidence, which brings a range of skills into play: the power to think critically, to analyse objectively, assess, extrapolate, deduce, evaluate, synthesize material and arrive at reasoned judgements. Through the exercise of such skills pupils ought to be steered away from blatant bias and prejudice. But as well as enabling people to understand their fellow human beings a little better, History teaches them to probe and question, sometimes to doubt people's words and motives, or their behaviour. So in studying the human condition young people should acquire a healthy scepticism in their pursuit of truth. That was undoubtedly why Nikita Khrushchev labelled historians as 'dangerous people'.

History teaching as outlined above has slowly taken root in Europe. In the early 1970s the enquiry approach was known in the UK as the New History. It was embodied in the Schools Council 13–16 History Project, which has continued to inform the theory and practice of History teaching in England and Wales to the present day. The question of whether a majority of pupils can exercise mature historical skills has been, and still is, a source of controversy – there will always be teachers who regard History merely as a repository of factual knowledge – but the enquiry approach has been steadily assimilated into schools. The movement towards a skills-based approach was also influential in the Federal Republic. Between 1954 and 1979 the number of secondary school students in the various *Länder* pursuing academic courses increased sixfold. There was an urgent need to develop appropriate History syllabuses and from this situation came a reformed discipline, based upon the subject methodology, known as History Didactics.[5]

In the wake of these changes, teachers became aware of the apparent tension between the priorities of method and content. If History is to be perceived as being concerned with development and change, the essential ingredients of chronology and continuity have to be built into pupils' learning. These methodological features have obvious implications for the content of European History syllabuses, as well as for teaching methods. Questions relating to syllabus content have preoccupied everyone with a professional interest in History since well before the emergence of the New History. From the 1950s to the 1980s the Council of Europe made provision for its experts to discuss History textbook resources, the formative themes and periods of European History and their implications for the whole History curriculum as well as for interdisciplinary courses of study.[6] Those inquiries and colloquia kept History at the forefront of the Council of Europe's educational agenda. Now, at the approach of 1992, there is a pressing need to review History teaching again, to establish how History can transmit specialized, relevant knowledge about Europe. In so doing, we need to be reminded of the particular problems of European history, to take note of new trends and decide how best to convey, through the careful selection of content, the distinctiveness of Europe's past.

HISTORICAL BIAS: PROBLEMS, IMPLICATIONS AND CONTROVERSIES

If History were an entirely rational and objective science, there would be no cause to discuss the subject of bias and prejudice. But since this is not so, we ought perhaps to heed the warning that 'Textbook authors and teachers must avoid value judgements, either explicit or implicit . . . They should be neither

; nor detractors. They must avoid projecting back into the past ay or personal values which would be anachronistic.'[7] In fact, individual teachers, writers or media producers may express preferences or harbour prejudices reflecting academic fashion, but explicit bias is usually occasioned by other factors. Since History curricula have become reflectors of social norms and values, they are affected by the inevitable time-lag between society's present and past priorities.

To identify the problems associated with bias and discrimination in History, the Council of Europe sponsored an extensive programme over three decades. In the first phase, school textbooks were the primary focus of attention because they were, and in many cases still are, the main source of information for pupils. Partiality in books profoundly affects not only the accuracy and balance of the content taught but the attitudes and values that are consciously or subconsciously promoted. Those aspects came under scrutiny at a CDCC symposium on Teaching about the Portuguese Discoveries in Secondary Schools in Western Europe, held in Lisbon in 1983. Experts saw this theme as a key model for eliminating undesirable ethnocentric tendencies and attitudes of racial and cultural superiority. They stressed the importance of treating the maritime voyages as part of a wider European phenomenon of contacts and exchanges between peoples, rather than as a national triumph. A fresh CDCC initiative on the standards and functions of History textbooks was scheduled for the autumn of 1990, as a joint venture with the Georg Eckert Institute for International Textbook Research in Braunschweig.[8]

It was revealed by CDCC experts that the most common form of bias up to the late 1960s was the 'national' interpretation of the past, which treated history as the rise and fall of great nations, echoing the earlier 'drum and trumpet' school. In the opinion of E. H. Dance, who was centrally involved in the initiatives for textbook revision, 'The national bias which has done most harm in Europe and its textbooks is the internal nationalism of the European states themselves.'[9] He cited the tendency of textbook authors to give undue emphasis to the achievements of their own nation. So both French and English histories dwelt on the victories of their forces in the Hundred Years' War and the colonial wars of the eighteenth century, just as they are concerned primarily with their nation's role in the emergence of democracy and representative government and the contribution of their inventors and merchant-capitalists to the Industrial Revolution in Europe. The discovery of America is claimed by Italy (Christopher Columbus's birthplace) and by Spain (whose monarch employed him). German textbooks describe Copernicus as a German; others say he was Polish. In many accounts of the origins of European democracy, little or nothing is made of the Swiss cantons, the medieval town republics or the Marxist version of democracy.

National bias in 1990 may be less crude, even less widespread, than in 1960, but where it exists it is strongly entrenched. A recent CDCC report confirms that 'the French were overwhelmingly convinced of the significance of their revolution for the world, of the superiority of their revolution compared with the American and Russian ones.'[10] National history is again being promoted in the UK: the new provision for History in England and Wales is a national curriculum in both senses of that adjective. In Eastern Europe and the Soviet Union the present resurgence of nationalism is likely to have educational implications. In some cases there are profound reasons why national history should retain its place. In Poland, for example, all secondary students over the age of 13 years are taken to view Auschwitz as part of their historical experience: the justification needs no explanation. In what was West Germany, on the other hand, the textbooks produced after 1945 were written in a climate of contrition and reconciliation. At a *Gymnasium* in Baden-Württemberg, for example, the subject of Jewish genocide, the Nazi concentration camps and other aspects of National Socialism were taught in the context of tolerance between majorities and minorities and the development of democracy, while teachers and students at schools in Hanover and Berlin set a precedent by holding an exhibition to mark the fortieth anniversary of the *Reichskristallnacht*.[11] So History classes can make political statements. That is why national bias was supported in the Soviet Union for so long, why in May 1988 History was thrown into crisis and History examinations were cancelled in every Soviet school for lack of reliable History books.[12] The ensuing reappraisal of Modern History graphically illustrates the dangers of state-controlled history, in which questioning and critical thinking are suppressed and historians are compelled to act as publicists and propagandists for a regime. But in the era of *glasnost* and *perestroika*, modern history may become a new Soviet industry, as the scale and nature of the Stalinist purges are subjected to close historical scrutiny.

Residual examples of the 'Great Power' mentality exist in History curricula but small states also have their idiosyncratic traditions. While students in France undertake in-depth studies of the French Revolution (at 15 and 17 years), in Denmark study is confined to the Thermidorean period. In England, the history of the First French Empire is usually treated as a series of anti-Napoleonic, European-wide campaigns, whereas the Danes focus on hostility to British naval aggression.[13] General priorities also vary. For example, in Scandinavian curricula there is a greater emphasis on Modern World History, whereas in Italy prominence is given to Ancient and Medieval. However, bias takes many forms. The tendency to think in stereotypes or to use words simplistically shows a disregard for objective accuracy. Many words used in History lessons (known in English as 'weasel words') are ambiguous: 'villein', 'orthodox', 'civilized', 'democracy', 'nationalism' – or even 'Germany'. Stereotyped thinking extends to whole ethnic groups or nations. For generations of French people England was 'perfidious Albion'. Although the Turks are among the *Gastarbeiter* of the German economy, in history they have been depicted as barbaric warriors, given to committing atrocities upon their Christian subjects. The Jews (if they were not entirely overlooked) were synonymous with money-lenders.[14] These stereotypes may have been excluded from recent publications but their residual influence still affects popular thinking. Yet in the last two decades international organizations have striven to rectify such prejudice, and in its resolution of October 1987 on the Jewish contribution to European culture and development, the Parliamentary Assembly of the Council of Europe highlighted the insidious nature of bias by omission.

Some of the neglected areas of European curricula are as surprising as they are serious. In Western schools, Russian and Soviet history is badly served. Interest is largely confined to patches of foreign policy involving the Western powers. So Peter the Great's Westernizing policies, Catherine II's expansionism, the Eastern Question, and the Eastern Front in two world wars are over-emphasized at the expense of significant domestic themes. The opening up of Siberia, the influence of Russian Orthodoxy on society, serfdom and the modernization of agriculture and industry, the revolutionary changes in the socio-political structures or the nationalities' issue do not receive the attention they deserve. Similarly, the histories of the Scandinavian and Balkan countries are by convention treated in discontinuous patches of time: the Viking age, the reign of Gustavus Adolphus, the Turkish incursions after 1453 and the nineteenth-century Balkan Wars. And there has been slow recognition of the fact that 'beyond Europe are four more continents, each with a history rich in lessons of politics and economics and religion and culture.'[15] Young Europeans should be aware that European history is not a saga of isolation but of constant cross-fertilization, of exploration, migration and multiculturalism.

This touches on a sensitive and sometimes controversial issue arising from the fact that Europe is a pluralist society. History teachers have to ask the question, 'In what ways should the History curriculum be different because we live in a multicultural Europe?'. Each school's answer will be implicit in its ethos, and the issue of giving an international dimension to the curriculum will be explored in a later chapter. But the problems and misunderstandings which can arise from cultural diversity must be faced. Some experts recommend a cautious approach in adapting History syllabuses; for example, they suggest that all potentially sensitive topics involving issues of race and creed, particularly in a conflict situation, should be treated in a remote time context. Others reject this strategy as a form of cowardice which does nothing to resolve cultural variances. Others again feel that local and regional history have important lessons to offer by underlining the cultural richness which can come from old diversities. Many communities in contemporary Europe represent cultures which flourished and showed great distinctiveness long before the age of European colonization. These ancient ethnic groups include the Basques, the Celts, the Lapps and the Gypsies. The point here is that difference is a fundamental feature of European history, and controversial issues, involving almost irreconcilable viewpoints, cannot be avoided altogether. However, while the mutual mistrust between Christianity and Islam, for example, can be explained in historical terms, this should not prevent teachers from trying to present the history of Islam with dispassionate objectivity.

There are two other issues which have been the subject of unacceptable bias. Most textbooks published before the 1980s relegated the female sex to the sidelines of history. Where syllabuses dealt with the subject of women, they largely focused on those few who exercised an exceptional leadership role: Boadicea, Joan of Arc, Elizabeth I, Christina of Sweden, Maria Theresa, Catherine the Great. Some attention has belatedly been given to the struggle for the enfranchisement of women, such as the Suffragette Movement, and to the theme of women at work in the domestic, industrial, medical and aesthetic spheres. However, for the most part there was a tacit assumption before the 1970s that the history of men adequately covers the history of all peoples. The explanation for this state of affairs is quite clear. It is not that men distorted the past as the authors of History books but that women did not have a dominating role in political, military and diplomatic history: consequently, they had no natural place in the 'drum and trumpet' account of the past. Yet in 1985 the Schools Inspectorate of the United Kingdom recognized that 'women have played a part as agents of change both within elite groups and as part of mass movements' and for this reason 'it was no longer acceptable to pay scant attention to women's lives in history.'[16] This view was recently endorsed by President Mary Robinson of the Irish Republic, who observed in her inaugural speech that 'As a woman, I want women, who have felt themselves outside history, to be written back into "history".'

In fact, women worked in many trades alongside men, as farmers, textile spinners, blacksmiths, pedlars and shopkeepers, in addition to acting as apothecaries and physicians and carrying out domestic responsibilities. Germain Greer has publicized the neglected creativity of countless female artists. Until recently the talents of seventeenth-century women playwrights of the English Restoration period were overlooked by literary critics, although novelists such as Jane Austen and Charlotte Brontë were admired in their lifetimes. Women participated in the revolutionary organizations of late nineteenth-century Russia, like the Land and Freedom Movement, and women workers began the strikes which led to the outbreak of the 1917 revolution in the capital city, Petrograd. The Ladies' Land Leagues became a focus of support for Irish tenants during the 1880s. In France women were involved in establishing Republican clubs during the French Revolution and took part in the 1848 and 1871 uprisings. Women have acted as rulers and regents, as well as patrons of the arts throughout the centuries. It is important, therefore, that History curricula in all European countries raise questions as to why limitations were placed on women, why restrictive laws and customs endured for so long, why the language of older books depicts women in the inferior or deferential roles and when and how the process of female emancipation took place.

This discussion brings us close to what has been called bias by proportion or disproportion. The charge is commonly made that European History generally gives too much prominence to conflict, wars, diplomatic crises and revolutions, rather than to peaceful initiatives and attempts to give international co-operation a legal and juridical framework. The irony is that many schemes for teaching Peace Studies are little more than apologias for war. And although the importance of social history is recognized today, the cultural and intellectual movements of European society are rarely treated in the depth that they deserve. As to the much neglected area of scientific achievement, Dance singled out Scandinavian History books as being unusually farsighted in their treatment of the history of science and their recognition of the importance of scientific advances in the history of human progress.

If science has engineered the major changes of the modern world, religion was the dominant force of medieval and early modern Europe. Yet in many secular quarters ecclesiastical history is a highly unfashionable subject. In the UK national curriculum, the Reformation may cease to be taught as a discrete subject in the 1990s. So it is worth recalling that religious bias, which stained so much of European history, produced its own versions of history. Catholic and Protestant interpretations are still alive in parts of Western Europe and it would be naive to assume that other religions in Europe's multicultural communities are above the fray of historical controversy. There could be genuine dilemmas here for History teachers. On the one hand, materialism and secularism, reinforced by state policy, have so undermined organized religion in many European countries that religious history has apparently become an irrelevancy. But the failure of Western curricula and textbooks to do justice to the history of the Orthodox Church and the Eastern Empire centred on Byzantium is a sad commentary on value judgements which have written off some 1200 years of history, culture and spirituality, and it does invite the reminder that:

> In all periods, religion has been a major component of society. To avoid teaching it ... is to be lacking in historical truth. Consequently, it is inadmissible that religion should have disappeared almost completely from most of the textbooks ... and from contemporary history syllabuses.[17]

What is now clear is that European History curricula twenty years ago were decidedly national, political, monocultural and ethnocentric. They were based on two premises. First, History was the history of Western European civilization, and contacts between Europe and the rest of the world, such as those in the Ages of Exploration and Colonialism, were taught in a Eurocentric way. Secondly, Western European civilization was presented as *étatiste*, its 1000-year history crowned by nationalism. It may seem negative, even irrelevant, to dwell on this situation, but in fact that is not so: first, because not all countries have succeeded in abandoning these perspectives, and secondly because they constitute a refuge for the more timid teachers who cling to deep-rooted conventions. Yet, ironically, when there was a move during the 1970s and 1980s to abandon the old conventions and come to terms with Europe as a complex society with strong interdependent, transnational, multicultural features, the cry went up that European History was becoming too Europe-centred. Obviously, a myopic Eurocentrism would serve History and pupils little better than hypernationalism; any overt bias is both undesirable and unwarranted.

In planning new European History curricula for the 1990s, it is essential that we start with an understanding of Europe that circumvents the pejorative charge of Eurocentrism. It is also necessary to establish the areas in which History has a specific contribution to make to pupil understanding of Europe.

THE CONTRIBUTION OF HISTORY TO EUROPEAN AWARENESS

History may be an awkward and controversial discipline in some respects, but almost half the twenty goals for teaching about Europe (see pp. 36–7) point to its symbiotic function in activating a sense of European awareness. History can contribute a knowledge of time, an appreciation of heritage, a sense of perspective and an awareness of Europe as a generic entity. Of these, the first is unique to History, and the continuum of historical time acts as a yardstick for the whole of European development.

The point that History should give the young a sense of time is fundamental. European History has the chronological spread to give substantive meaning to the concept of chronology, whereas national histories are a more variable medium. Europe also provides a useful resource for learning about the strength of continuity and the counter-force of change and to enable pupils to identify rates of development and explanations of cause and effect. The teacher's task is to provide progression of learning, since discontinuous study is a disincentive to European awareness. The achievements of classical Greece and Rome are important in Europe's prehistory but they cannot explain its subsequent evolution. Medieval Europe may demonstrate the continuity of Europe's economic or hierarchical systems and pupils may come to realize that change can be retrogressive as well as progressive; but from a study of medieval Europe only they could not appreciate the force of nationalism or of secular ideology on human action. And although a body of opinion favours twentieth-century studies for older secondary students, their knowledge needs to be based on a grounding of earlier periods of European history, for the obvious reason that contemporary issues are rooted in an historical context. For instance, issues such as the Irish question, German unification, the inviolability of Poland's frontiers, moves towards democratic government and the protection of human rights, neutrality and the neutral nations, the power of regionalism, the significance of areas of convergence – European 'crossroads', such as Belgium, Luxembourg, Alsace-Lorraine, southern Italy, Czechoslovakia or Hungary – can only be sensibly approached through a lengthy timespan.[18] So although History determines Europe today, pupils gain from a chronological understanding of Europe's past.

That point was implicit in the recommendations of two important Council of Europe gatherings. The 1965 Elsinor Symposium on Teaching History proposed twenty-five themes illustrating the development of Europe, and the conclusions of the CDCC teachers' seminar on The Viking Age, held at Larkollen in 1986, confirmed the principle of basing the curriculum on broad themes which display a chronological spread (Table 2 and Figure 3). Both sets of

Table 2 A comparison of the Elsinor and Larkollen themes

Twenty-five Elsinor themes	Twenty-three Larkollen themes and topics
What Europe owes to civilizations past and present: Greek, Roman, Byzantine;★ Judaism, Christianity, Islam, etc.	The relationships between local and European history; or how to use the local environment as a teaching resource about European history
The Great Migrations in Europe	Science and technology as a theme in teaching European history
Feudalism	
The Church	The emancipation of women in European history
Rural conditions and towns in the Middle Ages	Migration in European history
The Crusades	Banking and bankers in European history
Representative institutions and legal principles	The Jews in Europe
Medieval thought and art	Europe and the Arab world
Humanism: the Renaissance	Europe and Islam
The religious reform movements	The Mediterranean in European history
The voyages of discovery and expansion overseas	The Baltic in European history
	Southern Europe as a crossroads of cultures
The development of capitalism	The Danube in European history
The rise of the modern states	Classical Greece
Absolute government and representative government	The Romans in Europe
	Co-existence of Christianity, Islam and Judaism in medieval Toledo
Classicism and Baroque	The monastic orders
The age of Enlightenment	Pilgrims/pilgrimages in Europe
The Industrial/Agricultural Revolutions	The Crusades
Eighteenth- and nineteenth-century revolutions and liberalism/nationalism	The Hansa
Socialism	The Renaissance
Intellectual and artistic, scientific/technical developments of the nineteenth and twentieth centuries	The Industrial Revolution
	The French Revolution
	1848 in European history
European expansion in the world and the formation of colonial empires	
The two world wars	
Democracy, Communism and Fascism	
Europe in the world today	
Trends towards European unity in the different periods of European history	

★ Attention should be drawn to the place of Byzantine history in medieval civilization. Byzantine culture should be examined, and common elements, as well as differences between Western and Eastern history, should be observed.

recommendations include the contribution of Greek, Roman and Islamic civilizations to Europe and of particular peoples, such as the Jews and the Arabs; aspects of the medieval Church, such as the monastic orders, pilgrim movements and the Crusades; the impact of large-scale migrations; the development of banking, capitalism and trade in early modern Europe; the Renaissance; the importance of science and technology; the Industrial Revolution; and lastly the revolutions of the eighteenth and nineteenth centuries associated with the rise of liberalism, nationalism and democracy. If the Larkollen representatives placed greater emphasis on social history and the importance of specific groups of peoples, including women, in contrast to the abstract or political language of the Elsinor themes, this merely illustrates the change in historical priorities. However, by comparing these two lists sufficient compatibility of subject matter emerges to group them into areas of common European historicial experience and these could (indeed, one might argue, *should*) be taken into account in designing History curricula. Certainly, the Elsinor–Larkollen themes are the basis for further discussion if CDCC experts and European teachers would like to see a greater harmonization of History curricula. Furthermore, the correlated Elsinor–Larkollen themes provide the basis for either a discrete historical approach to Europe or an interdisciplinary approach, according to national or local preferences.

History's second important attribute is as a stimulus to the concept of 'heritage'. Until the 1980s there was little popular consciousness of the legacy of the past: it was largely the preserve of professional specialists such as archaeologists, antiquarians and art historians. That has now changed and there has been a revolution in attitudes as Europe's heritage has come into its own. People now appreciate that Europe's past is many-sided; it is to be valued and cherished as a source of personal and spiritual enrichment; above all, there is concern that it should be preserved for posterity. The inheritance of the history may be enshrined in a single building or may relate to the individuality of a locality or region; it may be the product of a movement or mode of creativity, evident within a wide area that crosses national boundaries, as the current Council of Europe initiatives on Cultural Routes illustrate. It may also be found in the realm of thought and ethics: although Christianity and the French Revolution left different legacies to democratic Europe, the impact of their ideas is as much a part of Europe's heritage as the artefacts and monuments made with human hands. It is one of History's functions to explain and evaluate such a diverse inheritance.

History also gives a sense of perspective to students' learning, which is one of the principal benefits of studying the subject in depth. The time perspective is the historical context in which we assess events, people and ideas, and it is vital that pupils build up a sense of sequence. But History is also concerned with spatial perspectives because there has always been an interaction between time and place. Some teachers believe that a concentric curricular model is an effective instrument for developing this combined perspective. The curricular starting point is local history because this often represents processes at work on a wider scale. By selecting localized examples, it is possible to develop a comparative approach to a topic, a strategy which is by no means new but has often proved effective.

In the interests of balance, it would be wrong to neglect the national perspective, with the proviso that whenever possible national developments should be related to local and European movements. In addition, when the themes being studied lend themselves to international or global treatment, the opportunity to exploit a wider perspective should not be missed. Some themes of European

51

history, such as exploration and colonization, are especially valuable as 'a window into other cultures'; that is to say, as introductions to the rich, contrastive civilizations of the Middle and Far East, Africa and the Americas, to which Europe is in various ways indebted.

Finally, European History can develop European awareness if teaching concentrates on the shared experiences and common environmental influences which unify Europeans. This is not a battle-cry against diversity, especially of a cultural and social kind. Nor does it imply that Brussels or Strasbourg should impose a single interpretation of European history by a blanket curriculum. However, there is a perverse tendency in some quarters to support the ideal of common European initiatives while decrying specific attempts to focus on the unifying features of the past; and sometimes this results in muddled thinking about goals and outcomes. If we accept the substance of Goal 18 from the list on pp. 36–7 ('To develop in pupils greater empathy and awareness of . . . a pluralist society, while drawing strength from those movements, organizations and aspirations promoting unity within Europe') then we should not be coy about the implications of unity in the classroom or lecture room.

As far back as 1953 the first Council of Europe Colloquy on The European Idea in History Teaching expressed the hope that 'a European view of history will emerge.' Echoes of this were heard in 1965 at the Elsinor Symposium: 'As far as possible, history should be presented from the European point of view.'[19] Much water has flowed under the bridge since those pleas for a synthesis of European history. Although the notion was attacked in the interim as an example of Eurocentrism, it was given fresh impetus by the recommendations of the 1983 symposium on Teaching about the Portuguese Discoveries, and in 1988 by the 39th European Teachers' Seminar on Teaching about the French Revolution in Secondary Schools. Both stressed the commonality of those legacies, suggesting that since the 1980s teachers seem willing to co-operate in seeking homogeneous interpretations of some of the seminal episodes of European history. There have been renewed requests for History textbooks for use across Europe. Not all authorities agree with such a policy, and some teachers might prefer investment in communication technology to facilitate the exchange of information and documentation. But representatives at the teachers' seminar on the French Revolution hoped for 'a co ordinated, large-scale operation, with the goal of producing a true "textbook of European history" . . . enabling national points of view to be placed in a wider setting . . . whilst working towards a broad consensus as far as possible on the way history should be written.'[20]

The subject of unity raises other questions. For instance, should teachers deliberately teach about European integration and co-operation? If so, how can these subjects be taught? Since 1965, when the Elsinor Symposium recommended the theme 'Trends towards European unity in the different periods of the history of Europe', the answer seems to be 'yes' to the first question, for Elsinor was followed by other conferences at which the theme of unity and integration was keenly explored. Yet in practice History teachers have had mixed success. An attempt to teach about The Move to European Unity in a UK national History project during the 1970s was not conspicuously appealing to the 13–16 year olds. In the stark sentiments of one secondary teacher, 'Post-war Europe is a boring subject.'[21] That kind of attitude places a good deal of strain on teachers' energies and imaginations, but it also poses questions about the ways young people learn and the difficulties of altering perceptions. A decade later, an international History project on The History of European Integration, which had a similar syllabus, resulted in somewhat more constructive attitudes, in the opinion of a Danish teacher involved.[22] The project evaluation produced an important clue to the more positive outcome: the pupils were fascinated by the idea of taking part in a common European venture. This suggests that unity and co-operation cannot be *taught* by formal means, but can perhaps be nurtured by example or experienced through active learning.

At the same time, the notion of unity can no longer be treated in the curriculum as the integration of Western Europe, much less the Community of the Twelve. Modern History syllabuses in the 1990s will have to catch up with political reality and abandon the old bifocal view of Europe in favour of an all-embracing concept. The exchange of information between countries, the resources for updating teaching materials and, most of all, the need for in-service training to expand teachers' knowledge of hitherto neglected areas of history, the knowledge of teachers in Western European of the history of Eastern Europe and vice versa, with special attention to historical themes and areas of common experience: these should be some of the priorities for the 1990s. The Council of Europe has anticipated these needs in its History programme for 1990–2. The fact that enquiry methods, active learning and the new information and communication technology are increasingly superseding traditional teaching methods has implications for teachers as well as students. In addition to encouraging contacts and exchanges, the number of extra-curricular activities with a historical dimension should increase, on the lines of the CDCC programmes for developing cultural routes and the UK Young Historians scheme to encourage students to undertake active research projects.[23]

There can be no doubt as to the singular contribution of History to European awareness. But three out of the four elements identified – awareness of unity (and diversity), sense of perspective and appreciation of heritage – are shared by other disciplines in the Arts and Human Sciences. In looking at the other two dimensions of Europe, we need to examine the nature and contribution of these other disciplines, seeking how the natural linkages can be exploited through multi- or interdisciplinary studies (Figure 3).

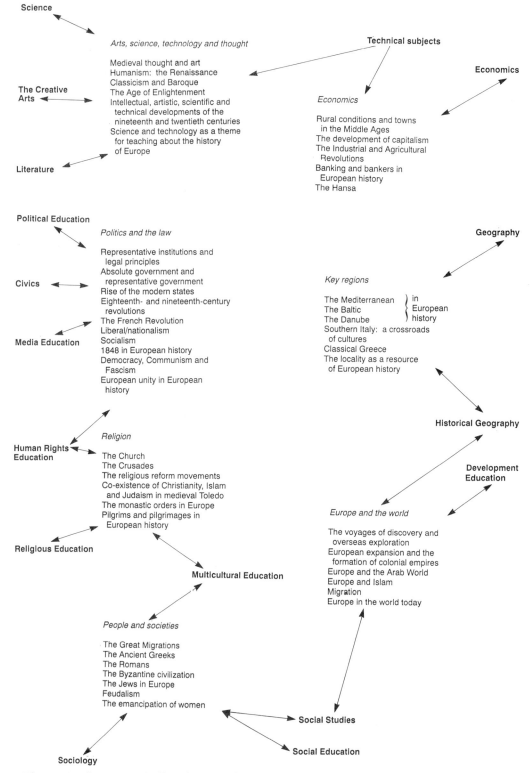

Figure 3 Elsinor–Larkollen themes of European history and cross-curricular links

---

SUMMARY OF PRINCIPLES FOR ENCOURAGING EUROPEAN AWARENESS THROUGH HISTORY CURRICULA

1 Syllabuses should reflect the distinctive character of Europe's past, and progression in complexity of subject matter.

2 Elements of shared experience common to parts or the whole of Europe should take precedence over divisive factors. 'Shared experience' should be interpreted widely; there should be no disproportionate emphasis on political unity.

3 European History should be seen as a synthesis of subject matter; for example, social, economic, cultural, artistic, spiritual, ethical and political.

4 The History curriculum as a whole should contain internal balance: Europe should not be seen in isolation but should be linked (for instance, by topics and case-studies) to local, regional and national developments and to the world context of other civilizations.

5 The teaching of European History should take account of discovery/enquiry methods, incorporating the main concepts of historical method, such as chronology, continuity, change, cause, consequence, impartiality, evidence and empathy.

6 Mechanisms for developing links with other subjects should be pursued, either in the History curriculum or in an interdisciplinary framework.

7 Active learning methods should take preference over formal methods and maximum use should be made of media, NICT facilities and extra-curricular learning in one or more European countries.

8 Modes of assessment and evaluation should concentrate on the encouragement of motivation and positive attitudes towards Europe, as well as on the understanding of concepts and the development of general historical skills.

NOTES

1 As, for example, in Goodson, I. F., and McGivney, V. (1985), *European Dimensions and the Secondary School Curriculum*, Lewes: The Falmer Press, p. 58. History will be spelt with a capital 'H' when referring to the school subject; when used in a general sense it will have a lower-case letter 'h'.

2 Symposium on History Teaching in Lower Secondary Education, held at Braunschweig, Federal Republic of Germany, 22–6 September 1969, reported in (1986) *Against Bias and Prejudice: The Council of Europe's Work on History Teaching and History Textbooks*, Strasbourg: Council of Europe, p. 33.

3 The commonest form of determinist bias is Marxism, but the reactionary-conservative tradition in Spain should not be forgotten: Montes, Rafael Valls (1983), *The Interpretation of the Spanish History and Its Ideological Roots Given in the Francoist Secondary Education System (1938–1953)*, University of Valencia: ICE.

4 Audoin-Rouzeau, Stephane (1988), *Report of the 39th European Teachers' Seminar on Teaching about the French Revolution in Secondary Schools in Europe, Donaueschingen*, Strasbourg: Council of Europe, pp. 4–5, indicates the effect on school History of the interpretations of the French Revolution by historians such as Soboul, Godechot, Furet, Cobb and Cobban.

5 This is explained in Rudeng, Erik (1979), *Report of the 4th European Teachers' Seminar on New Trends in History Teaching in Upper Secondary Education, Donaueschingen, May 1979*, Strasbourg: Council of Europe, pp. 32, 40–3.

6 The principal conferences on textbooks and symposia on History teaching were: The European Idea in History Teaching (Calw, 1953); The Middle Ages (Oslo, 1954); The Sixteenth Century (Rome, 1955); The Seventeenth and Eighteenth Centuries (Royaumont, 1956); The Period from *c.* 1789 to *c.* 1871 (Scheveningen, 1957); The Period from *c.* 1870 to *c.* 1950 (Istanbul and Ankara, 1958); Religion in School History Textbooks in Europe (Louvain, 1972); Co-operation in Europe since 1945, as presented in Resources for the Teaching of History, Geography and Civics in Secondary Schools (Braunschweig, 1979); Symposium on History Teaching in Secondary Education (Elsinor, 1965); Symposium on History Teaching in Lower Secondary Education (Braunschweig, 1969); Meeting of Experts on History Teaching in Upper Secondary Education (Strasbourg, 1971); Symposium on Teaching about the Portuguese Discoveries in Secondary Schools in Western Europe (Lisbon, 1983). There were in addition a number of teachers' seminars on aspects of History teaching, such as The Viking Age in Europe (1986) and Teaching about the French Revolution (1988). Plans have been made for a series of initiatives for 1990–3.

7 Summary of the *Report of the Symposium on Religion in School History Textbooks in Europe*, in *Against Bias and Prejudice*, p. 20.

8 Slater, J. (1990), *Report of the Educational Research Workshop on History and Social Studies – Methodologies of Textbook Analysis, Braunschweig, September 1990*, Strasbourg: Council of Europe.

9 Dance, E. H. (1967), *History Teaching and History Textbook Revision*, Strasbourg: Council of Europe, pp. 80–1.

10 *Report on the 39th European Teachers' Seminar on Teaching about the French Revolution*, p. 4.

11 Marict, F. (1980), *Report of the 8th European Teachers' Seminar on The Teaching of Human Rights in Upper Secondary Education, Donaueschingen, May 1980*, Strasbourg: Council of Europe, p. 22; Dance, *History Teaching*, pp. 76–7.

12 Recent political events in the USSR and in other parts of Central and Eastern Europe have also prompted an urgent re-examination of the centralized syllabuses and textbook approval. Slater, *Report of the Educational Research Workshop on History and Social Studies*, p. 6.

13 *Report on Teaching about the French Revolution*, pp. 13–14.

14 Dance, *History Teaching*, pp. 78–9, 91.

15 *Ibid*, p. 74.

16 Department of Education and Science (1985), *History in the Primary and Secondary Years: An HMI View*, London: HMSO, pp. 29–30.

17 *Against Bias and Prejudice*, p. 19.

18 For instance, on the teaching of Human Rights, Mariet reminds us that 'There is unquestionably a need for a historical approach . . . It is history, alas, which can best remind us how wide a gap there is between law and reality' (Report on the Teaching of Human Rights, p. 6).

19 *Against Bias and Prejudice*, pp. 10, 29.

20 *Report on Teaching about the French Revolution*, p. 8. We should also note a contrary, though arguably a minority, view that 'We should more readily anticipate a future where the role of textbooks may be diminished or marginalised', expressed in Slater, *Report of the Educational Research Workshop on History and Social Studies*, p. 14.

21 Goodson and McGivney, *European Dimensions*, pp. 74–5. A cognate point was made by Professor Louis Warzee (Belgium) at the CDCC course on Europe in Primary School, held at Gazzada (Varese) in 1983, when he suggested 'teachers, in general, are not interested in European problems': see (1983) *Report of the European Teachers' Seminar on Europe in Primary School*, Strasbourg: Council of Europe, p. 3.

22 Hojris, Orla (1987), 'An example of European teaching', in Shennan, M. (1987), *Report of the European Teachers' Course on Teaching about European Co-operation and Integration in Upper Secondary Schools, Ebeltoft, Denmark, March 1987*, Strasbourg: Council of Europe, pp. 11–19.

23 These will be discussed further in the context of extra-curricular activities, p. 93; also in 1990 the Wolfson Foundation offered financial incentives for evidence of good methodological practice by groups of students working on the theme of Cultural Links with Europe.

CHAPTER 4

The Spatial Dimension of Europe in the Curriculum

EUROPE AND THE NATURE OF GEOGRAPHY IN SECONDARY SCHOOLS

Most statements on teaching about Europe defer to the central importance of Geography.[1] The reason may seem obvious: it is a subject with a direct relevance to current events, enabling pupils to make informed judgements about the economic, political, social and environmental issues of everyday life. The justification can, however, be couched in simpler terms. Europe is a *place* – an area, a landmass and a continent – and Geography is first and foremost about area or place. Its association with that concept makes it the natural curricular medium for teaching about Europe.

To non-geographers this thesis has a natural logic, and most teachers committed to Europe in the curriculum would probably be grateful if their pupils continued to acquire a basic framework of knowledge about the physical structure and environment of Europe. In other words, the old-fashioned Geography syllabus, with its emphasis on physical features and regional variations within a national framework – rivers, mountain ranges, coastlines, lowlands, capital cities, products, crops and natural resources – served a useful purpose. It provided students with essential information, the 'nuts and bolts' of Europe. The fact that content was usually descriptive rather than analytical and that learning depended heavily on memorization of detailed fact is now considered a deficiency to be balanced against the knowledge acquired. But in its limited and mechanical approach, the 'capes and bays' method, which resembled the 'drum and trumpet' school of History teaching, prevailed until the 1950s.

In practice, traditional physical and regional Geography has had a varied fortune in European curricula. Through the knowledge explosion, the proliferation of the Social Sciences, and the influence of American child-centred education, traditional Geography syllabuses came under fire in parts of Europe, notably the UK and the Nordic countries. At the same time, the notion of 'the region' was criticized for signifying the continuity and uniqueness of 'place'.[2]

The weakness of the original premise (as a Belgian geographer implied recently) is that Europe and its regions are not cast in stone. Europe is a dynamic concept and there is increasing appreciation of Jean Gottmann's view of Europe. As a British geographer said in 1982, with the realities of the Common Agricultural Policy in mind, 'Mountains, rivers, valleys do not have the influence they did. The New Europe is even more man-made than the old. The beef mountains and wine lakes may be more significant in the long run than a real mountain and a real lake.'[3] Geography's contribution to an understanding of contemporary Europe is therefore considerably more complex than was thought in the past. Concurrently its scope has expanded to the point where it overlaps with several disciplines. The present subject includes urban geography (which has strong affinities with social history), environmental and development studies, political and cultural geography and aspects of geomorphology and climatology. It is hardly surprising that experts regard Geography as 'a field of study' rather than a discrete discipline.

However, there are good grounds for pleading that the physical and regional geography of Europe should be retained or reinstated in European curricula, as the case may be. Indeed, Physical Geography, with its classification of countries on physico-climatic criteria, the emphasis on frontiers and the physical divisions of countries into regions, held firm in France. It also continued to affect Geography teaching in countries like Spain, Switzerland and Belgium where the French school of Geography (derived from the great Vidal de la Blache) remained influential in curricular thinking.[4] There were echoes of this approach in a recommendation emerging from a recent major CDCC symposium on geographical documentation, that Geography's first contribution to education should be the development of 'an understanding of the location, configuration and diversity of physical and human environments of Europe'.[5] Yet, if the spatial dimension is still seen as Geography's base line, it is interpreted by experts in increasingly sophisticated terms. At the end of the same symposium, the rapporteur said in his summing up,

> The fact that the subject of geography now deals with the themes of spatial differentiation, spatial interaction and spatial organization, rather than static descriptions of states and regions, makes it particularly useful for developing in pupils and students an understanding of the dynamics of change in the Europe of the 1990s.[6]

So, accepting that school Geography is a protean area of the curriculum, the statement that teachers should use it to inform their students about Europe's basic physical and human resources is a welcome declaration.

Such a recommendation may help to give a common purpose to European teachers of Geography, many of whom have been diverted by other considerations in the previous decades. Certainly, the emergence in the 1960s of the New Geography, to which I have alluded, brought many changes in its wake. There was a growing debate on the balance of content and the relative significance of physical and human geography, but more significantly, the New

Geography was categorized as one of the Human Sciences and claimed to operate a scientific methodology. Emphasis was placed on skills, the use of spatial theory, models and quantitative data. Regional and Physical Geography lost out in countries such as England, Scotland and Sweden (as well as the USA) to in-depth study of general themes and sample topics or case-studies, chosen for their capacity to illustrate newly promoted concepts, exemplified by pattern and process.[7] There was tension between the relative importance of knowledge as against process or methods of learning, and before the 1980s some British teachers were expressing concern that *process* had become too prominent at the expense of the *content* of learning, a development which was particularly germane to the arguments in favour of teaching about Europe.

In the context of the New Geography, Europe was no longer considered an important subject of enquiry but had become a mere source of case-studies on which teachers could draw to illustrate global themes and topics. Michael Williams, himself an expert on European studies, crystallized the problem faced by teachers who saw the developments in geographical methodology as a threat to the European dimension then being actively promoted:

> Some geographers argue that the selection of which places to study is a secondary matter . . . The selection of place will be made on the basis that the places will most usefully serve the process of learning already determined. Thus, European places will be set alongside other places and these European places will not have any intrinsic value simply because they are located in Europe.[8]

Meanwhile, from the 1970s school Geography took different directions. In some European countries the subject ceased to be taught as a discrete discipline. In the Federal Republic of Germany, Norway and Sweden it was subsumed into multidisciplinary programmes and became a component of Civics or Social Studies. A different problem arose in Spain, where Geography has commonly been taught by historians or teachers of other disciplines. Pupils' perceptions of Europe were frequently inaccurate: a 1989 enquiry showed that 40 per cent of Spanish high-school students were unable to cite any city in the Netherlands, but many thought Brussels was in that country. Information about Europe in texts was fragmented.[9] From the other side of Europe, Yugoslavia, came the suggestion that Geography was too 'compartmentalized'.[10] Yet in the UK the once 'New Geography' was overtaken by different, sometimes radical, approaches which gave the subject a comprehensive rather than a restrictive function. Statistical method and the obsession with skills gave way to a renewed interest in the human, political and cultural aspects of society. The People–Environment theme, opening up issues and problems, gained popularity. This suggested that Geography had come full circle since a French government instruction of 1880 emphasized its affective role in encouraging empathetic understanding. Indeed, the geographer's concern with attitudes and with notions of culture as the behaviour of individuals, groups or institutions and the socio-cultural context of human interaction was restated in the opening address at the Utrecht Symposium in 1989.[11] However, there is still some way to go before Geography teaching is based on a broadly agreed European foundation, either in theory or in practice. The need to harmonize available information about Europe marks one stage in this process. A degree of progress was made by the European Standing Conference of Geography Teachers' Associations. A bulletin entitled *Eurogeo*, with documentation on geographical aspects of European countries, has been published since 1981 by a working group representing twelve states. Yet the resourcing of Geography teaching and learning by means of textbooks, atlases and the new information and communication technology is clearly a matter of continuing concern.

THE COUNCIL OF EUROPE AND GEOGRAPHY TEACHING

A quarter of a century ago the Council of Europe focused its attention on the quality of Geography textbooks and atlases and found them wanting. Four international conferences were held in the period 1961–4 to examine the printed materials used in teaching about the major European regions, and it was discovered that there were many common weaknesses: frequent examples of distortion and bias, a tendency to dwell on the exotic and to compress information so that it was inaccurate or misleading (as in the representation of the Netherlands as a land of windmills, clogs and cheese markets), and failure to explain the individuality of smaller countries (including Austria, Belgium, Denmark and Portugal). As a result of these criticisms and for the benefit of future authors, in 1967 the Council commissioned E. C. Marchant's work on *Geography Teaching and the Revision of Geography Textbooks and Atlases*, which included a 7-point code of practice. Teachers and writers of European Geography were urged in future to:

- think very carefully before omitting a description of any single country;
- avoid undue emphasis on the colourfully romantic elements of a country;
- beware of overemphasizing the difficulties of the physical environment, especially of giving the impression that little has been done to overcome them;
- ensure that statistics on which generalizations are based are up to date and accurate;
- in simplifying material for young pupils, avoid descending to untruths or half-truths, while refraining from prejudice in statements of opinion;
- try to empathize with other people while being fully informed about them;
- remember that in Europe no country is an isolated, self-sufficient entity, but every country is part of the common civilization of Europe.[12]

Yet there remains a need for vigilance in the matter of standards, and authors still bear a heavy responsibility.

Furthermore, since 1967 the scope of and access to geographical knowledge have been affected by the audiovisual media. However, since statistical information in textbooks can be out of date by the time it is published, a Danish authority, Professor Ove Billmann, suggested that authors ought to leave such data to information technology and 'concentrate on trying to develop in students images of place and country and of regional and global relations, conflicts and developments'.[13] Of other helpful works produced by CDCC experts to assist in the planning, teaching and assessing Geography curricula, mention should be made of a glossary of common geographical terms, published in six languages: Dutch, English, French, German, Italian and Spanish. E. C. Marchant's compilation of *The Countries of Europe as Seen by their Geographers* (1970) clarified the presentation of twenty-one countries in Geography lessons, and his edition of *The Teaching of Geography at School Level* covered both primary and secondary school Geography in twenty European states. A detailed curriculum study on Geography teaching at the upper secondary level was produced by J. W. Morris in the European Curriculum Studies series, a multi-volume project on curricula and examinations.[14]

During the 1960s the CDCC also embarked on a strategy for the collection and dissemination of accurate information, and this remains a high priority in its educational policy. In 1965 the Committee of Ministers passed a resolution for the creation of national information and documentation centres. The setting up at Utrecht of the Information and Documentation Centre for the Geography of the Netherlands (IDG) and the designation of the International Schoolbook Institute in Braunschweig as a European clearing-house for the exchange of information on Geography and History textbooks followed. These institutions supplement the work of various national organizations established at government or official level, or of private bodies such as La Maison de la Géographie at Montpellier in France. The impact of an institution like the IDG cannot be measured simply in the number of requests received for information. It is clear, from the example of the printed data gathered by the IDG on the Netherlands, that the availability of accurate material can greatly improve pupils' perceptions. The revision of published data, however, is a continuous process. School atlases may be better in technical terms than they were in the 1960s but publishers still need reminding that to meet the needs of the 1990s they should cover European themes – communications, trade, tourism, cultural features – as well as individual countries, to illustrate the interaction between states. Continuing concern that accurate data should be available to teachers led to the joint sponsorship by the CDCC and the IDG of the Symposium at Utrecht in September 1989 on Geographical Information and Documentation on European Countries. This provided a much-needed opportunity, not only to assess progress on the matter of data transmission, but to review on a European, rather than on a national, basis the effects on Geography teaching of the changes of the 1980s, the impact of the new information and communication technology, and, perhaps most importantly, the implications for establishing a European dimension in the curriculum.

In the event, this symposium should be seen as a landmark in Geography teaching. Agreement was reached on the use of NICT and on the pre- and in-service training of teachers facing an integrated Europe. The preparation of a handbook of sources of geographical information on European countries, a survey of Geography teaching and a new work to replace the study undertaken a generation ago by E. C. Marchant were also recommended. But of the three broad discussion areas on the agenda, the representation of the geography of European countries in the school textbooks of different countries was arguably the subject with the most direct curricular feedback. The participants shed light on what is being taught in European schools and what is still being omitted, the improvements in syllabuses, textbooks and atlases since the mid-1960s, and the areas which should be given greater prominence to meet both the changed social, political and economic climate of the 1990s, and also the requirements of the European Community and the Council of Europe with regard to a Euro-pean dimension. Their deliberations produced informal guidelines on two im-portant issues: first, the definition of teaching goals for Geography in t. e 1990s, and secondly, suggestions for appropriate European syllabus content.

TEACHING GOALS AND A EUROPEAN CURRICULUM

If Geography teaching is to play a useful part in European education, it has to respond to certain realities. The first is the complexity of Europe as a physical and human environment. Pupils need to know that there are various political groupings with different characteristics; and, for instance, the fact that the USSR stretches beyond the traditional confines of Europe affects its political and social complexion. Secondly, teachers and students must face the rapid integration occurring in Europe as socio-economic barriers are being disman-tled. The effects of integration are very much a geographer's concern. After 1992 there will be economies of scale and greater competition between large-scale corporations and national enterprises. It will be important for the young to learn at school about the geographical patterns underlying these develop-ments and to be well-informed about other countries before they undertake further education and training prior to entering the labour market.

In the past, change and economic competition have all too frequently led European nations into conflict. The lesson which has been learned since 1945 is that economic co-operation can and should override divisive competition. Students need to comprehend the challenge of change and develop the aptitude for co-operation with other Europeans to resolve mutual problems. This entails developing empathetic understanding for others, especially those whose ways of life are rooted in different cultural origins. It is a matter of appreciating both the common cultural elements and the rich diversity of cultures in such a way that bias and stereotyped thinking are eliminated and cultural identity is preserved in the New Europe. Geography is an essential curricular tool in this process. As the Director of the IDG observed, 'Sound geographical infor-mation is indispensable to the creation and dissemination of satisfactory "images" of the countries of Europe because geography provides the frame-work within which many economic, social and cultural activities take place.'[15]

At the same time, Geography teaching, like History teaching, must avoid being too Eurocentric. In the past, publishers of atlases were particularly guilty of this fault. A Dutch publishing manager urged a better balance, in line with the present trend in Belgium, Switzerland, Denmark, Finland and the Nether-lands, where maps of Europe constitute about one third (over 30 per cent) of the content of atlases.[16] In future, world maps should also illustrate various land distributions and projections on which Europe is not necessarily central. The global context would underline the interdependence of countries on which the relationship between Europe and the rest of the world is based. In the opinion of many Western educators, Geography is the subject best able to tackle world issues in the classroom and it is therefore most important for promoting international understanding.

Finally, Geography education is concerned with the development of skills. In addition to affective skills such as showing tolerance or empathy, students should acquire and apply a range of cognitive skills – analysis, evaluation, classification and synthesis, the application of concepts and theories – and the practical and participatory skills associated with undertaking fieldwork in another European environment. Although Geography teachers led the way in exploiting excursions, trips, exchanges and other means of active learning, they now recognize the potential offered by the new electronic media and interactive videos for establishing pupil contacts and facilitating joint school projects. In some cases, such as the European Studies Project of Ireland and Great Britain (which began in 1986–7 with two model projects to link students of 16–18 and 11–16 years in Northern Ireland and Belgium, extending by September 1990 to include the Republic of Ireland, England, Belgium, France and West Germany), the aim is to provide groups, classes and individual pupils with opportunities for collaborative work in Geography and History, combin-ing the use of E-mail (electronic mail) and residential contact. This kind of project involves training students in a set of information technology skills.[17]

So the aims of teaching European Geography follow the conventional requirements of learning, the acquisition of knowledge, skills, attitudes and values. Syllabus content ought to reflect the broad goals which have been identified, taking account of the age and ability of pupils. For younger second-ary pupils it may be more appropriate to emphasize affective skills in order to lay a foundation of interest in and concern for human issues, whereas for older students (16–19 years) the curriculum is more likely to focus on the evolving economic and political structure of Europe with emphasis on problem-solving and what a Dutch expert called 'practical knowledge relevant to a student functioning as a European citizen'.[18] For practical purposes, the goals will be subdivided into specific objectives selected according to levels of attainment appropriate to age and ability bands. How these are implemented remains a matter for national educators, although we are moving to greater internationalization of the curriculum. There is also a lobby in the European Standing Conference of Geography Teachers' Associations, committed to effective and regular exchange of information between European teachers of Geography, from which greater standardization of curricula is likely to develop.

However, since blanket coverage of the geography of every European country is an unrealistic target, the choice of content is crucial, and growing pressure to define the European dimension of all disciplines has helped to hone the selection process. A representative group of bilingual teachers asked their colleagues to reflect on certain questions. To what extent does Geography, for instance, reflect diversity on a regional/national scale or uniformity and identity in Europe? To what extent does it deal with common European solutions to overriding regional or global probems? To what extent does it stress the necessity of finding particular solutions in a specific region? To what extent does the subject underline the common European heritage and common links, and contribute towards mutual understanding? To what extent does it reflect the aspirations and problems of the developing countries of the Third World and emphasize the need for closer collaboration for development between Europe and the outside world? To what extent does Geography deal both with the common contemporary, social and economic problems and issues facing various countries in Europe, and with finding solutions to them through co-operative efforts?[19] Questions are one way of identifying priorities and in this case they point to certain concepts: unity, diversity, regionalism, change, heritage, pattern, process, co-operation, interdependence. These concepts are not unique to Geography and they can all be taught in an interdisciplinary framework (Table 3), but Geography can shed particular light on them through suitable themes (with topics and case-studies) and issues (in the form of questions and problem-solving exercises). Themes and topics have the advantage of being adaptable to different levels in a spiral curriculum. So the subject of energy, for instance, can be studied as a local, a regional or national issue, or as a Western European or a pan-European problem, in each case deploying a progression of skills.

In practice, European curricula already include a core of geographical themes and topics with a European dimension. Among the most common are:

- urbanization (structures, functions and problems of inner cities; for example, Paris, Hamburg, Glasgow);
- industrialization (patterns of production, location, change, specific industries, employment, unemployment and post-industrialization; for example, the Ruhr);
- land use (reclamation and development of coastal wetlands; for example, Scheldt-Rhine, Rhône delta, Venetia);
- agriculture (types, production, changes; for example, EC Common Agricultural Policy);
- population changes (migration, such as that of Turkish *Gastarbeiter* in Ger-

Table 3 The interdisciplinary approach: summary of suggested content for developing key concepts and themes

Europe: the spatial dimension	Europe: the time dimension	Europe: the cultural/social dimension

Key concept: Diversity

Themes	*Themes*	*Themes*
Variety of regional, national and local patterns in: (1) physical environment (2) climate (3) location, type and extent of natural resources (4) use of resources (5) human rural/urban settlement (6) artificial environments	Diverse political heritage of: (1) political theory (2) forms and practice: from extreme individualism to collectivism/centralized state control Legacy of historic rivalry and conflicts: (1) European authorities *v.* sovereign states; (2) extra-European relations Tradition of doctrinal, social and cultural schism between (1) Western Roman Christendom (2) Eastern Orthodox Christendom (3) modern Protestantism (4) other religious minorities	Variations in social patterns and experience: (1) wealth/poverty (2) class, status systems (3) ethnic minorities (4) multicultural communities (5) popular traditions and customs (6) language (7) religion

Key concept: Unity

Themes	*Themes*	*Themes*
Experience of co-operation through: (1) economic systems/agreements, such as Zollverein, European Community (2) communications – natural and artificial: rivers, canals, railways, ships, air (3) consumer economics (4) advanced technology, defence systems	Common heritage of: (1) Christian ethics – public/personal morality (2) colonial–imperial expansion (3) international relations – experiments in balance of power, co-operation/diplomacy (4) transnational movements and intellectual, cultural, artistic achievements	Co-operation/integration between: (1) governments; for example, European Union (2) growing uniformity of lifestyles between Europeans of comparable wealth and status (3) levelling effect of consumer society on taste, behaviour patterns (4) democratic systems (5) impact of youth culture

Table 3 continued

Europe: the spatial dimension	Europe: the time dimension	Europe: the cultural/ social dimension
	Key concept: Change	
Themes	*Themes*	*Themes*
Twentieth-century developments in:	(1) the Industrial and Agrarian Revolutions of the eighteenth and nineteenth centuries	(1) transformation of rural society into an industrial society with class structure
(1) environment		
(2) commercial structures	(2) evolution of scientific ideas and development of rational thought	(2) transformation of religious and social attitudes – role of women; children; family
(3) patterns of industry		
(4) communications		
(5) forms of energy	(3) development of sovereign states – nineteenth- and twentieth-century nationalism	
(6) land use		(3) growth of toleration, human rights and values
(7) patterns of employment		
(8) climate: potential of greenhouse effect	(4) post-war retreat from colonialism	(4) decline of organized religion/traditional Christian morality
(9) frontiers	(5) revival of social and political separatism	(5) rise of materialism and secularism
	(6) changing role of Christian churches/ ethics in European politics	(6) development of a multicultural society through migration

many; multicultural communities, such as Switzerland, France, the UK, the USSR);

● energy (forms and uses; for example, in France, the UK, Norway, Poland, the USSR);

● trade (port location and functions; for example, the Benelux countries);

● transport/communication (Flanders 'crossroads', the Baltic, the Danube);

● the environment (the Rhine, North Sea, Black Sea, acid rain in Norway, Dalyan Bay project, Turkey).

These in no way constitute a definitive list but are a sample taken from teachers' discussions. Since it is common practice to use case-studies, teachers should be encouraged to set their examples in a European context and to emphasize the broader scale in the European dimension. At the same time conscious attention should be paid to countering stereotypes.

Looking for a new approach, some geographers may feel sympathy with the request 'to be creative' and to bring the consideration of future scenarios into teaching.[20] Others believe that futurology is too esoteric and that the answer lies in extending the thematic approach from conventional themes to meet the changing concerns of European society. They would welcome more system-atic treatment of themes such as frontiers and changing political relationships (for example, in Berlin, Poland, Northern Ireland); the centre–periphery dichotomy (for instance, in the USSR, Moscow *v*. Vilnius; in Italy, Milan *v*. the Mezzogiorno); nuclear power (for example, the USSR and Chernobyl, France); leisure/tourism, alternative tourism, cultural tourism (for instance, the Mediterranean coastal zone; Languedoc; glacial geomorphology and sport in the Alps; the Danish farmhouse; the Greek taverna; the Austrian pension; room-letting in Polish fishing villages; European cultural routes and the rural habitat circuits of the Ardennes, the Eifel, French Lorraine, Luxembourg, the Moselle and the Saarland). Already pollution and conservation are familiar themes and ecology is likely to dominate the teaching of Geography in the 1990s.

To sum up, the Geography curriculum of the 1990s should focus on 'the realities, the problems and the opportunities offered by the New Europe'.[21] The most prominent realities appear to be the détente between Eastern and Western Europe (and consequently, the opening up of hitherto closed topics and sources of information), the maturing of the European Community and the emergence of a federation of united European states, perhaps by 1993. With the exception of the EC, these realities could not have been anticipated two years ago, making it certain that Geography textbooks will have to be rewritten to depict the New Europe accurately; the representation of Europe in three blocs – the Communist East, the European Community and 'the rest' – noted by a Spanish scholar at the Utrecht Symposium, is scarcely an adequate framework for study.[22] On the other hand, to understand the changing political geography of integration, there is a need to take account of the physical, human and economic geography of the Community member states. The role of Geography in informing students about political developments has perhaps been understated in the past, but it is now recognized that 'geography could play an important part in the political education of young people.' In particular, the topics of European unity, co-operation in Europe and democracy in Europe are part of the Geography teacher's brief because 'the integration of Europe will be better served by information about the realities of contemporary Europe than by clinging to the images of the past.'[23] Teachers may require some help in adjusting to the idea that they should deal with political ideas, but the Utrecht Symposium affirmed the importance of Geography in citizenship education, a practice already evident in Civics courses in Sweden.[24]

Despite the revival of interest in Human Geography, the cultural aspects of life in Europe have been somewhat neglected in textbooks. Some socio-cultural topics (such as sports, festivals, food, family life) have a place in multi- or interdisciplinary teaching at primary or lower secondary level, but greater play might be made of the diverse linguistic, ethnic, religious and social patterns in Europe and the cultural heritage through Historical Geography at the upper secondary level. In addition, the Council of Europe's initiative on European cultural routes indicates a particular role for Geography and underlines its appeal to young people as a subject which bridges the barrier between theory and practice through extra-curricular activities. In focusing on European awareness, however, the Council of Europe has stressed that preparation for life in an interdependent world requires subjects like Geography to present European themes and topics, whenever appropriate, within a global context. To illustrate the concept of international co-operation, for example, the Council of Europe has suggested certain geographical themes, such as the best use of energy and natural resources (for example, oil and water), the changing needs in communications and trade (for instance, Europe and the Pacific Rim states), relations with the developing countries (the North–South dialogue), the impact of migration on populations (intercultural policies) and the preservation of the ecological balance. The last theme, which is both a problem and an opportunity for contemporary Europe, is of prime relevance to the Geography curriculum. Indeed, in many secondary schools, Geography has become synonymous with Environmental Education.

ENVIRONMENTAL EDUCATION: A MULTIDISCIPLINARY APPROACH TO SPATIAL EUROPE

The European landscape is essentially artificial. Many features of our present environment, like many of its problems, have been forged in the twentieth century; and in the opinion of Gro Harlem Brundtland, not only will most of the great environmental battles take place in the 1990s, but it is imperative that they be won.[25] One of the 'battles' is to ensure that international resolutions to incorporate an environmental dimension into education are fully implemented by European governments. For two decades the leading international organizations have pressed for the inclusion of environmental awareness and stewardship in the curriculum. In 1971 the Committee of Ministers of the Council of Europe resolved that member states should introduce the principles of nature conservation and ecology into primary and secondary schools. This heralded a series of powerful statements in support of Environmental Education by UNESCO and the European Community, and in the opinion of one publicist, 'there is no immediately apparent reason why compulsory "Planet Care" education could not be on the syllabus of every school in Europe by 1992.'[26]

The UN recognizes that the exploitation and pollution of the environment and the destruction of ecosystems is a global problem. But for the industrialized countries of Europe, where many of these processes originated, the urgency and the responsibility for taking action are inescapable. One solution lies in securing intergovernmental agreements, such as the 1971 Ramsar Convention on the conservation of wetlands of international importance (the outcome of which is the official protection of the Baltic and North Sea coasts and all the Atlantic and Mediterranean coasts of Europe). Another is the adoption of specific strategies to reform the EC Common Agricultural Policy, such as through 'set-aside' schemes, or by introducing the concept of 'environmentally sensitive areas' and organic farming; for although the economic and social relevance of agriculture has declined, its importance for nature and the environment continues to increase. In the long run, however, it is just as important to convert the public to adopt positive attitudes and standards of personal and group behaviour which ensure that Europe's landscape, wildlife, flora and other natural resources are renewed and protected, and here the education of the young, both at primary and secondary level, plays an indispensable part.

During the 1970s Environmental Studies were established in the curricula of many European countries as part of a world trend. The International Environmental Education Programme (IEEP), launched in 1975 by UNESCO and UNEP (the United Nations Environmental Programme), brought over 130 nations and more than 260,000 pupils in primary and secondary schools into its activities. IEEP undertook over thirty pilot projects, which included pilot studies on Environmental Education (EE) methodologies for secondary schools in France and the Ukraine, on urban environment educational programmes in the UK, on comprehensive EE programmes for all school levels in Czechoslovakia, and on incorporating an environmental dimension into Biology and Geography education in Poland and Portugal. Subsequently, two United Nations reports on global ecology by UNEP and by the Bruntland Commission endorsed the crucial role of EE. As to the specifically European context, Recommendation No. 2 of the Fourth Conference of European Ministers of Education, organized by UNESCO in September 1988, was devoted entirely to the European-wide development of EE. As a follow-up, the IEEP promoted further seminars and symposia in 1989 and the Director-General of UNESCO was urged to give high priority to educational programmes for EE in 1990–1 and in the UN's medium-term plan for 1990–5.

The latter complements the specifically European initiatives of the EC and the Council of Europe. Following the initial EC pilot studies with primary pupils of 9–12 years (1976) and secondary students of 12–16 years (1982), the European Community policy and action programme on the environment (1987–92) gives priority to the promotion of education in environmental matters to every age group. In May 1988 the objectives and guiding principles of EE for all sectors of education were laid down by a resolution of the Council and the Ministers of Education of the EC. The goals involved increasing public awareness, ensuring that people are better informed and encouraging active participation in environmental protection. The translation of these general principles into curricula is seen by the EC as a matter for member states, but progress on national plans was reported in May 1990.

The Council of Europe's strategies are in agreement with those of the European Community. One of the nine areas of the Council's activity is the Heritage and Environment of Europe. By linking these two concepts, the Council has endorsed a holistic approach to safeguarding the 'space' of Europe for the future. In policy terms the heritage/environment continuum involves relating ecology, culture, values, economics and tourism, while the educational implications spread across the whole curriculum, from the Life Sciences to industrial archaeology (Figure 4, p. 73). The Council's Campaign for Urban Renaissance (1980–2) examined the cultural, social and environmental aspects of urban policies, from which came determined strategies for conservation and use of open spaces. Examples of good practice can be seen in Strasbourg, the 'green capital' of Western Europe, and around Mt Vitosha and the Bulgarian capital, Sofia.[27] Concern for the rural regions hit by change prompted the launching of the European Campaign for the Countryside 1987–8, which coincided with the European Year of the Environment organized by the EC. Many factors have contributed to the problems of rural communities, two being overproduction and the need for diversification, but the disadvantaged and declining areas have felt different stresses from those under pressure from intensive development. Rural Turkey, for example, is heavily populated but lacks infrastructure and services; the Scottish countryside is better served but parts have suffered from depopulation; while rural England is trying to stave off population pressure and urbanization. The European Campaign sought to prepare people for the European countryside of the year 2000 by identifying problems, anticipating solutions, and involving the young people of Europe's rural communities in these deliberations.[28]

So at the heart of the European Community and Council of Europe policies is the belief that their main educative goal must be *the development of environmental awareness in the young*. While EE should continue throughout life, it is at school that children and young people should learn that the environment of Europe offers precious assets which must be safeguarded and managed rationally, and that all aspects of the environment – land and sea, air and water, town and country, animal and plant life – constitute our common heritage. The matter of attitudes is therefore seen as the critical area of EE. The awakening of a child's curiosity in nature and interest in his or her surroundings, with evidence of respect for all living things, and a positive and sensitive approach to the natural world, are among the most valuable contributions that primary schools can make to the education of young Europeans. Without this foundation, the task of secondary teachers in conveying complex areas of knowledge and enabling older students to understand and explain a range of natural, scientific, economic, technological, legal and human problems relating to the environment, and their possible solutions, becomes more difficult. Moreover, the preservation of the European environment, the protection of human health and the safeguarding of the ecological balance depend on the constructive attitudes and responsible behaviour of those who will soon be adults.

The variety of material covered by EE demonstrates that it is not a single discipline in itself but a broad field of study involving the interaction between humans and their environment. Teaching is therefore only practicable in a multidisciplinary context, a point made by the Committee of Ministers of the Council of Europe as long ago as 1971 and reiterated by the Ministers of Education of the EC in 1988.[29] Multi- or interdisciplinary approaches, with the organization of subject matter around concepts, themes and topics, were widely canvassed in the 1970s, but it is equally possible to incorporate the relevant areas of ecology into a number of separate disciplines, giving each subject an environmental dimension. Whichever strategy fits a national or local system, the expertise of Geography teachers is likely to give them a central role in EE, either as the 'core' specialists in a social science programme of study or as co-ordinators with the task of cross-referencing knowledge and skills across the curriculum. The Council of Europe singled out certain areas of subject matter which Geography could contribute to the environmental curriculum: themes such as land formation and evolution; human impact on the landscape, rural and urban; development techniques; natural resources and planning. They also suggested that Geography might take on scientific topics like pollution and the water cycle. Certainly, Geography and EE are compatible areas, and in some schools they have been treated as interchangeable. However, the prevailing opinion is that EE is enriched by the contribution of a range of subjects and approaches. Environmental awareness can only come about through familiarity with botanical gardens, national parks, open-air and conventional museums, zoos and animal sanctuaries. An environmental dimension should therefore be incorporated into extra-curricular activities as well as into the formal curriculum (Figure 4).

THE CONTRIBUTION OF OTHER DISCIPLINES IN THE NATURAL AND HUMAN SCIENCES

The Council of Europe's resolution of 1971 on nature conservation in the curriculum made it clear that at secondary school level the Life and Earth Sciences had an important contribution to make in explaining environmental questions. Some scientific topics can be covered adequately in Geography lessons, particularly with younger pupils, but as Geography has moved towards a greater emphasis on human and social considerations, and scientific and technological advances have added to the volume and complexity of knowledge, it is clear that students do need a foundation of scientific learning if they are to be well-informed about environmental issues.

In the case of Biology, the 1971 recommendation includes in the list of proposed content the basic principles of ecology (the interdependence of living creatures and the physical environment; trophic chains; energy flows; population changes; natural balances and their dynamics; sequences, climates, ecosystems); the human effect on the distribution of species; the importance of protecting genetic assets; the significance and importance of nature reserves and other protected areas; and the effects of pesticides and other pollutants on the natural balance. Chemistry can contribute knowledge of synthesis and decomposition; the process of chlorophyll synthesis; the role of pesticides and nitrates; soil pollution; pollution of the air by sprays, smoke and sulphur; pollution of fresh water by phenols and detergents; pollution of seawater and marine life by oil spillages. With Biology and Chemistry, Physics sheds light on the water cycle and on the many types of pollution affecting, for instance, the North and Irish Seas and parts of the Mediterranean. Physics can also explain the impact of radiation, radioactivity and the production and disposal

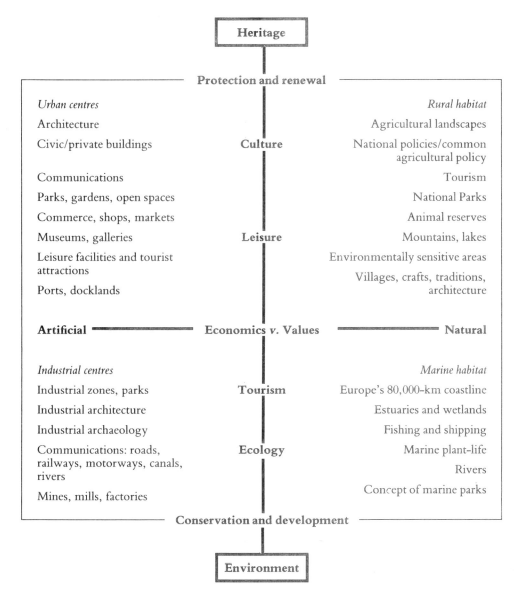

Figure 4 The heritage–environment continuum

of radioactive waste, with their stark relevance for certain European countries today.

Both the Council of Europe and the European Community also recognize the importance of Economics but acknowledge that it is still a minority subject, although aspects are taught in general social science courses. Since the 1960s, when the subject became established in upper secondary curricula in Western Europe, these organizations have pressed for more teaching about European economic structures rather than an emphasis on economic theory. In a 1972 survey in the CDCC European Curriculum Studies series, it was argued that:

> Europe can only maintain its living standards if it keeps its share of world markets, if it encourages innovation, if it manages its economic resources, better than its competitors. There is no better way of achieving these aims than in expanding Europe's economic expertise through the incorporation of economic studies into appropriate levels of its educational systems.[30]

In the 1970s the more progressive observers advocated compulsory study of the Western European economy which, with the expansion of the Common Market of the European Community, formed a distinct and substantial economic entity. The decade was marked by a number of significant inter-European initiatives in EC states in respect of Economics education for older secondary students.[31] However, the rise to pre-eminence of the Pacific Rim economies in the 1980s and the dramatic events of 1989 in Eastern Europe changed the perspective yet again. In anticipation of the single market from 1993, European Community policy has encouraged the study of European Economics, both through pilot schemes such as the History–Economics project for 14–16 year olds on European Integration and by recommending in a resolution of May 1988 that member states should include a European dimension explicitly in Economics curricula.[32] In the light of the East–West détente and the union of Germany, the economic prospects for Europe are set to change further in the 1990s. In addition, there is a view (which has given rise to a new form of study, Development Education) that equal attention should be paid to the increasing economic interdependence of the developed and less advanced countries.

Finally, we return to our starting point, the economic implications of the European environment. In discussing the problems facing urban and rural Europe, economic factors and examples of commercial pragmatism frequently have to be weighed against ecological or aesthetic considerations. Often the present-day economic factors also have to be set against matters of historical legacy (Figure 5). As we saw in the previous chapter, History is frequently the natural partner of Geography in studying the rural and urban environment. Human kind's increasing mastery of nature from prehistoric times to today's microchip society has to be set against the human capacity to disturb the balance of the environment through migration, war, disease, the exploitation and spoliation of resources. Some teachers of Geography appreciate the need to push back the parameters of their subject to include the techniques and subject matter of historical geography, industrial archaeology, vernacular architecture or ethnology. Sociology also has a role in environmental courses because its coverage of social structures and human problems is relevant to urban and rural development. Civics, Human Rights Education and Social or Personal Education may equally contribute to the ethical and behavioural issues raised by studying the environment of Europe, and some of these elements will be looked at later. My overall conclusion is that Europe's spatial dimension is

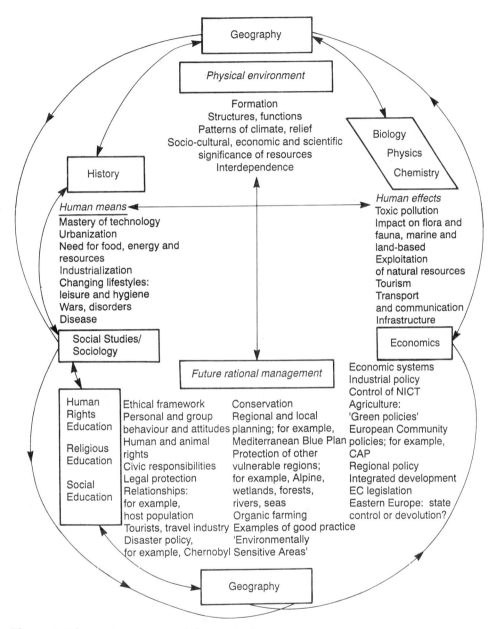

Figure 5 The environment and the curriculum

better served by flexible curricular arrangements that exploit the conceptual links between subject areas or disciplines rather than relying exclusively on the input of one or two subjects. To illustrate the point, there is no better example than a pilot project for about one hundred 15–16-year-olds from the Federal Republic of Germany, France, the Netherlands and Switzerland, sponsored by the Council of Europe in 1989 on the subject of 'A Frontier-Free Rhine'. The multilingual party travelled upstream from Rotterdam to Strasbourg, taking part en route in workshops that focused on architecture, writing/communication, ethnology/rural life and economics.[33] As an approach to Environmental and Heritage Education this kind of model deserves to be more comprehensively explored.

GEOGRAPHY AND THE EUROPEAN DIMENSION: SUMMARY OF PRINCIPLES FOR ENCOURAGING EUROPEAN AWARENESS THROUGH GEOGRAPHY CURRICULA

Knowledge

1 To develop pupil insight and understanding of the location, configuration and diversity of physical and human environments in Europe.

2 To develop pupil understanding of those values and other geographically relevant issues such as the protection of the European environment.

3 To promote understanding of the effects of European integration on the economies and societies of individual European states.

4 To develop practical knowledge relevant to participation as a future citizen of Europe.

5 To promote an understanding of the interdependence of Europe and the rest of the world.

Attitudes, aptitudes and values

6 To promote an awareness and empathetic understanding of the different ways of life existing within Europe.

7 To promote tolerance and eliminate stereotyped or Eurocentric perceptions of other peoples both within and outside Europe.

8 To develop awareness of the need to respond to change and willingness to co-operate with others in dealing with European problems.

Skills

9 To develop of a range of cognitive skills such as analysis, synthesis, the application of concepts and theories, and evaluation.

10 To supplement affective skills by developing practical, active and participatory skills of citizenship.

NOTES

1 Geography will be spelt with a capital 'G' when referring to the school subject; when used in a general sense it will have a lower-case letter 'g'.

2 Williams, Michael (1982), 'Europe in school Geography', *Teaching about Europe,* **9** (2).

3 Waites, B. (1982), 'Ways of teaching about Europe in school Geography', *Teaching about Europe,* **9** (2).

4 Graves, Norman (forthcoming), *Report of the Symposium on Geographical Information and Documentation on European Countries, Utrecht, September 1989,* Strasbourg: Council of Europe, p. 14.

5 *Ibid.,* p. 27.

6 *Ibid.,* p. 33.

7 Goodson, I. F., and McGivney, V. (1985), *European Dimensions and the Secondary School Curriculum,* Lewes: The Falmer Press, p. 80.

8 Williams, 'Europe in school Geography'.

9 Graves, *Report on the Utrecht Symposium,* p. 14.

10 *Ibid.,* p. 19.

11 *Ibid.,* pp. 7–9, 27, 32.

12 Marchant, E. C. (1967), *Geography Teaching and the Revision of Geography Textbooks and Atlases,* Strasbourg: Council of Europe, p. 100.

13 Graves, *Report on the Utrecht Symposium,* p. 13.

14 Morris, J. W. (1976), *Geography,* European Curriculum Studies, No. 10, Strasbourg: Council of Europe.

15 Meijer, H., '10 points for reflection', in Graves, *Report on the Utrecht Symposium,* Addendum 1, pt. 3.

16 Graves, *Report on the Utrecht Symposium,* pp. 20–1.

17 Austin, Roger (1989), *Report on The European Studies (Ireland and Great Britain) Project,* Strasbourg: Council of Europe.

18 Knoester, P. J. (Netherlands National Institute for Curriculum Development), in Graves, *Report on the Utrecht Symposium,* p. 19.

19 Peacock, D. (1982), *Report of the CDCC Symposium on Europe in Secondary School Curricula: Aims, Approaches and Problems, Neusiedl-am-See, Austria, April 1981,* Strasbourg: Council of Europe, pp. 32–3.

20 Graves, *Report on the Utrecht Symposium,* p. 19.

21 *Ibid.,* p. 33.

22 *Ibid.,* p. 14.

23 *Ibid.,* p. 9.

24 *Ibid.,* pp. 19, 26–7.

25 Brundtland, Gro Harlem (1989) (Prime Minister of Norway), *Naturopa,* **63,** Editorial, p. 3.

26 Anderson, A. (1989), 'Influencing behaviour', *Naturopa,* **61,** p. 11.

27 Rudloff, Marcel (1988), 'Strasbourg – the green capital'; Stoyanov, Dimitar (1988), 'Oxygen for Sofia'; both in *Naturopa,* **59,** pp. 10–12.

28 (1988) *Report of the Study Session of the European Committee for Young Farmers' and 4H*

Clubs, on Europe's Countryside for the Year 2000, March 1988, Strasbourg: Council of Europe.

29 Committee of Ministers of the Council of Europe: Resolution (71) 14 (30 June 1971) on the Introduction of the Principles of Nature Conservation into Education (this is being updated); the Council and Ministers of Education of the European Communities: Resolution (88/C177/03) of 24 May 1988 on Environmental Education.

30 Rust, W. Bonney (1972), *Economics,* European Curriculum Studies, No. 7, Strasbourg: Council of Europe, p. 18.

31 Ryba, R. (1977), 'The recent evolution of economics education in EEC countries at the upper secondary level', in Ryba, R., and Robinson, B. (eds), *Aspects of Upper Secondary Economics Education in EEC Countries,* Haywards Heath: Economics Association.

32 Shennan, M. (1987), *Report of the European Teachers' Course on Teaching about European Co-operation and Integration in Upper Secondary Schools, Ebeltoft, Denmark, March 1987,* Strasbourg: Council of Europe, p. 11; The Council and Ministers of Education of the European Communities: Resolution (88/C177/02) of 24 Mary 1988 on the European Dimension in Education.

33 (1989), *A Future for our Past,* **35,** p. 24.

CHAPTER 5

Europe's Cultural Identity

THE THIRD DIMENSION: THE CULTURAL PHENOMENON

Time and area are straightforward notions and readily equate with historical and geographical subject matter. Culture, the third dimension of Europe, is a different matter. It is a portentous concept which draws on many disciplines. Academics, therefore, tend to hedge their definitions with words of caution. The historian Douglas Johnson observed that 'cultural historians are distressingly vague when they explain what they mean by culture.'[1] Richard Pring, the educational philosopher, complained that 'the more one attempts to seek unity of European thought or culture in some overarching set of concepts or beliefs or cultural features the more one is open to criticism.'[2] Even an expert of the stature of Henri Janne, the former Belgian Minister of National Education and Culture, had to admit that 'culture is an extremely ambiguous concept . . . very difficult to apprehend in a "pure" state.'[3] For all that, the place of culture in the European curriculum has to be addressed. In the opinion of a former Chairman of the British Arts Council, 'If one wants to explore the possibilities of Europe's political future, one needs to examine the development of European culture.'[4] So it is the task of secondary school teachers to cut through the academic debate and find ways of translating cultural phenomena into pedagogical realities.

There are two fundamental interpretations of the concept from the standpoint of the curriculum. The first treats 'culture' as a by-product of time and history, the outcome of the civilizing process: indeed, for some the word is synonymous with 'civilization'. Matthew Arnold described it as 'the acquainting ourselves with the best that has been known and said in the world, and thus with the history of the human spirit', an interpretation with particular appeal to artists and humanists. Emerson, for one, believed 'Culture opens the sense of beauty', while the poet T. S. Eliot claimed that there is a common thread in an culture, 'an interrelated history of thought and feeling and behaviour, an interchange of arts and of ideas'.[5] From this line of thinking comes the tradition of 'High Culture'. Nurtured by the creative inspiration of Renaissance Italy, that impulse spread from the Mediterranean world into northern Europe by means of scholarship, literature, science, painting, architecture and music, bequeathing a legacy to future generations of Europeans, with all that that implies for today's school curriculum.

From the world of social science, however, has come a broader, all-inclusive interpretation. In the opinion of the American, Leroi Jones 'culture is simply how one lives', but Terry G. Jordan, author of a geographical study of Europe, elaborated on this terse definition:

Europe is a culture which occupies a culture area. Culture may be defined briefly as a community of people who hold numerous features of belief, behaviour, and overall way of life in common, including ideology, technology, social institutions and material possessions. A culture-area is any large area, usually contiguous, that is inhabited by people of a particular culture, a land upon which the visible imprint of that culture has been placed.[6]

This brings 'culture' closer to the idea of 'society', a concept very much in line with the definition of the Council of Europe's project group on Cultural Development Policies: 'Culture is the sum of the distinctive, material, intellectual, and spiritual values by which a society or group is characterised. It thus includes lifestyles and forms of production, values systems, beliefs and opinions, etc.' This implies that culture 'is dynamic and is the essential factor in quality of life ... in collective identity and consciousness ... [and] it is by definition "of the people", everyday "participating" and communal ... Cultural life is all embracing' and concerns the past, the present and the future.[7]

So what can be said about European civilization and its alter ego, European society? It has been said that the former has been comatose since the First World War when 'Europe experienced ... a simultaneous cultural, spiritual and political breakdown', and following the nadir of the 1930s and 1940s fell into a 'period of sedated convalescence' from which its peoples are only now emerging.[8] Whether Europe has recovered, and if so to what extent, are still matters of argument. In Henri Janne's opinion, Europe's cultural values have been irreparably obscured and eroded.[9] Other experts see Europe's decline in relative rather than absolute terms. Pointing to the buoyancy of the hybrid 'Atlantic' culture, which is an offshoot of Anglo-Saxon Europe, room for optimism has been found: 'If the present trend continues European culture may one day be world culture, as regional differences fade in an increasing acceptance of the European way of life', although even that cannot hide the fact that the 'dynamic leadership long held by mother Europe has ... passed to her overseas children'.[10] There is some truth in all these observations. In comparative terms Europe's authority waned in the post-colonial era, but in the past decade there has been a growing solidarity and revival of confidence in certain layers of European society which have enjoyed renewed prosperity and openness. Many Europeans are increasingly coming to terms with their inheritance of unity in diversity.

None the less, for some while experts warned of dangers to the integrity of European culture, and their concern led to reappraisals of European society and its values. For instance, the cultural identity of Europe was the subject of a major Council of Europe colloquy at Delphi in May 1980, at which the nation-states were urged to look to the quality of life of their citizens, a quality threatened with erosion by soulless materialism. European cultural attitudes were examined in the light of four conceptual polarities: liberty and security; materialism and spirituality; rationality and emotionality; nature and production or organization. The overall conclusion was that European culture patterns swing like a pendulum between extremes; but whichever is in the ascendant, Europe always experiences tension and an inclination towards paradox and change.

On the matter of liberty and security, it seems that Europeans wish to live in well-ordered societies where the security of their community is effectively protected; but in practice, they also expect guarantees of certain personal liberties, such as choice, expression, privacy and conscience. This pressure between the individual and the community is not only a recurring theme of European development, it gives rise to very subtle tensions, such as that implicit in Rousseau's theory of the General Will or the dictum 'Freedom is obedience to the law.' And another unique aspect of this culture pattern is the adherence to highly sophisticated theories of the state.

As to the dichotomy between materialism and spirituality, Europeans have by tradition inclined to ideals and to spiritual or socio-cultural utopias based on various principles, Christian, socialist or liberal. Yet latterly they have become members of an economy-orientated society, dependent on technocratic and ever more centralized systems. On the question of rationality and emotionality, it was argued that since the eighteenth-century Enlightenment, reason has been the cornerstone of both European culture and the advanced industrial society. The logic of reason, however, usually places efficiency before liberty, systems before people, so that the countervailing free play of imaginative and creative forces (so brilliantly displayed in Europe's past, in movements like Romanticism) has to be given constant encouragement. Finally, with regard to the fourth paradox, while Europeans recognize the importance of industrial production, they are also becoming steadily aware of the imperative of protecting the environment and preserving a symbiotic relationship with nature, attitudes which have historic precedents in European culture.

A year after the Delphi colloquy, Henri Janne presented his seminal paper on *Europe's Cultural Identity* to the Neusiedl Symposium on Europe in Secondary School Curricula. His personal commentary on the issues raised at Delphi and his interpretation of what he called 'the cultural phenomenon' make invaluable reading for teachers involved in European education. As a sociologist he took the view that culture is the sum of human activities, values and relationships specific to a society. In the case of Europe, it could be argued that the regions and nations have their own cultural characteristics based on historical experience. Certainly, Europe has been variously influenced by four historic cultural areas: the Graeco-Byzantine–Slavonic circle, the Roman–Carolingian–Gallic circle, the Iberian–Islamic–North-African circle and the Scandinavian–Celtic–Anglo-Saxon circle,[11] and to these one should perhaps add the West-European–North-American–Transatlantic circle which has been so influential in the twentieth century (Figure 6). Yet Europe's social systems have many features

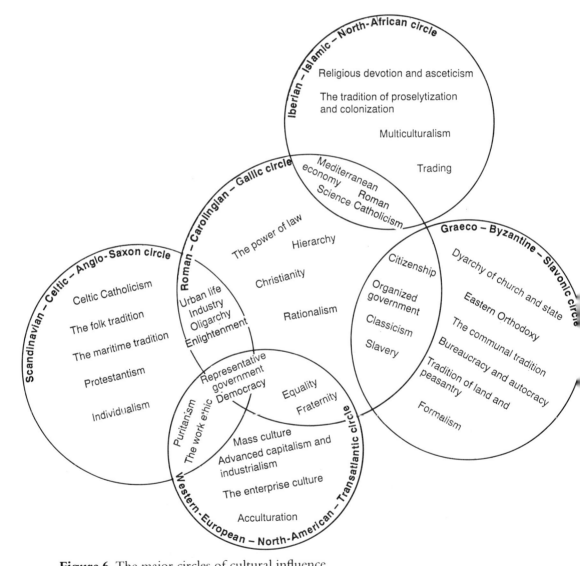

Figure 6 The major circles of cultural influence

in common (the hierarchical tradition has a long history), so that it is still possible to study Europe's cultural profile as an entity.

Indeed, Europeans share a wealth of experience based on eight cultural elements: namely, currents of religious experience; a mode of rational, scientific thinking; sophisticated political ideologies; a range of artistic movements and forms of expression; liberal principles of individualism; the socio-economic philosophy of capitalism; the capacity for linguistic communication; and, most recently, concern for the global environment (Table 4). However, these

Table 4 A cultural framework – Europe

A civilization Eight elements of cultural experience	A society Five circles of cultural influence
1 Currents of religious experience	A Graeco-Byzantine–Slavonic circle
2 Mode of rational scientific thinking	
3 Sophisticated political ideologies	B Roman–Carolingian–Gallic circle
4 Range of artistic movements and forms of expression	C Iberian–Islamic–North-African circle
5 Liberal principles of individualism	
6 Socio-economic philosophy of capitalism	D Scandinavian–Celtic–Anglo-Saxon circle
7 Capacity for linguistic communication	E West-European–North American– Transatlantic circle
8 Concern for global environment	

elements are also subject to flux and distortion. For example, reason, that most specifically European cultural feature, cannot be considered European any longer for it belongs to the whole of the industrialized world. The enterprise culture, which should provide the *means* of social improvement for Europeans, has in fact become society's intrinsic *end*. At the same time, official obsession with economic expansion means that 'that portion of culture which is resistant to commercialization is relegated to the sidelines.'[12] This situation also explains the general disregard for humanist values and Renaissance ideals which had been absorbed into Europe's cultural tradition. And the tensions and self-doubts do not end there. With the widespread questioning of socialism in East and West, the crisis in science and industrialization and the faltering of Christian ethics, Europe's cultural identity appears (not for the first time in its history) to be endangered. Looking ahead, Janne said pointedly: 'Europe, having invented reason, must rid itself of reason's contradictions: that is, for Europe, the cultural challenge.'[13]

The solution to Europe's identity crisis – if there is one – will lie in its inclination to pluralism and co-existence. Toleration came slowly to Europe, and it was Roy Wake's guess that 'perhaps more has been achieved from the cynicism and indifference that comes from temporary exhaustion than from passionate conviction.' Anti-Semitism, he pointed out, is a European phenomenon; so for the most part is racism.[14] Religion was another prime cause of bloodshed in the sixteenth and seventeenth centuries. However, since diversity has always been present, Europeans learned in time to accept difference out of necessity, and from 1648 a degree of public toleration was underwritten by international guarantee. The irony is that in the last thirty years, just as tolerance has become a popularly accepted cultural norm, the multiplicity of cultural differences has radically increased. A new question-mark hangs over Europe's cultural identity, and the underlying problem is the development of a value-system in tune with a multicultural society. That is a matter for discussion in a later chapter. For the moment, we need to look at the indigenous elements of European civilization.

RELIGIOUS CURRENTS IN EUROPEAN CULTURE

The first of the cultural elements mentioned by Janne was religion. As we have observed, religion is an uncomfortable subject in a laicized society. Many Europeans regard Europe as a purely secular concept and the spiritual dimension to be outside the sphere of education. Indeed, religion and religious education were specifically excluded from the educational agenda of the Council of Europe. In bringing these facts into the open, there is no intention of being contentious. It would be regressive to revive old disputes about the power of church and state or nineteenth-century Catholic interpretations of history which assumed that 'The Faith is Europe and Europe is the Faith.' However, it would be equally obtuse to ignore the part played by religion in the development of European values. Allowing for the fact that boundaries and terminology are transient, Christendom was the historic precursor of Europe, just as Greece and Rome were the precursors of Christendom (as Paul Valéry, the French poet and essayist, noted); and though the separation of the post-Roman world into two Christian empires was followed a millennium later by greater divisions with the Protestant Reformation, the theory of a universal, indivisible commonwealth of the faithful was never eclipsed, any more than was the secular notion of the unity of Europe.

The power of religion to influence human behaviour and its impact on the development of society are bona fide themes of European history. Countless examples could be cited, but two will perhaps suffice. Celtic imagery from the Bronze Age on, which has been discovered throughout Europe, is thought to symbolize the sophisticated religious and philosophical ideas at work in a non-literate society;[15] and the Parliamentary Assembly of the Council of Europe recognized 'the very considerable and distinctive contribution that Jews and the tradition of Judaism have made to the historical development of Europe in the cultural as well as other fields'.[16] In medieval and modern Europe the Jews were (to use Hoggart's mixed metaphor) 'the pollinating bees for ... artistic and intellectual activity ... acting like yeast in the somewhat stolid, unintellectual and unartistic societies in which they settled'.[17] In principle the Council of

84

Europe approved further discussion of Jewish influence in Europe. In the spirit of this resolution and where state provision for Religious Education allows, it ought to be possible to include Judaism in courses of comparative religion and ethics, while remembering that:

in the 19th and 20th centuries Einstein, Heine, Lassalle, Marx, Felix and Joseph Mendelssohn, Max Reinhardt, were Jews as well as Germans; . . . Bergson, Bernhardt, Rachel were Jewish as well as French; . . . Epstein and Ricardo (not to mention Disraeli) were Jews as well as Englishmen; . . . the Rothschilds, who belonged to so many different nations, nevertheless belonged all of them to the nation of the Jews; and . . . in earlier centuries still the achievements of giants like Maimonides and Spinoza shall not be forgotten.[18]

The view that religion is an outmoded issue in the 1990s is a shortsighted one. Religion is hardly a spent force in Ulster or the Ukraine. And consider some recent developments and their implications for the political and social future of the continent: the visit of President Gorbachev to the Vatican; the release of Soviet Jews and other religious dissidents; the discussions between the Archbishop of Canterbury and Pope John Paul II on church unity; the debate on the ordination of women; the support among the Catholic clergy of Poland for the Solidarity movement; the strength of European Muslim hostility to Salman Rushdie's *The Satanic Verses*; and the challenge to the Christian churches posed by the revival of Islamic fundamentalism. These are not isolated or haphazard developments; they are potentially significant strands in the cultural transformation of Europe by the year 2000. Meanwhile, the 900th anniversary of the birth of St Bernard of Clairvaux, founder of the Cistercian order, was celebrated in 1990, a landmark in Europe's religio-cultural heritage. Yet the problems associated with teaching about spiritual phenomena in Europe, past and present, have not yet been solved. With a few exceptions – Ireland, Denmark, Sweden and the United Kingdom, where Religious Education has a role in the curriculum – the subject of religion in European culture, which those responsible for eduction are inclined to ignore, will remain at the mercy of History curricula, thus consigning it to an increasingly uncertain fate.

THE ROLE OF SCIENCE AND TECHNOLOGY IN EUROPEAN CULTURE

On the other hand, teachers are more inclined than they were a generation ago to acknowledge that science and technology are fundamental to European culture. From the Renaissance to the twentieth century, European technical prowess demonstrated the continent's intellectual and inventive monopoly, 'the providence of God and industry, as it were conspiring the European good', according to the Rev. Samuel Purchas. Not surprisingly, this seventeenth-century cleric overlooked the contribution of other civilizations to mathematical and technical knowledge, but he highlighted two aspects of a scientific surge and a 'technological "great leap forward" that stamped Europe on the world in a way that the world was never stamped on Europe'.[19] These two fields were the navigational and maritime improvements of the sixteenth century and the development of firepower for military purposes, a continuous process leading to the nuclear missiles of today. A number of historians have pointed out how European culture, like political power, came out of the barrel of a gun. But once the empirical scientific tradition was harnessed to technology, the effects proved far-reaching. Having embraced the techniques and assumptions of an advanced industrialized society, Europeans find themselves propelled inexorably towards the incalculable experience of post-industrialism.

For these reasons students at secondary school level need to comprehend the scientific basis of European society. Obviously it is vital for the physical and natural sciences to figure prominently in their own right in the secondary curriculum so that pupils develop skills and knowledge of rational principles and scientific data in the traditional way. But the imaginative and intuitive aspects of the reasoning process, displayed by great scientists (from Newton to Einstein), should also be recognized. Young people ought to learn about the personal and scientific contexts of the great discoveries as part of the cultural baggage of an educated person.

A quarter of a century ago, History teachers were advised to adopt an 'entirely revolutionary approach to their subject', and to leave aside the influence of monarchs, statesmen, generals and economic forces in favour of developments in science.[20] However, when the Schools Council tried to lower the barriers between Arts and Science in the UK during the early 1970s, by promoting the historical approach to science with a programme for 14–16 year olds on the subject of medicine, the project team was criticized by traditionalists who apparently failed to appreciate that 'Science has done more for humanity than any other human activity.'[21] In the 1990s pupils would unquestionably benefit from knowing more about the changing state of the sciences, the enigmas that baffle learned minds and some of the solutions which have come through research. Students might also find it interesting to glance down the cul-de-sacs of science, such as alchemy and astrology. There is a strong case for approaching scientific advances through the lives and work of the greatest scientists and inventors, 'the great dead who framed our culture'. Then pupils would understand that the history of the nineteenth century should be interpreted through the work of Faraday, Dalton, Darwin, Mendel, Mendeleyev, Pasteur, Lister, Röntgen and Curie; and that of the twentieth century through Einstein, Planck, Rutherford and Bohr.[22] And finally, the curriculum should provide opportunities for learning about ethical and environmental issues which have emerged because of developments in, for example, drugs, genetic engineering, energy production and other industrial and commercial activities affecting the quality of life.

How can young people acquire this scientific 'cultural baggage'? Specialist science teachers should be encouraged to teach about cultural aspects in the

science curriculum, because too often subject matter in the inters
curriculum tends to fall to the lot of teachers of the humanities or the sɔ͟
sciences. In addition to History, Literature can help to stimulate the interest of
senior secondary students. For instance, the story of Francis Crick and J. D.
Watson's discovery of the structure of DNA (deoxyribonucleic acid), the genetic coding of life, told in Watson's best-selling paperback, *The Double Helix*,
makes compulsive reading. Television also can play a valuable part through
dramatic, factional and documentary programmes (*The Double Helix* was later
adapted for TV drama), by presenting in an intelligible way the fundamental
achievements of science and the outstanding challenges facing scientists as the
twenty-first century approaches.

THE CREATIVE AND FINE ARTS IN EUROPEAN CULTURE

For many people, the fine arts, architecture, music, literature, scholarship and
film are the substance of European culture. Through these areas of activity men
and women gave expression to their creative individuality, and some Europeans achieved a level of excellence rivalling (and in certain respects exceeding)
the accomplishments of people in other civilizations.

The cradle of European civilization was Italy, whence the classical heritage
of Greece and Rome was transmitted to a barbarian Europe and the papacy
propagated the Christian faith. Italian primacy in science, literature, painting,
architecture and ideas was maintained until the sixteenth century, and thereafter the honours were shared between nations, between France, Germany,
Britain, the Netherlands, Spain and others. To choose between the individuals
or the nationalities who were most influential in shaping European consciousness is bound to be an arbitrary, not to say a flawed, exercise; the purpose here
is merely to indicate a few possibilities and stimulate teachers to think through
their own alternatives.

Leaving aside Italy, whose pre-eminence was unchallenged in the medieval
and early modern periods – the Italy, that is, of St Francis, Dante, Aquinas,
Michelangelo, Columbus, Leonardo da Vinci, Machiavelli or Galileo – there
seems no direct correlation between political and cultural influence, except,
perhaps, in the case of Louis XIV's France. In its golden age imperial Spain's
was substantially a spiritual leadership, personified by St Teresa and Loyola,
though Cervantes and Velásquez prove that a cultural flowering also occurred;
while the Netherlands, mere provinces of the Spanish crown, produced Erasmus and Rembrandt (and in a much later age Van Gogh). Scotland, a relatively
impoverished state, rivalled France in the field of philosophy during the Age of
Reason. In the last century and a half, Russia has contributed Pushkin, Tolstoy,
Stravinsky, Lenin and Eisenstein. Ireland has James Joyce. In addition, some
individuals left a different mark on their domains during their lifetime. Perhaps

in this category we might place Charlemagne, the Medici, Napoleon, Queen Christina of Sweden and Christian IV of Denmark.

Britain's influence was probably strongest in literature, political economy and science, with Chaucer, Shakespeare, Byron, Dickens, Bacon, Locke, Newton, Adam Smith, Malthus and Darwin. The Germanic peoples gave Europe Gutenberg, Luther, Bach, Haydn, Mozart, Beethoven, Wagner, Goethe, Hegel, Marx, Einstein and Freud, and the French (with French-speaking Switzerland) produced Montaigne, Descartes, Racine, Molière, Voltaire, Rousseau, Hugo, Manet, Cézanne and Le Corbusier, ranging over ideas, science and the arts.

This cultural burgeoning was neither continuous nor concerted and the strength of national traditions and mentalities, which was reinforced by the French Revolution, has to be reckoned with. However, there was also a degree of homogeneity and continuity so that art forms transcended national boundaries, making it possible to speak of specific European 'schools' or movements: Romanesque, Gothic, Renaissance, Humanism, Neo-Classicism, Baroque, Rococo, the Enlightenment, Romanticism, Impressionism, Naturalism, Symbolism, Realism, Cubism, Surrealism, Modernism and so forth. In addition, Europeans evolved particular forms and styles. In music we find the motet, madrigal, chorale, symphony, concerto and sonata; monophonic music gave way to polyphonic, and in the twentieth century electronic music developed from instrumental. In painting, the development of linear perspective and realism in the portrayal of the human form and of the natural world were pioneered by Italian and Flemish artists of the Renaissance. The theatrical arts evolved far earlier, with the tragedies of Aeschylus, Euripides and Sophocles, and the comedy of Aristophanes. Though the medieval mystery plays and popular theatre of the Commedia dell'Arte were less sophisticated models, dramatic art rose to new heights in Shakespeare and Molière, Ibsen and Brecht.

For 400 years the printing press ensured the supremacy of the printed word in the 'cultural baggage' of Europeans. The novel, in particular, developed as a genuinely European literary genre, for it 'has explored in exceptional richness and depth those experiences, principles, assumptions and prejudices which have made up the texture of European life'.[23] Who, we might ask, are the giants of European literature and which are the seminal works? Literary experts will differ, but a well-known British authority singled out Jane Austen, *Mansfield Park*; Honoré de Balzac, *La Peau de chagrin*; Herman Bang, *Tina*; Charles Dickens, *Bleak House*; Fyodor Dostoevsky, *The Brothers Karamazov*; George Eliot, *Middlemarch*; Gustav Flaubert, *Madame Bovary*; James Joyce, *Portrait of the Artist as a Young Man*, *Ulysses* and *Finnegan's Wake*; Franz Kafka, *The Trial* and *The Castle*; Thomas Mann, *Buddenbrooks*; Alessandro Manzoni, *I Promessi Sposi*; Marcel Proust, *Remembrance of Things Past*; Ignazio Silone, *Fontamara*; Stendhal, *The Red and the Black*; Leo Tolstoy, *War and Peace* and *Anna Karenina*; and Ivan Turgenev, *Fathers and Sons*.

However, movements and names (even of the great and the good) do not tell the whole cultural story. A vast range of visible evidence survives within

Europe's cities and through its rural heritage. The latter is being celebrated in an ongoing Council of Europe scheme, Architecture without Frontiers. In 1987 the European Campaign for the Countryside was inaugurated at Lisbon to preserve and promote the treasures of the rural habitat. Urbanization is also a unifying experience, although Europe's towns and cities vary in age, layout and purpose. Some grew up on the sites of Roman *castra*; some developed haphazardly with the increase in medieval commerce or around ecclesiastical communities; others were planned on the initiative of local rulers or secular authorities. For obvious military and economic reasons, walled townships were widespread in medieval Europe, but topography and climate made for differences in appearance. Buildings varied in style and construction according to the natural materials of the region. Thus to the human eye there are stimulating contrasts as well as similarities between the walled cities of Tuscany like San Gimignano, the rugged Old Town of Edinburgh and the fortified port of Aigues Mortes. The same judgement could be made of twentieth-century architecture (although contemporary construction depends on industrial technology rather than on nature for materials). Age should not be the determining factor in assessing the heritage-value of urban architecture; recognizing this, Council of Europe experts are anxious to win agreement on a set of principles as guidelines for a conservation and restoration policy.[24]

In the course of centuries a wealth of architectural styles has emerged in Europe. From the temples of classical antiquity (preserved in the Doric style of the Parthenon in Athens and the circular rotunda of the Pantheon in Rome) to the domed basilicas of the Byzantine world or the medieval cathedrals of Catholic Europe (Romanesque or Gothic, and sometimes, as with St Peter's, embellished by artists of genius during the Renaissance and Baroque periods), European architectural designs and structures were to assume international influence. However, the churches were not sole patrons of the arts. Secular monuments rose in equal abundance: fortresses such as Hradcany, Rheinfels or Château Gaillard, or the *castillos* of New Castile; the fortifications built by Hadrian, Edward I, Vauban or Maginot; imperial or royal palaces: Versailles, El Escorial, Schönbrunn, the Winter Palace and the *châteaux* of the Loire; the villas of Veneto; market squares and town halls symbolized by the fifteenth-century Grand Place in Brussels. While there is an understandable mystique about these structures, we should not forget that industrialization brought its own architectural monuments: the dockland warehouses and lighthouses of maritime Europe, the factories, cooling towers, hospitals, housing estates, bridges and the ubiquitous railway station, like Budapest's Keleti Palyautvar, with its memorials to Stephenson and Watt, all combining 'techniques and aesthetics, art and industry'.[25]

The legacy of European 'High Culture' was left by the wealthy and cultivated, a social and political aristocracy, whose tastes were served by the phenomenal talents and energies of an indeterminate number of artists and master craftworkers – architects, painters, sculptors, stonemasons, wood-carvers – some of whom, like Michelangelo or Bernini, Lebrun or Mansart, did achieve recognition in their time, while the rest worked anonymously for posterity. In more recent times, patronage has been exercised by a thrusting industrial and commercial meritocracy or an all-powerful state machine. The new craft-workers are architects, engineers, steel-workers, brick-layers and steeple-jacks, the employees of large construction companies. In this changed climate some Europeans seem indifferent to the achievements of the High Renaissance. A minority, perhaps, are even alienated by the aesthetic demands of, for instance, the medieval or seventeenth-century arts. Yet the increasing popularity of theatre-going, and the growing numbers who flock to cathedrals, stately homes, art galleries and museums of art and industrial archaeology, suggest that a sizeable number of Europeans recognize that they are custodians of a precious heritage.[26]

The problem for teachers is how to explain the aesthetic values of great art in such a way as to make it intelligible and appealing to the young. The task is formidable, for teachers face a generation of school pupils whose lives are completely pervaded by a counter-culture promoted through the media. Teachers of art (more than teachers of music) have been left to devise their own pedagogical solutions. But this matter of visual culture is absolutely crucial if we are to produce thinking people whose senses have been developed as fully as their cognitive skills.

In 1981 a group of French-speaking teachers argued that images, whether of a painting or a drawing, a film or a television picture, ought to be a stimulus to the eye and a means of familiarizing it with visual culture. An image can be 'a powerful illustrator, valuable as simile, as symbol and in terms of imaginative appeal'; it also acts 'as a motivating force, by virtue of its close association with the emotions.' Pierre Corset, of the Institut National de l'Audiovisuel in Paris, reiterated this self-same point, drawing attention to a serious methodological vacuum and the consequent deficiencies in much classroom practice. He argued that 'There is a profound disparity between the two ways of gaining knowledge – the one based on the written word, with well-known learning methods, and the other dealing primarily in sensory perception, which calls the emotions into play but in respect of which few learning methods have been established.'[27] We need to give all pupils an awareness of the 'language of pictures' and to establish teaching methods for sensory education, involving image and sound or combinations of the two. This can only be achieved by first highlighting the problems, then analysing the limitations of current methods of teaching in the Creative Arts and finally bringing together experienced teachers and experts to undertake a collective revision of teaching methods and learning strategies (comparable with the advances made in communicative language learning), prior to putting forward a set of practical recommendations.

The main thrust of Council of Europe policy on the Creative Arts has been to arrange set-piece events aimed at broadening public appreciation of the European cultural heritage. In the hope of promoting cultural democracy the CDCC organizes regular exhibitions of European art. Twenty of these major events have been held so far. They focus on the great movements and creative periods, on some of the patrons of the past or on historical themes. The exhibitions mounted during the 1980s demonstrate the artistic variety presented to the European public. The city of Florence was the venue for the 1981 exposition on Tuscany and the Medicis. In 1982 two exhibitions were organized, one in Lisbon on the subject of The Portuguese Discoveries and Renaissance Europe and another in Istanbul on Anatolian Civilizations. Two years later, in 1985, Lisbon hosted another event, the first 'exhibition-dialogue' on Contemporary Art. In 1989 Paris was the scene of the exhibition entitled The French Revolution and Europe. For teachers of Art and History the value of these large-scale exhibitions is that they make available catalogues of the works of art, together with slide-packs and video films for use as resources for teaching about European culture. Meanwhile a more complex initiative was launched in 1988 by the Council of Europe to co-ordinate a multinational celebration of the Baroque movement as part of the Cultural Routes project. It is expected that this will have practical repercussions for education at secondary level. Two major events, the European Summer of Baroque and the Queluz Colloquy, opened proceedings in Western Europe. However, the interest shown by the authorities in Central and Eastern Europe (Hungary, Poland, Czechoslovakia and Yugoslavia) and their desire to participate, exemplified by Yugoslavia's hosting of the Belgrade–Ljubljana Seminar in 1989, underline the international character of the Baroque style as an influence on the major art disciplines.

Like art, music is a form of international communication. It is therefore ironic that it has also been a manifestation of the diversity of Europe's national cultures, particularly during the nineteenth century when nationalism was at its zenith. By broad consent the music of Dvorak and Smetana is unmistakeably Slavonic, that of de Falla is Spanish. Arguably, too, there is an Italian quality to Verdi and a distinctive French character to the music of Ravel or Debussy, matched only by the Englishness of Elgar and Vaughan Williams. And yet the universal appeal of music can transcend its origins, a fact demonstrated by the adoption of Beethoven's rendering of Schiller's 'Ode to Joy' as the European anthem.

It was partly to broaden access to music for all young people and to reinforce music education that 1985 was designated European Music Year (as well as International Youth Year) on the joint initiative of the European Community and the Council of Europe. By coincidence 1985 also marked the tercentenary of the birth of the three European baroque composers J. S. Bach, G. F. Handel and Domenico Scarlatti. Among the special events of European Music Year (EMY) were a giant performance of the *Messiah* in Gothenburg by 3000 singers from five nations, the London Handel Week, the Bach Festival in Stuttgart, the Scarlatti exhibition in Portugal and Spain, and the European Music Youth Festival in Munich. Most activities were organized at national, regional or local levels, but a European Organizing Committee was set up to co-ordinate a Europe-wide programme, the participants being drawn from every walk of musical life. On New Year's Day, EMY opened with a Vienna Philharmonic concert broadcast on Eurovision with the support of the European Broadcast-ing Union (EBU). Some of the musical projects (such as the Norwegian musical, *The Keys of Paradise*, and Switzerland's 'evening of silence') were highly original, and others promised long-term benefits (such as the changes in Greece's system of music education and the translation at the initiative of Liechtenstein of the complete works of Carl Orff into braille).

The Council of Europe supported many events, including the Open House Music Day on 22 May in the Palais de l'Europe and a tour by a Youth Orchestra of European countries. The European Parliament likewise lent its support to the European Harp Week, which was organized by the Europäische Kulturinitiative. EMY also drew interest from some of the Eastern European countries, notably Czechoslovakia, Hungary, Poland, the USSR and the former German Democratic Republic. Perhaps the most ambitious popular event, however, based on an idea of the French national committee, was the multinational European Music Day, celebrated on 21 June, which involved some 10 million Europeans.[28] More recently, 1991 marks the celebration of Mozart's bicentennial and his contribution to European culture.

POPULAR CULTURE AND ITS EDUCATIONAL IMPLICATIONS

'Popular culture' is another all-embracing term meaning the achievements, values, occupations, activities and lifestyles of the people. The expression is often applied to modern culture: in other words, to denote the sociological face of contemporary Europe. This can be misleading: mass culture is in no way circumscribed by time, as is testified by the Icelandic sagas of the *Flateyjarbók*, the medieval mystery plays and the Arts and Crafts movement. Indeed, the surviving evidence of mass culture provides historians with invaluable sources by which to measure social vitality. There is another school of thought, how-ever, which interprets 'popular culture' as the antithesis of 'high culture' and inferior to it, since mass culture is non-discriminatory. This encourages the idea that popular culture should not be taken seriously because it is mere *kitsch*.

Popular culture has none the less enjoyed a revival, stimulated by increasing opportunities for leisure and a preoccupation with the cult of nostalgia. As long ago as 1964 a Council of Europe working party anticipated the value of the historical legacy left by popular culture. In a report entitled *Collective Awareness of European Cultural Highlights and their Incorporation into the Leisure Culture*, it noted that each era of European civilization experiences a 'modern' phase; so, in their time, the cathedrals of the Middle Ages were just as spectacular an achievement as today's nuclear research centres. Since the mid-1980s the Council of Europe has pursued a number of strategies to encourage awareness of the cultural geography of Europe – 'lifeseeing', rather than 'sightseeing', as the Dane Axel Dessau called it. By sponsoring restoration projects and encour-aging regional identity, but most of all by promoting the concept of cultural

routes, the CDCC expects to make Europe's cultural identity more
and better appreciated by the European public; to safeguard and enh
cultural heritage as a means of improving daily life and as a source o.   ..er
development; and to enable the public to experience fulfilment in their leisure
time. The term 'European cultural route' refers to any 'route crossing one or
more countries or regions, organised around themes whose historical, geographical or social interest is patently European'.[29] Two examples have already
been mentioned in passing – the Rural Habitat scheme, which was launched in
Luxembourg in 1987, and the Baroque Routes, a theme providing significant
linkages between the Catholic countries of Western Europe and the Orthodox
countries of Eastern Europe. Meanwhile, two other transnational routes are
being developed. The Silk Roads, which have particular relevance for the
history of France, Italy, Spain, Turkey and the United Kingdom, indicate the
importance of that valued commodity of silk in the exchange of styles, populations, technology, finance and culture. However, the prototype for the whole
notion was the identification of the ancient pilgrim routes to St James of
Santiago de Compostela in northern Spain, which illuminates many aspects of
Europe's spiritual, cultural and economic heritage. The pedagogical potential
of these routes will not be lost on History and Geography teachers familiar
with history trails, simulations and fieldwork. The UK Young Historians
scheme plans to implement the notion of cultural routes for secondary school
students, and already the St Jacques Centre of European Cultural Classes, in
the Royal Abbey of St Jean d'Angély in France, has initiated a multidisciplinary, extramural programme for 14–18 year olds to study the St James pilgrim
route. Its themes, to be treated either briefly or in depth depending on the age
and level of the students, are as follows:

1 *Compostela:* places of pilgrimage, popular piety, pilgrims and pilgrimages;
2 *Journey:* journey and routes, the horse, alms, assistance during the Middle
  Ages;
3 *Romanesque art:* Cathedral of St James of Compostela, the pilgrimage
  churches, Romanesque art in the region and in the West;
4 *Economic relations:* salt and wine, ships (evolution), trade in the Atlantic,
  shipping laws, the trader during the Middle Ages;
5 *A common civilization:* Christianity, borders, the emergence of 'national' languages, the emergence of names, the beginning of 'national' feelings;
6 *How do we see the Middle Ages today?*: the historical novel, the historical film,
  comic strips;
7 *A world of pictures:* in sculpture, in tapestry, in wall painting, in illumination;
8 *Emergence and development of towns:* ancient 'cities', new cities around abbeys
  and castles, with economic activity.

Archaeology, both classical and industrial, has also played a part in establishing exhibition and teaching centres where students can see and handle for
themselves the tools and artefacts of earlier technologies and sample, albeit
vicariously, the lifestyle of past generations. Vernacular architecture is another

aspect of popular culture with a high potential for secondary education. Renewed interest in the environment is leading to greater awareness of where and how people lived, and the traditional styles of domestic architecture which evolved from indigenous building materials: what can we learn, for example, about ways of life from the low-pitched roofs of Mediterranean houses or the steeply pitched chalet homes of the mountainous regions; the stepped and tiled gables of northern seaboard towns and the elaborate timbered or half-timbered 'magpie' facades of the north European hinterland? As to twentieth-century developments, the Design and Technology curriculum should incorporate 'popular' developments and major influences, typified by Le Corbusier or the Bauhaus school.

Popular traditions of the past and the present also have a strong human interest for younger secondary children. Folk songs, folklore and fable (in which Scandinavian and Central–Eastern Europe are particularly rich), folk dancing, traditional folk costume, re-enactment of local customs, participation in festivals, fêtes and sports can appeal to the imagination, test skills and provide an introduction to the cultural dimension. For adolescents the medieval mystery play is a theatrical alternative to walking the pilgrims' way to Santiago de Compostela or Glastonbury. The needs of the younger secondary pupils differ little from those of the primary child, and we would do well to remember that, although European culture encompasses civilization, literature, the sciences and the arts, 'for a primary child its practical manifestation is through his everyday life: his family, his house, his playground, his friends, his neighbours, the school, the parish, the village or the neighbourhood.' Culture, in the opinion of one primary expert, is nothing to do with aristocratic life-styles, not 'a mummified ritual' but 'a living, evolving force ... our way of life, our spiritual outlet; in other words, our European ideal'.[30] If that is so, it is vital that the diversity of European cultural material is fully exploited to counter the alternative modern subcultures or counter-cultures such as punk or acid house, which attract some young people away from their heritage cultures.

Industrialization has turned Europe into a market-oriented, consumer society with leisure to participate in cultural activities. 'The vestiges of European tradition ... have been painted over with a heavy varnish of "consumer society" life-style', warned Henri Janne. 'The cultural particularities which inhabit the collective memory and consciousness of Europe and without which its identity cannot be perceived, must be brought back to the surface through this varnish (it covers both national expressions of culture and the cultural identity of Europe).'[31] The lessons of the recent past suggest that progress does not lie with national cultures. The culture of consumerism gives Europe a veneer of unity, but whether the uniformity produced is advantageous remains to be seen. Apart from that uniformity (exemplified by the use of English and the ubiquitous blue jeans), consumer-culture is characterized by material abundance, inbuilt obsolescence, instantaneousness and, some would argue, superficiality. It is a culture that is both transnational and transatlantic. Like industrialization itself, this culture, once the popular culture of Europe, was transmitted to North America, transformed there and boomeranged back in the twentieth century.

Europe's reaction to this process has been half-hearted and ineffectual, in the opinion of Richard Hoggart and Douglas Johnson. In point of fact, the only response has been withdrawal into the least edifying symptoms of Europe's own popular leisure-culture. 'The key word today is . . . triviality. The masses of the population are on the receiving end of opinions, impressions and amusements . . . There is a new unity of Europe expressed by the Eurovision Song Contest . . . by interminable sporting contests and soap operas and now by satellite TV.'[32]

The exploitation of popular culture in the media, especially through television, is a profound educational issue. Young Europeans are children of the media; it has been estimated that they spend an average of 12–18 hours a week in front of a television screen, apart from the time spent listening to cassettes and radio. The audiovisual media constitute a growing influence on their judgement, taste and choice, as well as throwing down a challenge to teachers and educational administrators to put a higher priority on sensory education. Experts fear, however, that the young are receiving 'a mosaic culture' or *'un savoir en miettes'*. As consumers they have been further exposed to the products of the 'culture industries', companies producing media products such a videos and cassettes, while as the 1980s progressed, the smaller nations of Western Europe, like Denmark, felt that through TV their adolescents were being increasingly subjected to the influence of the national cultures and language of the richer or larger European states, such as France and Germany. The even greater danger, however, heralded by the advent of cable and satellite TV, is the total supremacy of the 'burger-culture', symbolized by the arrival of McDonalds in the Piazza di Spagna, one of Rome's most prestigious squares, and most recently in Pushkin Square, Moscow, not to mention the establishment of Euro Disneyland on the outskirts of Paris. If this is 'popular culture' and if it is the *only* kind of culture with which young Europeans can identify, then the whole concept of a *European* cultural dimension may soon be in serious jeopardy.

Recent Council of Europe activities indicate that it takes this threat seriously. In addition to the Cultural Routes programme, the CDCC launched a new activity in 1987, an examination by European experts of national and regional cultural policies, beginning with the French. A conference held at Florence in 1987 on Culture and the Regions sought to encourage regional cultural co-operation and the development of specific policies, and Lisbon was the scene of a major colloquy on Culture arising from the North–South Campaign of 1988. It is easy, however, to overlook the cultural revolution brought about by technology in popularizing art forms. In 1988 a series of colloquies was organized for European Cinema and Television Year (ECTVY) to mark the hundredth anniversary of the invention of cinematography and the fiftieth anniversary of television. Finally, we should not overlook the paperback

explosion which enables everyone to enjoy the masterpieces of European literature either in their original form or in translation. There is but one proviso:
much more should be done to persuade publishers to undertake the translation
and diffusion of this precious cultural heritage.

SOME CURRICULAR IMPLICATIONS OF EUROPE'S CULTURAL IDENTITY

It should be apparent that the cultural dimension is no longer an optional area
of the curriculum which European schools can choose to ignore or explore at
will (see the summary on pp. 98–9). Nor is it a passing fad, for in 1954 the
European Cultural Convention spelled out the need for education to include
the study of European civilization. Throughout the 1980s the pressure to find
ways of developing a coherent policy of Aesthetic Education, both at primary
and at secondary level, was inherent in the policy statements of the Council of
Europe and the European Community.[33] Teachers were urged to adopt a
number of strategies. Whenever the opportunity presents itself in the classroom or lecture room, European values – such as the principles and practices of
individualism, democracy and pluralism, and concern for the environment –
should be explained to pupils. Unifying cultural experiences should be emphasized in preference to divisive manifestations. Curricula should be modified to
include European themes and topics such as the conservation of Europe's
cultural heritage.

Inevitably these recommendations have implications for the structure of
curricula. If 'culture' is defined in the broadest terms, most subjects can make a
contribution towards the understanding of European cultural development,
including the Natural Sciences, Physical Education, Sport and Dance, although
the Human or Social Sciences, Modern Languages and Creative Arts have a
more important function. To translate this heterogeneous list into reality,
teachers may prefer to keep to conventional disciplines while taking account of
the universal elements of cultural experience put forward by Council of Europe
experts (Table 5). As an alternative, schools may develop a multidisciplinary
programme in the nature of Cultural Studies, to which specialist and generalist
teachers contribute. The opportunity could be taken to explore European
culture by means of the 'circles of influence' or through crossdisciplinary
themes such as that of Europe's Cultural Routes (Figure 6, p. 82, and Table 5).
A third strategy may also be considered, using the multidisciplinary courses of
modern Social Studies already functioning in a number of national systems and
in which it is established practice to deal with aspects of contemporary European society and politics. It should be possible to expand these programmes,
incorporating (where necessary) additional scientific, environmental and economic material, into a body of content reflecting the cultural input of the Human
and Natural Sciences. Parallel courses, focused on the Audiovisual Arts (with
History, Media Education and Classical Studies) on the one hand, and on

Table 5 The cultural dimension of Europe and the curriculum

| A civilization* | A society* | The curriculum | |
		Primary subjects	Secondary subjects
1	A B D	Religious Education History	Multicultural Education
2	A B C D	Sciences History	Political Education Technical Education Literature
3	A B C E	Political Education History	Media Education
4	A B C D E	Art Music History Literature	Craft and Technology Media Education
5	A B C E	Human Rights Education Political Education	History Multicultural Education
6	C D E	Economics Social Studies Human Geography	History
7	D E A B	Modern Languages NICT	Classics Media Education
8	C E	Environmental Education Geography	History Development Education Social Studies

* See Table 4, p. 83.

Modern Languages and Communication skills on the other, would provide for the remaining cultural elements of significance.

These suggestions imply a need for further curriculum reorganization and development at a time when European teachers are being asked to integrate new information and communication technology into their teaching and meet more sophisticated standards of assessment and evaluation. However, while the problems associated with teaching about European culture should not be underestimated, they are not insuperable. The work undertaken at the European Academy in Berlin over a quarter of a century indicated the value of child-centred strategies, but the principle was carried to excess in some courses of European Studies in the United Kingdom, where cultural content eschewed high culture in favour of popular culture, which was interpreted as 'what appeals to the taste of adolescents'. So some syllabuses came to depend on elementary sociological topics adding little to the substantive knowledge of European culture: pop stars, horoscopes, camping holidays, food and drink, advertisements, sport, clothes and cartoons.[32] This kind of subject matter can stimulate discussion by motivating students to speak in Modern Language classes, but it points to a recurring dilemma: how far should cultural content, whether 'high' or 'popular', be selected on its interest-value and affinity to student lifestyles, and how far in reference to Europe, and particularly to European distinctiveness? Good practice confirms the need to build on the foundation of pupil experience, but the greater priority must be to broaden pupils' cultural perceptions.

Finally, although emphasis has been given in this discussion to the cultural features which have brought a unifying influence to the indigenous cultures of Europe, popular culture has flourished amid demographic diversity and there are considerable variations within nation-states, from Italy to the United Kingdom, Belgium to the USSR. The fact that Europe has come under so many 'circles of influence' shows that it is a multicultural civilization. However, immigration and the movements of people in the twentieth century have been on a different scale from the past. Some of the ethnic minorities came from poorer to richer areas of Europe: Portuguese workers and their families moved to France, Yugoslavs to what was West Germany. But the majority of immigrants came from further afield, bringing with them distinctive, non-European values, religions and lifestyles, and the new multiculturalism challenged long-held social and educational assumptions. However, it also underlined the words of the 1968 European Charter of Education of the European Association of Teachers: 'Education must respect the diversity of our peoples and the variety of their cultural and spiritual features, which together make up our European heritage.'

SUMMARY OF REASONS FOR A EUROPEAN POLICY ON CULTURAL/ AESTHETIC EDUCATION

1 Young Europeans today live in a more sophisticated cultural environment than ever before. They are constantly exposed to a vibrant visual culture – through film, television, videos – which they do not always understand. They need to develop skills of visual perception and discrimination.

2 Young Europeans today live in a world of sound and noise. They need to develop their aural skills and learn to discriminate between the aural experiences offered by the latest audio media. They also need to become sensitive to the sounds and songs of the natural world.

> 3 European education seeks to develop in young Europeans a deeper awareness of Europe's cultural and environmental heritage. This is a responsibility of schools, working in partnership with other authorities to exploit the audiovisual experiences offered by art galleries, museums, special exhibitions, nature walks, reserves, parks, zoos, theatres, stately homes, cultural routes, historical sites and places of outstanding natural beauty.
>
> 4 Aesthetic education offers unique possibilities for personal fulfilment, satisfaction and life-interests, which assuredly benefit the development of an individual personality.

NOTES

1 Johnson, Douglas (1972), 'Odd man in', *New Society*, 28 December, p. 727.

2 Pring, Richard (1973), 'Integrated studies in the secondary curriculum' (Lecture given at York Conference on European Studies, 13 April), p. 9.

3 Janne, H. (1981), *Europe's Cultural Identity*, Strasbourg: CDCC, p. 2.

4 Rees-Mogg, William (1989), 'Disturbingly quiet on the Western front', *The Independent*, 2 October. Some of these ideas are taken up in the section on the creative and fine arts in European culture.

5 Eliot, T. S. (1948), 'The unity of European culture', Appendix to *Notes towards the Definition of Culture*, London: Faber and Faber, p. 119.

6 Jordan, Terry G. (1973), *The European Culture Area: A Systematic Geography*, New York: Harper and Row, pp. 2–7.

7 Cited by Blackledge, R. C. R. (1982), *Reflections and Observations on the CDCC Project No. 1 Preparation for Life*, Strasbourg: Council of Europe, p. 33. Additional comments of value, by Reinhard Schindehutte of the European Youth Centre, may be found in (1986), *Report of the Study Session of Young People for Democratic Action in Europe (Jeunes pour une action démocratique en Europe – JADE) on Training for Europe, EYC, Strasbourg, 1986*, Strasbourg: Council of Europe, pp. 15–16.

8 Rees-Mogg, 'Disturbingly quiet'.

9 Janne, H., *Europe's Cultural Identity*, pp. 5–7.

10 Jordan, *The European Culture Area*, pp. 15, 364–5.

11 Wake, R. A. (1980), 'Europe in the curriculum', unpublished paper, p. 12.

12 Janne, H. (1981), 'Europe's cultural identity' (paper for the Symposium on Europe in Secondary School Curricula: Aims, Approaches and Problems, Neusiedl-am-See, April 1981), Strasbourg: Council of Europe, p. 6.

13 *Ibid.*, p. 10.

14 Wake, R. A. (1980), 'The idea of Europe', unpublished paper, p. 9.

15 Green, Miranda (1990), *Symbol and Image in Celtic Art*, London: Routledge.

16 Resolution 885 on the Jewish contribution to European culture, 39th ordinary session of the Parliamentary Assembly of the Council of Europe, 5 October 1987.

17 Hoggart, Richard (1987), *An Idea of Europe*, London: Channel 4 Television Publications, p. 11.

18 Dance, E. H. (1967), *Bias in History Teaching and Textbooks*, Strasbourg: CDCC, pp. 91–2.

19 Wake, 'The idea of Europe', p. 7.

20 Dance, *Bias in History Teaching*, p. 101.

21 *Ibid*.

22 *Ibid*.

23 Hoggart, *An Idea of Europe*, p. 15, where he also cites the list of European novels which follows.

24 Saas, Marie-Laure (ed.) (1989), 'Introduction to 20th century architecture', *A Future for our Past*, **36**, p. 2.

25 Ballester, Jose Maria (1989), 'Editorial on Bridges', *A Future for our Past*, **35**, p. 3.

26 For a discussion of the importance of museums, see the report of the symposium on *Museums and the European Heritage: Treasures or Tools?* held in Salzburg, Austria, in September 1990.

27 Corset, Pierre (1981), *Report for the Symposium on The Secondary School and the Mass Media, Grenoble, France, June–July 1981*, Strasbourg: Council of Europe, p. 29. The views of the group of French-speaking teachers, quoted above, can be found on p. 18.

28 (1986), *Final Report of the Organizing Committee on European Music Year 1985, Strasbourg*, Strasbourg: Council of Europe.

29 Directorate of Education, Culture and Sport (1989), *Secretary General's Memorandum on European Cultural Routes*, Strasbourg: Council of Europe, p. 7.

30 Candidi, M. Corrado (1983), 'Methods and techniques for arousing in 6–12 year old children an awareness of a European dimension', in *Report of the European Teachers' Seminar on Europe in Primary School, Gazzada (Varese), Italy, May 1983*, Strasbourg: Council of Europe, p. 14.

31 Janne, *Europe's Cultural Identity*, p. 6.

32 Hoggart, Richard, and Johnson Douglas (1987), *An Idea of Europe*, London: Chatto and Windus, p. 81.

33 The Council of Europe: Recommendation R (83) 4 of the Committee of Ministers; Resolution (85) 6 on European Cultural Identity; Recommendation 1111 (1989) (1) on the European Dimension of Education; the EC General Report on the Activities of the European Communities on Heightening Awareness of the European Dimension, 1985; Resolution of the Council and the Ministers of Education, 24 May 1988 (88/C 177/02).

34 Goodson, I. F., and McGivney, V. (1985), *European Dimensions and the Secondary School Curriculum*, Lewes: The Falmer Press, pp. 29, 27–57.

CHAPTER 6

Language Learning and Communication

THE LEGACY OF EUROPEAN DIVERSITY

For a millennium the map of Europe has been a jigsaw of ethnic and linguistic groups, although the historic precedence of one language over all the rest enabled diplomatic communication to take place between courts and conclaves. Latin was the language of the Roman Empire, the Christian Church and medieval Europe, serving as the guardian of high culture and communication and the instrument of religion, administration and scholarship. The advent of nation-states and the emergence of national languages produced the decline of Latin in the last three spheres. In the extended period between the Renaissance and the eighteenth century, French superseded Latin as the cultural *lingua franca* of continental Europe and became the language of international diplomacy. German enjoyed a certain prestige in the nineteenth century as the international language of science, and in the last fifty years Russian has been the influential language of Eastern Europe. Since the mid-twentieth century, however, English has dominated in science and technology, as well as in the business, industrial, commercial, entertainment, travel, educational and information fields in the West. The growing influence of English in educational systems suggests that it may become a universal second language, although this trend is opposed by the international agencies and by the French in favour of multi-lingualism and multiculturalism. Meanwhile, regional languages, many of which survived the rise of the nation-state, continue to decline as means of communication, though they are increasingly cultivated as badges of identity.

Language, although the most important, is only *one* constituent of ethnicity: among the others are mentality, religion, territory, customs and perceptions of history. Thus much of modern European history charts the way ethnic groups have exploited these various facets of ethnicity to achieve self-determination and statehood. Nationalism was their spur and language frequently fuelled nationalist spirit. The latterday Holy Roman Empire was *'das heilige römische Reich deutscher Nation'*, and the feeling of ethnic unity among German speakers

101

was to bolster Hitler's power-base, as well as facilitating the extraordinary speed of German reunification in 1990. Yet affinity of language does not automatically act as an ethnic or a political catalyst (even if it makes for easier day-to-day communication). German, for example, is spoken not only in Germany but in Austria, Luxembourg, Liechtenstein and Switzerland, and by ethnic minorities in eastern France, southern Jutland, Eupen-St Vith in Belgium, South Tyrol, Transylvania and scattered parts of the USSR. In fact there are six major or 'high status' European languages: English, French, German, Italian, Russian and Spanish. The first two are the official languages of the Council of Europe, but the European Community has nine in everyday use. In reality we are some way from dismantling the hotch-potch of language barriers that continue to present obstacles to unity for many European citizens, despite the advances in high-tech communication. The learning of modern languages is therefore a sensitive issue and a priority area of European education policy.

To many people the extent of European heterogeneity is surprising. A recent taxonomy shows that there are sixteen full-scale sovereign nation-states in the West, each with its own literary language; there are eight political nations without their own literary languages, twelve 'ethnic nations' with no state but with their own literary languages, and in addition twelve special ethnic groups without literary language or statehood. Eastern Europe follows a similar pattern. Here seventeen full-scale nation-states or federated states exist, two political nation states which have no separate literary languages, twelve ethnic nations and one special ethnic group, the Yugoslav Muslims.

Of Europe's literary languages, the Romance tongues are spoken by some 175 million people; c.185 million speak the Germanic languages and c.215 million the Slavonic. There are also c.20 million speakers of other Indo-European languages, of whom 4 million speak one of the Baltic languages, c.2 million the Celtic tongues of Breton, Welsh or Irish, and 14 million Greek or Albanian. In addition to these, 21 million Europeans speak the Finno-Ugric languages and 13 million the Turkic-Tartar tongues, while over a million people speak either Maltese or the Basque language, Euskera. Europe's literary legacy is therefore preserved in many national tongues, which in the course of time produced many distinctive literary forms. Norway and Greece each have two distinct literary languages. In numerous states, such as Switzerland, Yugoslavia, Czechoslovakia and above all the USSR, citizens accept the need to be multilingual. Yet other nations with proud monocultural traditions can be divided from their neighbours by a deep linguistic gulf. Until recently, for instance, only 4 per cent of English people could speak French and only 10 per cent of French people spoke English.[1]

Traditional divisions have been complicated since 1945 by the emergence of the cultural minorities already mentioned. Guest workers, migrants or immigrants who are foreign-born now total over 20 million in Western Europe. In the city of Luxembourg almost 55 per cent of schoolchildren are of foreign parentage and, at the final count, over 180 languages were spoken in the schools of the former Inner London Education Authority, many being non-

European. To meet the diversity of needs, UK experts have current plans to introduce a range of languages into the secondary curriculum, including Chinese, Japanese, Hebrew, Arabic, Turkish, Hindi, Punjabi, Gujerati and Sylhet. In Sweden there is 'home language teaching' provision in over seventy languages. Europe contains both immigrant and emigrant countries; for instance, many people came from Portugal to France for employment, just as Yugoslavs seek work in Austria and the Turks are the most prominent *Gastarbeiter* in the Federal Republic of Germany. As a result, many schools in Europe have been effectively transformed into international institutions.

LANGUAGE AND THE PRESERVATION OF THE IDENTITY OF MINORITIES

To such migrant groups, as well as to all the other ethnic minorities with literary languages of their own, language is an important symbol of ethnic identity, both of the individual and of group membership, especially in an age of increasing rationalization from the centre.[2] The Council of Europe was quick to respond to the argument that language is a valuable common resource to be protected and developed. For some ethnic communities on the geographical margins of Europe, such as the Basques, Welsh, Bretons, Sardinians, Faroese and Lapps (or more correctly, the Saami), the vernacular is still a vital reality, despite the centripetal force of the nation-state. For these peoples, aware of their isolation, language is the bedrock of self-respect and independence. A Breton student at a *lycée* in Brest explained: *'Finistère, le nom de notre département, signifie littéralement la fin de la terre, le bout du monde quoi!'* But during a spontaneous discussion of national attitudes to cultural minorities, another girl spoke up for the majority of her fellows by insisting, *'Il faut garder nos différences.'*[3] And some thirty years ago, it was recognized by bodies like the Council of Europe that national policies and techniques of language teaching would have to respond to social change if Europe's minority languages were to survive, much less flourish, in the twenty-first century.[4]

A beginning was made in 1971 when a group of CDCC experts embarked on an investigation into a theoretical framework for learning languages, leading in due course to the definition of a range of 'threshold levels'. One of the underlying principles of their research was that language learning should help citizens to be 'autonomous', that is to say, to be free, self-reliant communicators and socially responsible individuals, aware of their cultural heritage. In other words, recognition of the cultural role of language in binding a community of individuals together is consonant with international doctrines on human rights. The 'threshold level' model was applied in individual projects to the learning of some twelve European languages, including those which are less widely used, such as Dutch, Norwegian and Portuguese, and two regional languages, Catalan and Basque. The purpose of the programme entitled Nivell Llindar, commissioned by the Generalitat or principality of Catalonia, is to restore the use of Catalan in public life and secure its teaching as a second language for non-speakers resident in Catalonia. The project Atalase Maila seeks to help the indigenous population to use Basque in everyday life. Council of Europe experts assisted with this work and the organization gave its stamp of approval to the preservation of dialects and minority and regional languages such as these. The recent adoption of the European Charter for Regional and Minority Languages by the Standing Conference of Local and Regional Authorities of Europe was a further important statement in defence of Europe's linguistic diversity.[5]

The linguistic heritage of the children of Europe's migrant workers cannot be left out of this discussion of minority languages. The question of 'heritage' languages is obviously part and parcel of the wider question of education for a multicultural society, a subject to be discussed in a later chapter. However, the children of Europe's new ethnic minorities often had to grapple simultaneously with psychological and educational problems, and underachievement was a common result. The ability to talk, to explain and make themselves known was a common practical difficulty. Thus the educational and communication needs of these pupils became one of the major targets for intergovernmental action, specifically through the Council of Europe's special Projects Nos. 4 and 6 (1977–81), and in more general terms, in the CDCC Second Medium-Term Plan of 1981–6. From the mid-1970s, when Western governments took stock of their educational policies towards migrants or immigrants and their children, the principles of equality of educational rights and the importance of linguistic communication for integration were recognized; additionally, there was growing acceptance that migrant children should have the opportunity to study the mother tongue and culture of their country of origin: the principle laid down by the Bullock Report (1975) that 'no child should be expected to cast off the language and culture of the home' was echoed in other national policy statements (though not always so clearly in practice). However, national strategies varied in response to local circumstances and to the immigrants' perceived needs.

Bilingual solutions aimed at integration were adopted by Sweden and the Netherlands, for example. In the case of the former, bilingual education was guaranteed by law from 1976–7, and research into language learning and the adult sector, published in *Threshold Level Swedish for Migrants*, produced useful benefits for the schools sector.[6] Multilingual states such as Belgium and Switzerland, however, evolved more complex models relating to the territorial dominance of language.[7] France, the Federal Republic of Germany, Sweden and the UK undertook pilot projects in language learning under the aegis of the Council of Europe's Project No. 4, and on their completion the CDCC continued to support language learning programmes. A colloquy at Strasbourg on Migrant Culture was followed later in 1983 by the Delphi Symposium on Language Teacher Training. As a result of these deliberations, a series of thirty-seven international workshops for teacher trainers was launched. Three, held in Norway in 1985 and in Sweden and Portugal in 1986, were devoted to migrant education. These workshops focused on a range of host country languages, including Catalan, Dutch, Norwegian and Swedish, together with the European, African and Asian languages of the migrants themselves. The solutions adopted have produced reasonable, though varying, stability; however, by 1988, it was becoming clear that the language learning needs of many former migrants had changed. Language for 'survival' was increasingly superseded by the vocational requirements of second generation immigrants, while language education as a whole was poised to proliferate in response to the pressures of European integration and the needs of the 'new migrants' taking advantage of easier mobility after 1992. In this situation many teachers feel that the most useful service the Council of Europe could perform in the 1990s is to accelerate the dissemination of information among European institutions and provide a regular forum for exchanging experiences and solutions to foreign language teaching, particularly in multinational classes.[8]

In concluding these remarks, it should be said that the work of the CDCC has been complemented since 1977 by directives of the European Community on initial teaching in the language of the host country, on social integration and on the organization of the teaching of the mother tongue. Within the framework of its educational programmes and with subsidies from the European Social Fund, the EC has supported a series of pilot studies and projects designed to improve teaching methods and help young migrants preserve their cultural identity while settling into their European environment.

LANGUAGE FOR COMMUNICATION AND UNDERSTANDING

'Heritage' languages may be precious for preserving group identity and culture in the 1990s, but the fundamental importance of language is as a means of interpersonal communication, a tenet reflected in the aims of the Council of Europe's mainstream activities in the field of Modern Languages. The Council has sought to promote mutual understanding, leading to respect and tolerance, to further co-operation and good working relations and to facilitate personal mobility, access to information and mutual enrichment between Europeans: in effect, to promote the multifarious aspects of communication. And so, as a corollory, the primary objective of modern language teaching is the development of pupils' communication skills, notably of personal expression and comprehension of written and spoken texts of all kinds. In the current climate of greater European unity and mobility, the value of developing such abilities should be obvious to all. Certainly, since a resolution of the Committee of Ministers called in 1969 for an intensified modern language programme, there has been a steady and marked improvement in levels of language competence throughout Europe, due to the advances made in the field of communicative language teaching.

The major shift of emphasis has been from the structure of language to the learner. Traditional methods prevailing into the 1960s were modelled on the teaching of the classical languages, notably Latin and Ancient Greek, and placed heavy emphasis on the memorizing of vocabulary and the application of grammatical rules to the translation of texts. This approach served students badly by failing to develop their aural and oral skills, leaving them ill-equipped for conversation or the practical demands of travel, business and everyday life. The working out of a new learning model based on 'threshold levels' was a significant achievement of the 1970s because it enabled a learner to develop the ability to communicate in a foreign language, by identifying specific objectives appropriate to the student's needs and capabilities. The descriptive model devised for English usage was matched by a French version, 'Un Niveau-Seuil', developed by a team at the Centre de Recherche et d'Étude pour la Diffusion de la Langue Française (CREDIF). Versions have now been produced for twelve languages of member countries.[9] Teaching and learning techniques were then elaborated in a series of pilot projects within the CDCC's major Project No. 4 on Modern Languages. One outcome was that learning was recognized as an active process, while teaching methods were changed accordingly, so that by the early 1980s there was 'a movement away from absolute control by the teacher to group work and pair work where the pupils communicate with each other. We also notice a movement away from closed questions to which the teacher already knows the answer and towards questions requiring speculation and the expression of feelings'.[10]

The communicative methodology was taken up initially by schools in eleven states – Austria, Denmark, the Federal Republic of Germany, Finland, France, Ireland, Italy, Portugal, Sweden, Switzerland and the UK – and in 1982 their findings were reported to an international conference at Strasbourg under the rousing banner, 'Across the threshold towards multilingual Europe – Vivre le multilinguisme européen'. Out of the Strasbourg recommendations came the second major CDCC Project, No. 12, Learning and Teaching Modern Languages for Communication (1982–7), indicating that the needs of the school sector were being treated in the 1980s as 'priorities among the priorities'. In particular, in 1982 the Committee of Ministers of the Council of Europe requested governments of member states to make provision for the learning of

> at least one European language other than the national language ... to pupils from the age of ten or the point at which they enter secondary education ... in such a way as to enable them by the end of the period of compulsory schooling ... to use the language effectively for communication with other speakers of that language.[11]

and to encourage the use of the new language-learning systems developed under the auspices of the CDCC.

Secondary school students were not the only target group of Project No. 12, but the prominence given to the school sector can be gauged by the fact that twenty-two out of its thirty-seven international workshops for teacher trainers were focused on school-based issues, from Communicative Language Teaching in the Classroom, held in Finland in 1984, to *Insegnare a Comunicare in Italiano – Problemi di Competenza Testuale*, which ran in Siena in 1987, while the majority related to the teaching of French and English in secondary school. There was broad consensus among those who took part in Project No. 12 that the principal aim of Modern Language teaching is to promote international communication.[12] A large measure of agreement was also reached on the form of language examinations, the reform of syllabuses, curricular guidelines and textbooks. In particular, the Schools Interaction Network, which had been started in 1979 under Project No. 4, developed further as the result of fourteen formal visitations to thirteen member countries made during the period 1984–7; some of these were for the purpose of establishing contacts for the first time (as in the case of Belgium, Spain, Greece, Iceland, Malta, Norway and the Netherlands); others were 'intensive' visits to investigate the working of the objectives procedures. Teachers' language proficiency and their appraisal of pupils' skills came under scrutiny, as did the use of specific goals to stimulate pupil motivation (evident in the UK graded language tests). The Interaction Network was inadvertently instrumental in extending the 'threshold level' specifications to several national and regional languages (Dutch and Portuguese, for example) and in disseminating new and effective teaching strategies and materials. Educational research projects were also promoted and their findings published; some were of a theoretical nature, others rooted in classroom situations, such as the study by Joe Shiels of the Linguistics Institute of Ireland, Dublin, on communicative classroom practice and procedures, which drew on textbooks in French, German, Italian, Spanish and English. Finally, since language teachers were one of the target groups of the project, a major programme of workshops for those responsible for pre- and in-service teacher training was included, with the express purpose of strengthening European co-operation in this field.[13]

THE ADVANCES OF THE 1980s

In retrospect, the 1980s were a period of considerable progress in Modern Languages education. In addition to the proven efficacy of communicative methodology and objectives procedures, the identification of transferable skills was a step in the direction of tailoring language courses to vocational or occupational needs. Through the initiative of the Federal German Ministry of Education, case studies into vocationally oriented language learning (VOLL) were commissioned in Austria, Denmark, France, the Federal Republic of Germany, Sweden, Switzerland and the United Kingdom, with interesting results. We might, for instance, note the UK schemes, Foreign Languages at Work (FLAW) and Technical and Vocational Education Initiative (TVEI), to prepare young people for the world of work. By the end of the decade four other broad trends were apparent. First, foreign languages were in regular use in the classroom and there were noticeably higher levels of attainment, due to the success of communication techniques and to the increasing opportunities enjoyed by young people to practise oral and aural skills on visits, exchanges, work schemes, holidays and so forth. The Project No. 12 team noted examples of conspicuous success in the bilingual teaching of some North Rhine-Westphalian *Gymnasien* and in the teaching of French in Andalusia.

Secondly, as a consequence of this, Modern Languages now make a high-profile contribution to the European dimension and to the development of European awareness and that more elusive phenomenon, 'European consciousness'. This trend reflects the basic assumption of CDCC and EC policies, that in stimulating awareness of other European peoples, the knowledge of foreign languages is a key element in the construction of Europe. By the 1970s both organizations were committed to the compulsory learning of at least one European language in addition to the mother tongue. By the mid-1980s the member states of the EC were ready to support the requirement that secondary students should have a working knowledge of two languages in addition to the mother tongue, on the grounds of the prime importance of language for international co-operation and integration, while the 1982 recommendation of the Council of Europe urged that authorities should ensure available facilities 'for learning as wide a range of languages as possible'. That policy was not confined to the secondary sector. In 1983 a CDCC working group endorsed a second language for primary children 'as a means of discovering Europe'.[14] Some eight or nine member countries are currently engaged in the introduction of languages into the primary school curriculum, which has been made a priority sector in the new CCDC modern languages programme.

Evidence of the advances made in foreign language competence by certain types of institution was put forward at a joint EC/CDCC conference on Secondary Schools and European/International Education, held at Namur in Belgium in May 1990 and organized with the co-operation of the International Baccalaureate Office and the European Schools. The linguistic needs of secondary students in a multicultural Europe came under scrutiny, along with the organization of a multilingual curriculum, the use of foreign languages as media of instruction for other subjects and examples of 'good practice' of the kind found in schools with Bilingual and International 'Sections'. In fact, it was revealed that there is considerable diversity of provision and strategy in schools. Small countries, such as Luxembourg and Malta, and certain frontier regions like Alsace and Nordschleswig, introduce their two main languages at primary school level, and consequently introduce a second foreign language at the beginning of secondary education. Special bilingual schools, represented by the École Active Bilingue in Paris, teach the first foreign language from kindergarten level. The European Schools, established to educate the children of officials in the European Community, also teach a foreign language from the first year of the primary school, and in several countries projects are under way on similar lines, as are a number of bilingual pilot schemes. Alternatively, where foreign language learning begins at the secondary school stage, intensive study (six or seven periods a week) is a normal procedure, a policy which was developed from the early 1970s in the Federal Republic. Bilingual classes are a feature of about seventy-five schools in the German *Bundesländer*, of an unspecified number of Dutch schools and also of French institutions, such as the Collèges Jean Monnet and schools in the region Nord Pas de Calais. Specially intensive language education is provided in trilingual classes of schools in Alsace, the International Sections of secondary schools following International Baccalaureate Organization (IBO) programmes, and separate state foreign-language schools, where pupils may learn up to four European languages. Similar opportunities, however, are open to Swiss *Gymnasium* students, of whom 15 per cent learn four modern languages, and also to many German pupils, for instance, in Baden-Württemberg and North Rhine-Westphalia.

A number of lessons can be learned from these experiences. Language learning benefits from starting at an early age, from daily contact between teachers and pupils and from continuity between the school sectors, since in this way pupil motivation can be most successfully sustained. High levels of competence are attained by gifted children in the 'Bilingual Sections' of secondary schools and through the use of one or more foreign languages as the teaching medium for pupils of 12+ in a number of subjects, notably History, Geography, Biology, and the Social and Political Sciences.[15]

The European Community, however, has a responsibility for the language competence of *all* its citizens. Thus the Commission took a quantitative policy line in 1989, putting forward to the Council of Ministers two proposals for promoting foreign languages through the LINGUA programme, one for post-secondary education and the other for the compulsory stage, giving

> a common framework of principles directed towards the promotion of Community languages in schools. These include encouragement for all school pupils to study at least one Community language in addition to their mother tongue, and to have the opportunity of studying in a second; increased priority in school curricula for communication skills in Community languages . . . and the inclusion, where appropriate, of evidence of competence in another Community language as a condition of entry to higher education. The pursuit of these principles is to be supported by . . . financial aid to support the intensification of language teaching in schools.[16]

The LINGUA package, which it was agreed should be backed by 100 MECU for the period 1990–4, was greeted with enthusiasm by most EC governments and by the European professional bodies such as the European Secondary Heads' Association, whose Dutch president spelled out what was at stake:

> We grown-ups cannot miss that opportunity for guiding our young people into Europe. Language is the key. That is why our association is ready and willing to play an important part in the LINGUA programme

... No country, no school, no secondary head would be wise to stand aside when LINGUA knocks at the door.[17]

The third broad development to emerge from the 1980s is the recognition by educators that Modern Languages Education has extended learning horizons. It is now appreciated that communication is a complex process involving the development of a large range of skills that in turn reflect different aspects of human activity and several areas of the curriculum (Table 6 and Figure 7). Language learning alone draws on skills and competences within the audio, visual, written, cognitive, physical and social areas, demonstrating that language-communication is multipurpose. In the unified, multicultural Europe of the post-1992 era, the communicative power of language will need to facilitate understanding, personal mobility, access to information, and the capacity to co-operate at work or at leisure with fellow Europeans, to exercise the rights and obligations of European citizenship, to understand and be involved in the social and cultural experiences which Europe has to offer, and finally, to appreciate Europe's environment. The Council of Europe's language experts have insisted that 'Communication is not confined to the routine business of daily life. For human beings to communicate, each must have an understanding and awareness of the socially shared attitudes, values, beliefs and knowledge which underlie the surface behaviour of the other and are encoded in language and the way in which it is used.'[18] Happily, most young Europeans today can accept this sophisticated interpretation of communication. As multimedia consumers they realize that attitudes, information and mood can be conveyed in a host of ways, ranging from body language to electronic systems. Louis Porcher made a similar point in another CDCC report:

When we say communication we do not mean by words alone: gesture, mimicry, movements, etc. form part of the mastery of communication and there is no justification for neglecting them in education, as is too often the case. The essential aim is to build up what linguists call 'communicative ability'. This ability is needed in every act of social life ... Communication is a social practice which includes language, itself a social practice.[19]

Finally, the innovation which is likely to affect the 1990s even more than it has changed the 1980s is the power of the new information and communication technology (NICT). Although language is the primary tool of communication, other communication media – film, television, newspapers and photographs – are constantly used by European teachers as stimulating visual aids in the classroom. However, the revolution in electronic communications has altered the scope and meaning of the word 'communication', and linguists have been in the forefront of this development since the advent of language laboratories and computer-assisted language learning (CALL). The advantages of multimedia systems, satellite TV and video have been apparent to language specialists for some time, and initiatives for teaching migrants have been helped by

Table 6 Communicative skills

Development skills needed for good communication		Media	Process skills practised in the process of communication
Audio	Hearing Listening Distinguishing Interpreting sound/ language/nuance	**Human voice** Radio broadcasting	Sympathetic listening Interpretation
Visual	Seeing/looking Interpreting sight Reading Scanning Appreciating	**Television** **Film** **Artistic media**	Entertaining Advertising Summarizing Artistic presentation
Oral	Questioning Answering Speaking Translating Conveying information	**Telecommunications** **Theatre**	Formal speech/verbal presentation Persuasion/promotion Artistic performance Informal conversation Other kinds of oral response Lobbying
Written	Spelling Punctuation/syntax Writing Drawing Paraphrasing Composing	**Books** **Letters** **Documents**	Research/collecting/collating information Scripting
Cognitive	Comprehension Conceptualizing Assimilating Memorizing Formulating responses Interpreting all media Articulation	**Electronic systems** Fax E-mail **Computers** Software and hardware	Formulating information Conveying information Storing information Accessing information
Physical	Touching Controlling Manipulating Simulating Acting	**Personal physique**	Motor skills Co-ordinating Adapting Demonstrating
Social	Facial expression Sensitivity to nuance, feeling Poise, self-confidence Selllllllf-reliance Maturity	**Body language** Gesture Mime Kinesies Proxemies	Displaying interest and desire to interact Non-verbal responses Fostering autonomy

teaching materials produced by bodies such as the BBC, Swedish Educational Radio and Television, and the Adolf Grimme Institut, the multimedia institute of the German Volkshochschulverband. One of the most influential multimedia productions was the Council of Europe's English language learning

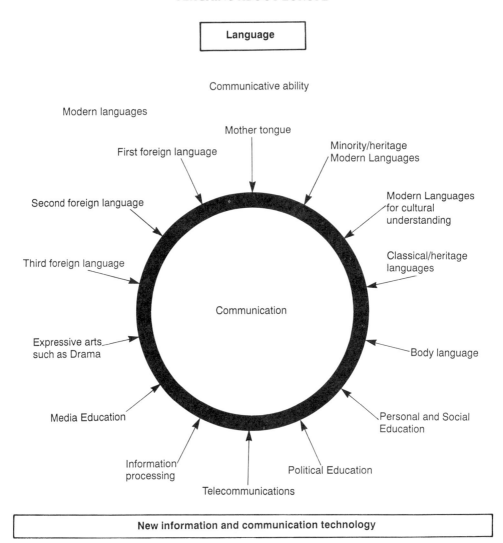

Figure 7 Fourteen keys to communication

programme for beginners, *Follow Me*. Produced by broadcasting authorities of the Federal German *Länder* and the UK under the Council's aegis and inspired by its threshold strategy, *Follow Me* set out to facilitate European co-operation. It was a conspicuous success in that it was followed by some 500,000,000 viewers in seventy countries. In fact, in the wake of the audiovisual revolution has come a dramatic language development: the steady increase in the use of English.

However, the advantage of the new communication technology is that it is truly international: it can be used effectively for the benefit of all audiences, speaking any language. Similar multimedia language courses were launched in 1990 for learning Catalan (*Digni, digni*) and Spanish (*Viaje al Español*). Meanwhile the BBC Continuing Education service has maintained a rolling programme in Italian, French, German and Spanish since the 1960s, and has sometimes included Russian, Greek and Portuguese. In view of the appeal of the audiovisual media to the young, considerable opportunities remain to be exploited. Television has already done much to remove the barriers of ignorance between people of one country and another: while demonstrating how a 'foreign' language is a natural part of the 'foreign' way of life, it also reduces the sense of alienation and makes participation seem a possibility. A group of British experts recently confirmed this by recommending that 'understanding television in a foreign language should be seen as a legitimate goal of language teaching.'[20]

LANGUAGE POLICIES FOR THE 1990s

The European Community's LINGUA initiative emphasizes the importance of Modern Languages for European understanding and the socio-cultural context of language learning. In their strategies for a European dimension, the Education Ministers also attach great weight to student study visits 'both for improving linguistic proficiency and for gaining knowledge and experience on cultural, scientific and technical matters.'[21] Equally, they accept that language teachers need more time for study abroad and a guaranteed flow of up-to-date information. The expansion of extramural opportunities during the 1980s (the subject of Chapter 8) is a policy area in which the European Community and the Council of Europe have already collaborated. European co-operation in language teaching has also been set in motion by the Schools Interaction Network and encouraged by organizations such as the Association for Teacher Education in Europe (ATEE), the Foundation for European Languages and Educational Centres (Eurocentres) and the newly constituted Association for Language Learning (ALL). Greater harmonization in matters of curricula, evaluation, materials, resources and teacher training is a clear prospect for the 1990s.

Raising the level of 'language awareness' is another priority for the coming decade. It requires better dissemination of information, linking education to the world of work, new teaching strategies and the imaginative extension of language festivals and competitions. The European Schools Day Competition is a long-standing event,[22] but recently the notion of a Festival of Languages has been tried out in Belgium, the Federal Republic of Germany, Portugal and the United Kingdom. These festive occasions give opportunities to display language talent in a variety of ways (through performances, original writing and videos). On the well-established precedents of music and poetry festivals, prizes are awarded to raise pupil interest and motivation. A European Festival of Languages, organized by the Council of Europe, would be the logical extension of what has proved a successful initiative for increasing public awareness.

Linguistic awareness would also be helped by a fuller understanding of the communicative approach. There should be greater emphasis in classrooms on the genuine *use* of foreign languages, rather than mere practice. Use of language involves multi-skill tasks rather than limited transactions, and pupils need to improvise to cope with the unexpected. Teachers therefore have to devise and implement an integrated skills approach in the classroom, including reading programmes and courses of study which incorporate progression and continuity of learning. They must be able to promote and manage a range of situations where there is pupil interaction. And last but not least, classroom strategies should maximize the teachers' use of foreign languages. The practice of teaching and learning other subjects in a foreign language stimulates linguistic competence in both teachers and pupils, and although there are acknowledged difficulties in enlisting teachers with sufficient expertise, the problem can be eased in various ways. As was suggested earlier, considerable use can be made of foreign language media – TV news and feature programmes, films and music – and interactive networks, while after 1992 in all EC countries the number of resident speakers of other European languages should increase noticeably, some of whom may be enlisted into service in schools.[23] In addition, the EC General Directive on equivalence of qualifications, operative from February 1991, should allow for a much greater mobility of teachers.

Accepting the necessity of maintaining progress in Language Education, the CDCC's present priority is to develop the strategies of Languages for Communication to meet the needs of Language Learning for European Citizenship. One of the successes of Project No. 12 was the marked improvement in lower secondary language education; hence the next CDCC Modern Languages programme will focus on the primary and upper secondary sectors. Special attention will be paid in the coming decade to a number of areas. First, educational research should focus on a range of matters: how learners (across the ability range) learn a foreign language, and whether, and if so how, learning one foreign language facilitates the learning of a second; the nature of linguistic difficulty; the nature of progression in communicative language learning/ teaching; learner autonomy; the role of grammar; curriculum modelling; motivation in language learning; the integration of visits and exchanges into the curriculum.[24] Secondly, given the challenge of 1992 and the new dialogue between East and West, it is vital that Europe has a highly trained, multilingual teaching force ready for the twenty-first century. The idea of a European model for teacher training in Modern Languages has much to commend it. However, this would require an extended programme of international workshops to build up teacher confidence in communicative methodology, backed by school-based INSET with multimedia packages, self-evaluation modules, videos and interactive support materials. The aim must be to give teachers linguistic, cultural, pedagogical and technological skills, with 'recognition that modern language teaching requires a firm technological base'.[25] Thirdly, this point turns the discussion from the subject of traditional language-communication to that of advanced electronic communication.

EDUCATION AND THE NEW INFORMATION AND COMMUNICATION TECHNOLOGY (NICT)

The revolution in advanced technology in Western Europe gained a new momentum in the 1980s. Although the direct effects were primarily economic, in the long run there are deep socio-cultural implications. Reference has already been made to the influence of audiovisual media, especially television, on Europe's cultural identity, and we shall return in the following chapter to the media as a subject area of the curriculum. It is necessary, however, to make a distinction between Media or Communication Studies, which deal with the socio-cultural values area, and the use of the media as teaching resources and tools of communication; for, put another way, 'the use of the media for educating the citizen, and educating the citizen in the use of the media, are quite discrete, distinct and separate, one from the other.'[26] We are here concerned with the latter, with the development and use of mechanisms of communication. But within this spectrum there are other distinctions to be made. We should not confuse the 'conventional media', the principal sources of information up to the 1980s – press, radio, cinema and TV – which provided uni-directional communication, with the new interactive media systems, combining audiovisual elements with microcomputers, which are a feature of Europe's fully fledged information society.

A 1989 report on education in the Federal Republic of Germany reminds us that information or knowledge is said to be doubling every five or six years; that in the Western *Länder* of Germany the information sector accounted for one job out of every two, and that the boom in IT (information technology) markets and services means that by the end of the twentieth century 70 per cent of the active population are likely to be concerned with the new data-processing techniques.[27] It is worth reflecting therefore on the danger of European society being divided between those who can understand and participate in the processing and communication of information – the 'computer literate' – and those who suffer by age, class, gender, ethnicity and handicap from the disadvantage of what has come to be called 'computer illiteracy'.[28] Education for European citizenship must include the measures to minimize the social injustice of media poverty, and it is important to note that there have been numerous national and international educational initiatives to address the problem.

In the last decade all Western governments have reviewed their policies and most have already taken steps to promote technological education, though their achievements have varied.[29] Some stepped up their provision for technical education and media or communication studies or targeted certain sectors. Distance learning was pioneered in Denmark and Portugal but has also been developed in France, Austria and the other Nordic states. Other states launched fresh major initiatives, among which were the Netherlands Information Stimulation Plan of 1984 (INSP) and Norway's Programme for Action on computer technology, Italy's 1985 National Plan for computing in secondary education and Spain's New Technologies Programme of 1987. It is perhaps significant that smaller countries like Iceland, Luxembourg, Malta, Switzerland and San Marino have demonstrated that they are equally committed to NICT. From 1989 a new sixth-form subject, Systems of Knowledge – the philosophy, history and practice of communications – has become part of the university entrance requirements in Malta.

The educational issues arising from NICT have also been studied at length by the major international organizations. UNESCO set the pace by monitoring progress in media education from the 1970s,[30] while the European Commission's programme for young people, Community in Education and Training for Technology (COMETT), emphasizes training in NICT for the post-secondary sector, just as LINGUA encourages telecommunication links between classes of students. The European Ministers of Education meeting in Turkey in 1989 under the Council of Europe's aegis sought an overview of the impact of the new technologies on education to meet the challenge of the information society.

Information technology has been described as 'the great enabler'. Primarily, it enables the process of communication to take place.[31] As an invaluable tool of learning it enables us to access and process information quickly, accurately and objectively; it enables people to extend their powers of perception, thought and articulation through numerous activities which include writing, solving mathematical problems, formulating the visual image, making music and speech and communicating the results. With the linking of microcomputer technology to telecommunications, we are enabled to transmit information almost instantaneously to another person or institution within the same country or across the globe. However, since telematics services allow the individual selective access to knowledge, there is also considerable scope for individualized, autonomous learning. The potential for educational use now becomes apparent.

NICT enables teachers to achieve a number of educational goals:[32]

- to achieve existing goals more effectively by using new methods, such as video presentation and computer-assisted learning (CAL);
- to enable new goals to be taught within the current curricular framework of subjects; for example, through television or computerized database;
- to learn about society and its technology, with a possible futures orientation;
- to learn to use NICT as part of a general programme for developing information and communication skills;
- to acquire knowledge and skills appropriate to vocational training for a specialist occupation;
- to develop a critical approach to the use of NICT from a variety of perspectives;
- to use NICT for creative purposes of personal communication and self-expression.

Not only does it enable *existing* goals to be carried out more effectively, using methods such as video presentation and CAL, it also opens up the possibility of *new* curricular goals. Videodisc technology allows easy transition from stills to moving picture sequences, the facility to freeze or repeat, retrieve and follow up needs for information. These techniques can add a new dimension to the services of the uni-directional media, which can be critical in a subject like Literature. As the UK National Curriculum English Working Group argued, the media as a whole can play an important part in developing English (as an example of a literary language and mother tongue) by enabling pupils to understand how the various media, especially literature, film and TV, construct meanings and textual interpretations, how they throw light on different genres, narrative information, fiction, documentary exposition, and concepts such as author, editor, audience and stereotype. Using NICT in Literature lessons it will be possible to compare dramatic performances and extend the facilities for critical analysis. As to other disciplines, History teachers have realized that with the appropriate software they can make use of a variety of evidence, from archaeological finds to portraits and manuscript material. There are many advocates of the potential value of the electronic media for History teaching. A Danish expert demonstrated the use of the ECHO databases to a European Teachers' Seminar of historians and social scientists in Ebeltoft in 1987; an Anglo-Dutch electronic mail link-up of twenty-four primary schools, sponsored by Shell UK in recognition of the tercentenary of the Glorious Revolution (1689), provided a focus for historical studies and the countering of stereotypes; the European Studies project for 11–16-year-olds uses E-mail, and the museum of Flag Fen in Cambridgeshire, England, launched a UK E-mail scheme in 1989 which it is planned to extend to mainland Europe.[33] These examples indicate the use of communication technology in History teaching, but continuing progress depends on the availability of suitable software.

However, apart from Science and Mathematics the subjects which grasped the NICT nettle most readily were Geography and Modern Languages. At the joint CDCC–IDG symposium held at Utrecht in September 1989 on Geographical Information and Documentation on European Countries, specialists from nineteen European countries discussed a range of new developments, including the importance of electronic media.[34] The experts took account of the pioneering work carried out by the Information and Documentation Centre for the Geography of the Netherlands and urged the development of Geographic Information Systems as Educational Tools (GISET) and the general adoption of videodisc technology. It was admitted that there was some disparity between those European teachers still using traditional teaching aids and those who were already provided with interactive videodisc technology to process, store and access information, and were therefore equipped to exploit the interconnected use of graphs, diagrams, statistics and photographs, and provide simulated situations for pupil exercises. E-mail is also being used to conduct joint environmental projects by students in different countries – the European Studies Project and the Anglo-Dutch project involve studies of the local environment – and this is an area where geographical learning stands to benefit considerably.

Teachers of Modern Languages also have at their disposal a range of audiovisual material (including original version films) to develop aural skills, stimulate pupil imagination and hence promote language in speech and writing. (As a good example, foreign language classes in Lower Saxony have successfully compiled a newspaper in English using a database accessed through electronic mail.) In fact, the concept of the programming language in IT software is an interesting aspect of the Language and Communication axis, which should establish a special affinity between language teachers and learners and the computer. It is worth noting that the San Marino report of 1989 to the European Ministers of Education testified that the study of the artificial language PROLOG acted as a spur to discussions on the nature of language and communication; and the official German view is that 'No media education can exist without language education. A language used solely for processing and transmitting data can be just as important as the language used for complex human communication (with all its ambiguities, ironies and paradoxes).'[35]

Within the general curriculum, electronic communications allow students to undertake simulations and acquire up-to-date information from external sources, about weather patterns (for Geography) or current affairs (for Civics) or economic trends (for Economics). Using database and numerical data-processing facilities, students can then undertake more sophisticated data analysis and problem-solving than was once possible. Such exercises fulfil another educational goal of NICT: reinforcing the development of general study skills, graphical, information and communication skills. And lastly, the creative potential of NICT in enabling students to create a video, a newspaper or a computer programme is sometimes overlooked, but it can serve as a natural source of self-expression in written form, art, music or technological design. It has been argued that 'having to construct a communication develops a deeper understanding of the content of that communication'.[36]

The special needs of disabled young people can also be met through new technology. Advances in robotics have resulted in the development of sophisticated prosthetic appliances for those with motor handicaps, and it is now clear that NICT can help those with sensory handicaps. In the UK a government-funded centre uses information technology to help children with severe communication problems arising from cerebral palsy and injury. Norway has a NICT course for trainee teachers of the disabled, France has pioneered teaching aids for handicapped children, and a number of other countries, including the Federal Republic of Germany, the Netherlands, Sweden and Switzerland, have advanced pilot schemes in operation. Computer technology also enables teachers to provide for the differences in capability and work rate between individual pupils. The flexible and personalized learning opportunities can be beneficial to both slow learners and exceptionally gifted pupils. Through their Computers for Success project, the French have found that slow-learning second-year secondary school pupils can understand concepts in subjects of the general curriculum.

In a Council of Europe paper on policy options, three routes for incorporating NICT into secondary curricula were suggested. Most teachers and experts seem to favour the first, using NICT as a tool across all the subject areas of the existing curriculum. Alternatively, it can be inserted into a new subject or subjects for all pupils as, for example, Media Education or Computer Literacy; or thirdly, it can be treated as a Computer Studies option for older secondary students.[37] In fact, NICT has been introduced into European secondary education through various arrangements, too diverse to describe here. However, in Germany, where elementary IT courses form part of the curriculum of all pupils, certain criteria have been established, similar to those put forward by the new National Curriculum in the UK. Teachers elsewhere may find the checklist helpful in determining their own strategies. The courses aim to give every student the following basic knowledge and skills:

- analysis of individual experience of IT;
- instruction in the basic concepts of IT;
- hands-on instruction in the use of computers and peripheral devices;
- instruction in the possible applications of and methods of using IT;
- introduction to the use of algorithmic diagrams in problem-solving;
- familiarization with the development of electronic data processing.[38]

In addition, the courses cover certain values-related issues and competences to which we shall return in the context of Media Education.

Despite its obvious uses, some educationists urge caution in regarding NICT as a panacea for all educational ills.[39] Some teachers undoubtedly feel threatened by IT hardware, and most experts would agree with the OECD Report of 1986 that 'We need to train, as rapidly as possible, the entirety of the teaching profession to use the new technologies.'[40] The implications for pre- and in-service training are enormous. As a basic necessity, UK language experts recommended that Language students and serving teachers should be familiar with computer-assisted language learning, data retrieval, word processing and the uses of satellite TV and video as elements of communicative methodology.[41] The Utrecht Symposium of 1989 made similar recommendations for Geography teachers.[42] At the same time, we might note that a number of countries, such as France and the Nordic states, have made substantial headway in this area. Denmark, for instance, has completed a five-year programme of training for all its upper secondary teachers.

Teachers also need to be informed of the range of possible pedagogical strategies and to study 'good practice' initiatives. Some of the most interesting examples of communication in practice consist of school links established by electronic media – fax, videotext, E-mail, satellite and teleconferencing. A number of schemes have operated on a purely national basis, such as the MINERVA project involving some 237 schools in Portugal, and NETWORK INTER-ACTION, a pilot communications scheme based in London, linking 1500 youth clubs and schools in the UK. Mention has been made elsewhere of an international communications programme, the European Studies Project, linking upper secondary school students from England, Northern Ireland, the lic of Ireland and Belgium by E-mail with the aim of developing infor- mation and foreign language skills. A data communication project was devel- oped in Kalmar to link Swedish and British schools by E-mail, and another Anglo-Scandinavian plan is the European Comparative Local and European Studies (ECLES) involving ten schools in Stockport, UK, and Copenhagen in a joint environmental studies project. Networks have been created between schools in Sèvres, Madrid, Naples and Lisbon, debates taking place with the use of teleconferencing. Additionally, French schools have telematic links with Italy through the FORTUNAT network and have conducted bilingual tele- conferences with German pupils in Lower Saxony. UK primary and secondary schools have been active in using E-mail and satellite communication to link with schools in other European and overseas countries for the purpose of projects across the whole curriculum. Since 1986 teacher groups have been active in discussing the mechanisms for establishing a European schools network.[43] Recognizing that there are technical barriers such as compatibility of trans-European computer links, there are nevertheless encouraging examples of interschool co-operation, which suggest that progress has been made towards finding a communications model where 'with the help of electronic mail and other computerized systems one might see develop an international network of schools based on clusters of three to six schools co- operating in the elaboration of joint studies and the preparation of pupils for life and work in a multicultural and multilingual society.'[44]

If this ideal is implemented in Europe, there will be massive implications for schools, for investment in hardware and software and trained personnel, for changes in curricula, in teaching methods and styles, school organization and community relations. The potential for enriching the curriculum and for devel- oping international awareness and understanding is beyond dispute. In these circumstances, communication in all senses of the word would become the key activity in schools; in which case the aphorism that 'Education is both more and less than communication' becomes a good deal more meaningful.[45]

NOTES

1 Krecji, Jaroslav, and Velimsky, Vitezslav (1981), *Ethnic and Political Nations in Europe*, London: Croom Helm, *passim*. My thanks are due to Professor Krecji for giving me updated statistics for this study.

2 Bliss, I. (1989), 'Language and language teaching in plural societies: an agenda for discussion', *European Journal of Teacher Education*, **12** (2), p. 60.

3 Livet, Eve (1988), 'L'Europe en trainant les pieds', *Le Monde de l'Éducation*, **152**, pp. 72–7.

4 For example, Welsh was in danger of extinction and even as late as the 1950s was regarded as an anachronism. Since the 1970s the trend has been reversed, Welsh has proved both successful and popular as a teaching medium, and in the new National

Curriculum it will form part of the compulsory element in the curriculum in Wales for pupils up to 16 years. See Bliss, 'Language and language teaching', p. 62.

5 Girard, Denis, and Trim, John (1987), *Final Report of the Project Group (Activities 1982–87) on Project No. 12: Learning and Teaching Modern Languages for Communication*, Strasbourg: Council of Europe, pp. 9–15, 49–50; (1988), *Report of the Secretary General, M. Marcelino Oreja, to the Parliamentary Assembly on Problems of Education and Training in Europe, May 1988*, Strasbourg: Council of Europe, p. 14.

6 Porcher, Louis (1981), *The Education of the Children of Migrant Workers in Europe: Interculturalism and Teacher Training*, Strasbourg: Council of Europe, p. 148; Bliss, 'Language and language teaching', p. 60; Salin, S., 'Language learning by migrants: a follow-up study', in Girard and Trim, *Final Report of Project No. 12*, p. 54.

7 Bliss, 'Language and language teaching', p. 63; Banks, J. and Lynch, J. (1986), *Multicultural Education in Western Societies*, London: Holt, Rinehart and Winston, p. 142.

8 The importance of the European Documentation and Information System for Education (EUDISED) was noted: Rey, Micheline (1983), *General Report on Migrant Culture in a Changing Society: Multicultural Europe by the Year 2000*, Strasbourg: Council of Europe, p. 4; Girard and Trim, *Final Report of Project No. 12*, pp. 65–7.

9 Girard and Trim, *Final Report of Project No. 12*, p. 22.

10 Starkey, Hugh (1984), *Report of the CDCC Symposium on Human Rights Education in Schools in Western Europe, Vienna, May 1983*, Strasbourg: Council of Europe, p. 22.

11 Recommendation No. R (82) 18 of the Committee of Ministers of the Council of Europe to Member States concerning Modern Languages.

12 Salter, Michael (ed.) (1989), *Languages for Communication: The Next Stage*, London: DES and CILT, p. 2.

13 Girard and Trim, *Final Report of Project No. 12*.

14 (1983), *Report of the European Teachers' Seminar on Europe in Primary School, Gazzada (Varese), Italy, May 1983*, Strasbourg: Council of Europe, pp. 10–12.

15 DES (1985), *The European Schools and the European Baccalaureate*, London: DES papers presented to the EC/CDCC Namur Conference on European and International Education in Europe, May 1990.

16 (1988), *Bulletin of the European Community*, Strasbourg: Council of Europe.

17 Van Rooijen, Anton A. (1989) (President of the European Secondary Heads' Association), reported in *The Observer*, 21 May.

18 Girard and Trim, *Final Report of Project No. 12*, p. 75. A group of UK specialists stated that in addition to basic transactional communication, pupils 'also need to acquire the language which will enable them to: communicate in the classroom, express personal feelings and opinions, talk about the life and culture of their own and the foreign country, give an account of everyday experience, express themselves imaginatively in speech and writing, and in general communicate spontaneously in unrehearsed situations' (Salter, *Languages for Communication*, p. 7).

19 Porcher, *The Education of the Children of Migrant Workers*, p. 82.

20 Salter, *Languages for Communication*, p. 9.

21 (1988), 'Resolution of 24 May 1988 of the Council and Ministers of Education on the European dimension', *Official Journal of the European Communities*, C177, **31**.

22 This event is discussed in Chapter 8.

23 Salter, *Languages for Communication*, pp. 17–18. The same suggestion emerged from *Quelle école pour l'Europe? Rapport du Forum Européen Organisé à Lyon par EUROPE EDUCATION*, January 1989.

24 Salter, *Languages for Communication*, p. 20.

25 *Ibid.*, p. 17.

26 Corset, Pierre (1981) *Report for the Symposium on The Secondary School and the Mass Media, Grenoble, France, June–July 1981*, Strasbourg: Council of Europe, p. 19. The report by Professor Francis Balle, 'The information society, schools and the media', given to the Standing Conference of European Ministers of Education at Istanbul, October 1989, gives a succinct explanation of the information communication revolution in post-industrial society. Balle's report is reprinted in Eraut, M. (ed.) (1991), *Education and the Information Society*, London: Cassell.

27 de Landsheere, Gilbert (1989), *Report for the 16th Session of the Standing Conference of European Ministers of Education, Istanbul, October 1989: The Information Society and Education: Synthesis of the National Reports*, Strasbourg: Council of Europe, pp. 13–14.

28 Cerych, L., and Jallade, J.-P. (1986), *The Coming Technological Revolution in Education: Report for the Netherlands Ministry of Education and Science on the Potential and Limitations of New Media and Information Technologies in Education*, Paris: European Institute of Education and Social Policy.

29 The policies of European governments are summarized in the twenty-six National Reports on *The Information Society – A Challenge for Education Policies?* for the Standing Conference of European Ministers of Education, Strasbourg: Council of Europe, 1989.

30 For example, (1977) *The Study of the Media in Education*, Paris: UNESCO; (1982) *Report of the Grunwald Symposium on Education of the Public in the Use of Mass Media*, Paris: UNESCO; (1984) *Media Education*, Paris: UNESCO; Masterman, L. (1986), *Report on the Impact of Mass Communication Media on Curriculum Development and Educational Methods*, Paris: UNESCO.

31 Carpenter, J. P. (1989), *Report of the Colloquy on Computerised School Links, on Using the New Technologies to Create Links between Schools throughout the World, Grossmead Conference Centre, Exeter, Devon, UK, October 1988*, Strasbourg: Council of Europe, p. 2.

32 These are elaborated in Chapter 1 of Eraut, M. (1989), *Report for the 16th Session of the Standing Conference of European Ministers of Education, Istanbul, October 1989: The Information Society – A Challenge for Education Policies? Policy Options and Implementation Strategies*, Strasbourg: Council of Europe. Reprinted in Eraut, M. (ed.) *Education and the Information Society*, London: Cassell, pp. 171 ff.

33 The demonstration by the Danish expert, Johann Nielsen, is reported in Shennan, M. (1987), *Report of the European Teachers' Course on Teaching about European Co-operation and Integration in Upper Secondary Schools, Ebeltoft, Denmark, March 1987*, Strasbourg: Council of Europe, p. 5; see also Austin, Roger (1989), 'Report on the European Studies Project, Strasbourg: 1989', *The Times Educational Supplement*, 8 December.

34 Graves, Norman (forthcoming), *Report of the Symposium on Geographical Information and Documentation on European Countries, Utrecht, September 1989*, Strasbourg: Council of Europe, pp. 24, 34–5.

35 (1989), *Report of San Marino to the 16th Session of the Standing Conference of European Ministers of Education, Istanbul, October 1989, on The Information Society – A Challenge for Education Policies?*, Strasbourg: Council of Europe, pp. 148–9; de Landsheere, *Report: The Information Society and Education*, p. 21.

36 Eraut, *Report: Policy Options*, p. 34.

37 *Ibid.*, pp. 37–9.

38 (1989), *Report of the Federal Republic of Germany to the 16th session of the Standing Conference of European Ministers of Education, Istanbul, October 1989, on The Information Society – A Challenge for Education Policies?*, Strasbourg: Council of Europe, p. 60; *Report of the United Kingdom*, pp. 199–202.

39 Balle, 'The information society', p. 19; Eraut, *Report on Policy Options*, p. 44.

40 (1986), *New Information Technologies: A Challenge for Education*, Paris: OECD/CERI, cited in Eraut, *Education and the Information Society*, p. 59.

41 Salter, *Languages for Communication*, pp. 11, 17.

42 Graves, *Report of the Utrecht Symposium*, pp. 33–4.

43 Carpenter, *Report of the Colloquy on Using the New Technologies, passim.*

44 *Ibid.*, pp. 16–17.

45 MacBride Report, Pt I, Chapter 2.5: cited in Corset, *Report for the Symposium on The Secondary School*, p. 33.

PART 3

EXTENDING THE PARAMETERS OF EUROPEAN EDUCATION

CHAPTER 7

Preparation for Life in European Society

A CHANGE OF DIRECTION

Earlier in this study the distinction was made between the three aspects of European education: that of informing young people and children *about* Europe, educating them *through* the medium of Europe and preparing them *for living in* a world in which Europe represents their extended family home. The first two are manifestly concerned with the formal curriculum and in particular with the knowledge and skills to be gained from studying the established disciplines – Geography or Modern Languages or Science. However, the review of Communication as a highly complex aggregate of skills (the point at which the last chapter concluded) serves as a bridge between learning *about* and *through* Europe to the equally important area of education *for life in* Europe. Here the primary emphasis falls on the affective area of learning, on attitudes, values and competences rather than on knowledge *per se*, although clearly the European context is the experiential backcloth against which all pupil learning is bound to be set.

In leaving the broad theme of preparation for life and citizenship in Europe to the later stages of this study, there is no suggestion that it is less important. On the contrary, here we come to the essence of European education. It is about learning to live amicably alongside other Europeans and accepting common responsibilities towards the rest of the globe; it is a matter of learning to make the most of the equal social and economic opportunities which now present themselves; of meeting new political realities and technological challenges; and finally, of enjoying together the experience of a unique cultural and environmental heritage. These were the major areas designated by the Council of Europe's project on secondary education. Preparation for Life (1978–82), which provides us with a convenient framework.[1] Now we turn from Europe as a historical idea and a cultural area to Europe as a socio-political entity, to examine the educational implications of preparing the young to live in European society in the 1990s and beyond.

THE HIDDEN CURRICULUM: SOCIAL INFLUENCES ON THE YOUNG

In the progression from adolescence to adulthood, the young are subject to a number of external influences. These pressures can be more significant in shaping their attitudes and ways of behaviour than classroom learning. Whatever their ethics or quality of life, it is the members of the family who tend to provide the young with their first formative models, but pupils also have to come to terms with their own peer group at school and in the neighbourhood. Beyond that, their lives can be affected by their environment and the community at large; church membership or affiliation to some other organization can prove profoundly important. Sometimes there are contradictory forces at work too. For many adolescents the world outside their home – town centre supermarkets, sunshine resorts or the streets of the beckoning capital city – assumes the character of 'the real world' through persistent portrayal on the TV or video screen. School then seems an artificial world, all the more so because it is responsible for compulsory education and is involved in the pupil's well-being and instruction. Indeed, the external world operates a 'hidden curriculum'. In coming to terms with these various influences, the young prepare themselves for life while also being prepared by others (whether intentionally or subconsciously) to be independent adults, parents and citizens.[2]

Family life is still the foundation of European society, despite the changes that have occurred in family structures, particularly in the industrialized regions. As the 'nuclear family' has replaced the traditional pattern (except in certain regions, such as southern Italy),[3] working parents spend less time at home and children generally leave home earlier. The break-up of families is much more common and the number of one-parent families is increasing rapidly (though it is interesting that the nomenclature 'family' is still used); so too the incidence of the 'new extended family' of step-relatives as the result of divorce. Predictions of 'crisis' and 'danger' have beset the family since the 1960s, yet it sustains intergenerational attitudes and continues to transmit a code of practice, central to which are traditional religious affiliations and moral principles. The family is still a caring institution for most young people and provides the main support; in effect, it provides an informal curriculum. In the opinion of Professor Klaus Schleicher, 'there has been a growing awareness in Eastern and Western Europe ... that the family is irreplaceable because of its educational, social and economic function.'[4]

However, the family's capacity to influence the adolescent is sometimes limited by the emotional hold of the peer group. In a study entitled *Preparation for Personal Life and for Life in Society*, the Norwegian educationist Edvard Befring examined the importance of peers to young people, since 'the adolescent is dumped into a society of his peers, a society whose habitats are the halls and the classrooms of the school, the teenage canteens ... and numerous other gathering places.'[5] These vary from one country to another, but among the environments which bring young people together are the disco, the youth club, sports arenas, local parks and the street corner. This does not mean that adolescents lack worthwhile values in their pursuit of leisure: many are imbued with caring and idealistic instincts. But there can be a dark side to adolescence, reflected in the development of a distinct and sometimes aggressive teenage culture and industries geared to adolescent needs. There can also be insidious social pressures to conform, which, at the worst extremes, sponsor gang rule verging on dictatorship. To counter these, schools can offer counselling and personal and social education.

At school the peer group remains an important means of contact and influence. Students are brought face to face with an organization, based on certain systems and rules, which determines what and how they learn. Their daily experience is affected by the way the authorities interpret the curriculum not only in terms of syllabuses, teaching methods and priorities, but also over pupil participation or the relationship between the school and the local community. Indeed, some sociologists regard the key element in the 'hidden curriculum' to be the relationship between all members of the school, from the school board and teaching staff to the pupils and cleaners. This relationship reflects the school ethos, the prevailing assumptions and attitudes governing personal behaviour and the exercise of professional duties; the ethos in turn can have a profound effect upon the young. In addition, since schools are seldom closed communities but serve and are served by others in the locality, it has become normal practice for adolescents to make a social contribution while they are still at school, by undertaking voluntary tasks or part-time work, by becoming involved in work experience, cultural or sporting activities, or by gaining experience with adults in the community, such as the elderly.

Since the 1960s all these influences – family, peers, school, community – have had to withstand the impact of the mass media. In the opinion of one expert, 'the popular media ... constitute a "parallel" school – a place of education after school or parallel to it.'[6] If one takes this statement at face value, it suggests that individual teachers have limited authority to influence the young; so, for that matter, have family, friends, neighbours and peers. In truth, Europe is sufficiently large and diverse for the media to reflect many indigenous traditions, while at the same time having a widely varying effect on adolescent tastes and attitudes. Yet TV, video and radio are also sufficiently formative media for us to ask some leading questions. For instance, how 'European-orientated' are they? Are the mass media likely to encourage or play down feelings of European identity in favour of a determinedly nationalist or nebulously transatlantic culture? Will they help to stimulate European consciousness or act as a negative force in a unified Europe? Again, we turn to the expert for an answer – and for some reassurance. Perhaps the counter-influences of school, family, peers and local community on adolescent attitudes should be taken more seriously than is implied above, because it seems the media 'respond to expectations, interests or curiosities which have already been aroused at school or elsewhere ... people watch on television and read in the papers what they have learnt to appreciate and understand elsewhere ... This is the reality behind the maxim that people get the papers or programmes they deserve.'[7]

In this study we are concerned primarily with the influence of school and the current provision for preparing the young for European society. If the Council of Europe brought many issues affecting young people of 14–19 years to international attention through its work on secondary education, its recommendations found echoes in the resolutions of the European Community for a 'People's Europe'.[8] The conjunction of policy on social and educational matters between the two major European organizations has already borne fruit and promises to make further changes in regions with entrenched social traditions.

PERSONAL AND SOCIAL EDUCATION

Since secondary education stretches from childhood to the onset of adulthood, it has to cater for variations of maturity apropos of pupils' physical, sexual, emotional and mental development. At the end of compulsory schooling or its voluntary extension, choices and decisions have to be made about the future. As they approach full citizenship, and in some cases military service, young people may be on the verge of marriage or cohabitation, parenthood and property ownership. Without personal and social education at school, they will find it harder to make autonomous decisions.

The starting point for social education is the individual. Until the doubts which plague a good many adolescents are resolved, they cannot fulfil society's expectations and behave as responsible, integrated social beings. As it is, the young can easily become the frontline victims of unsatisfactory educational methods and market forces. The fluidity, alienation and economic uncertainties of life add to the private difficulties of the substantial number of pupils with special needs.[9] Although the situation varies from one country to another, it has been estimated that 20–40 per cent of young people in Europe probably fail to achieve their potential and should therefore be a cause for concern. Yet the research undertaken by Edvard Befring for his study of the personal development of young people suggests that many of them yearn for a set of fundamental values. School, it is suggested, should help adolescents to acquire those values and enable them to reflect upon their own socialization, to be aware of their sex and partnership roles, and to recognize changing family structures.[10] During secondary education pupils should also achieve the capacity to solve their own problems on the basis of self-discovery and self-discipline. Through social education they should be able to define their own identity and gain a degree of autonomy. They should establish positive interpersonal relationships and at the same time find a measure of personal enrichment and satisfaction.

Personal education, then, is about developing into a balanced person; it is about learning to make the most of one's abilities and qualities and knowing how to enjoy living, goals which obviously embrace the whole curriculum (Figure 8). Aspects such as the individual's involvement with organized society

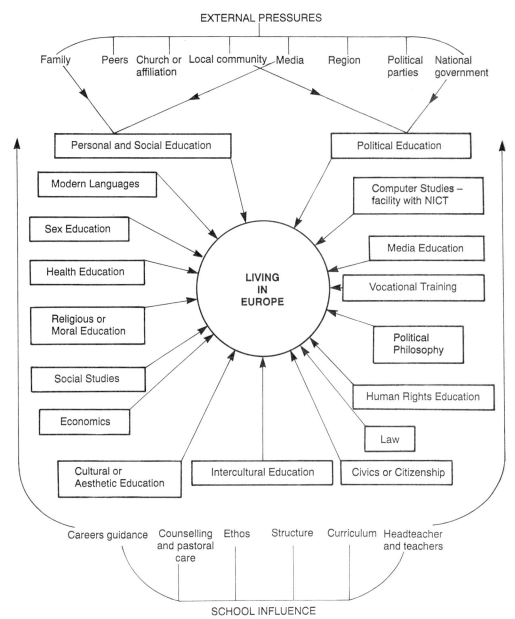

Figure 8 Preparation for life in Europe

are matters for citizenship or political education which we shall look at shortly. Particular and strictly personal difficulties cannot be dealt with in the class or group situation, but there are certain areas of common personal experience which should be dealt with in school. These are of the relational type – personal and sexual relationships, coping with emotions, bullying and antisocial behaviour, friendships, caring for other creatures such as pets, and child care – and of the ethical and developmental kind. Although many educational systems make no provision for religious instruction (nor is this a matter for discussion here), there are many deep ethical or moral questions which young people feel the need to discuss with others, whether they belong to the Christian church or any other faith or none: questions such as life after death, the purpose of life, fate or divine intervention, the ethics of war and peace, disarmament, pacificism, abortion, birth control, euthanasia, medical issues such as surrogacy and *in vitro* fertilization, coping with personal problems – depression, grief, bereavement and rejection. There are also many matters affecting the development and normal maturing of the individual that overlap with personal relations and ethics. These include matters of safety (self-defence, road traffic, first aid), business and industrial awareness, health and health-related subjects (drugs, addictions, AIDS, abortion, problems of puberty). Physical fitness, sport and health are increasingly recognized as 'necessary for a state of well-being' and make an important contribution to 'each person's own self-knowledge and . . . to the educative process generally'. With this in mind the Committee of Ministers of the Council of Europe recommended in 1987 that a set of Eurofit tests should be adopted for assessing the physical fitness of European pupils in the 6–18 years age-range.[11]

Development also depends on emotional enrichment, and here too there is growing acceptance by schools that they have a responsibility to prepare young people for cultural life. Europe's cultural heritage was discussed in Chapter 5, but one fundamental point bears repetition: the creative and performing arts are not a luxury, nor are they reserved for an elite. On the contrary, they should be integrated into school programmes to prepare the young for future participation in cultural activities. This suggests a need for a rounded policy of aesthetic education in Europe, not only to preserve the culture and environment of our civilization, but to open up proper opportunities for personal fulfilment and assist in the personal development of pupils' senses and aesthetic powers (see pp. 98–9).

Personal development therefore depends on both the official and the hidden curriculum. In an ideal world personal and social education would be carefully tailored to each student's age and requirements, but in reality the best we can hope for is that learning takes place in small groups and that teaching is consistent with the pupils' level of development. A decade ago the Council of Europe Symposium at Solna on Social Education for Teenagers produced helpful recommendations on the aims, methods and content of social education and how they should be implemented.[12] It was agreed that didactic methods are counterproductive; instead there should be student participation and consultation, work methods which advance the socializing process, such as group-work, simulations, socio-drama, role-play, projects and debates. Social skills and behaviour do not develop by chance: they need to be consistently encouraged. These include the ability to express oneself clearly, to think analytically, argue logically and make rational judgements, to use the different media with discernment, to accept or challenge rules and regulations thoughtfully, to take a stand on issues but to tolerate the views of others, to co-operate and disagree with others in an open and constructive way, to participate and delegate, to display sound common sense by practising rules of safety and to live a healthy life.

Most teachers involved in social education believe that teaching through single disciplines should be supplemented by cross-curricular and experiential learning; also that it is vital to integrate the young 'outsider', such as the handicapped or the newcomer, to promote the value of every child regardless of achievement level, and to build on the connections between the school, home and local community. So far as the Council of Europe is concerned, throughout the 1980s its policy was to stress that young people should be given first-hand experience of problem-solving, decision-making, planning, setting priorities, managing and creating, and this is the message for the 1990s. Since these kinds of experience cannot always be provided in the classroom, schools are urged to establish a wide range of contacts and external links to extend their pupils' opportunities for social learning.

Outside contacts are also vital in preparing young people for working life. Preparation for the world of work constituted one of the five areas of youth experience examined by the Council of Europe's experts during the Preparation for Life project. The survey by Yves Deforge into a cross-section of European systems for training young people during and after compulsory schooling anticipated many of the general developments of the 1980s.[13] Despite the diversity of national provision and high youth unemployment in the recession of the early 1980s, the decade was marked by more positive attitudes towards industry and business as part of the lead-up to working life. A recommendation of the Council of Europe's Committee of Ministers laid down that during compulsory secondary education, young people should be given 'a broad perspective on working life', including theoretical studies of the nature and forms of work, and opportunities for work experience, but that specialization in technical and vocational learning should not take place at the expense of breadth of understanding.[14] Following this recommendation, closer links were forged between teachers and representatives of industry, producing more sponsorships and work schemes for pupils and work exchanges for teachers in addition to the establishment of liaison committees between schools and industry. For their part, schools have also made efforts to provide training in the kind of practical and technical skills needed by industry and the cognitive skills associated with communicative language and IT competence. One outcome has been the rise in status of technical and vocational education in relation to the conventional academic disciplines. But in view of the economic pressures to produce students with high technological skills, compulsory schooling should still focus on traditional knowledge, skills and attitudes, lest education become too utilitarian and functional at the expense of the humanist values enshrined in life skills.[15] This brings us back to personal and social education as the means of turning young people into flexible and responsible workers.

However, there is no common European pattern of personal and social education. It seems that local traditions, pressure groups and the powers of Church and state can all influence practice. In Catholic countries and in Muslim communities there are many who feel that religious teaching as it affects personal choice and conduct – central features of personal development – is specific and non-negotiable. At the same time, some interesting work has recently been carried out with 16–18 year olds, casting new light on personal and social development by bringing together peer groups from once irreconcilable communities.[16] For the most part, however, it is left to the conventional curriculum and to teachers of the Human Sciences to include personal and social elements in their syllabuses. Topics such as sex, abortion, marriage, parenthood, hygiene, health, financial management, citizenship and human rights, understanding the media and the laws, are treated in a variety of subjects: Religious Education, Home Economics, Biology, Social Studies, Economics, Philosophy, History and Civics, Physical Education. None the less, new discrete subjects have also been developed – Health Education, Sex Education, Child Care, Consumer Education, Media Studies and Personal, Social and Health Education – and to these one should add the role of careers guidance and the counselling or pastoral systems, where they have been developed. In a number of countries, interdisciplinary courses deal with a spectrum of social issues. Recent curriculum changes in Portugal have produced an integrated treatment of social subjects (such as human rights), but the practice is well-established in other states. The Scottish educational system, which differs in many respects from the English, has evolved a multidisciplinary course of Contemporary Social Studies; Dutch-speaking Belgium has its *Sociale Vorming*, the Walloon part of Belgium has *Cours d'histoire et de formation sociale*, France and Luxembourg have *Instruction civique*, Norway has *Samfunnskunnskap*, the Federal Republic of Germany has the *Sozialkunde* or *Sozialwissenschaften* and *Politische Bildung und Gemeinschaftskunde* (Figure 9).

Although no distinction should be made on grounds of sex in the way these subjects are taught, the content of some courses has implications for the female role and for the personal development of girls. The tradition in Europe has been that 'productive work is more highly valued than the caring work which holds the fabric of society together.' At a CDCC seminar on Sex Stereotyping in Schools it was recognized that 'if sexual equality is ever to become a reality, the work of caring for others must be shared by men. The values of individual achievement which underlie men's careers must be challenged – true sexual equality implies major changes in our way of life.'[17]

Attitudes to sexual equality undoubtedly changed in Europe during the 1980s and at the same time governments, as well as some industrial and com-

Year 1
A newcomer to secondary
   school
Looking forward
Making new friends
Your family
Behaviour and
   responsibilities
Learning to cope with
   problems: fighting,
   bullying, jokes against
   you, cheating and anti-
   social behaviour
Self-control
Differences in people
Self-image and cleanliness
Changing appearances
Feelings and moods
Personal tastes
Hobbies, leisure-time and
   pets
Computers and games
Forming good habits
Projects and library skill

Year 2
Outside friendships and
   family relations
People and stereotypes
Looking after your body
Temptations and
   addictions, such as
   smoking, slot machines
Safety and first aid
Equal opportunities
Codes of conduct
Advertising and images
Building up your skills:
   study, homework, tests
Computers and technology

Year 3
Teenagers' interests and
   concerns
Personal relations
Self-reliance, self-discipline
Decision-making
Developing your study
   skills
Addictions, such as alcohol
First aid
Equal opportunities
The media's images
Racism
People's religious beliefs:
   Muslim, Hindu,
   Buddhist

Year 4
Two weeks' work
   experience
Family, home relationships
Child care
Friendships with the other
   sex
Opinions and attitudes
Addictions, such as drugs
Health and fitness
Business and industrial
   awareness
Simple financial
   management
Caring and causes
The Christian churches and
   other religions, such as
   Judaism
Crime, punishment, the
   law and the police

Year 5
Industrial awareness
Preparing and applying for
   a job or planning a career
Personal relations with the
   other sex
Sexually transmitted
   diseases
Safety and self-defence
Your life and coping with
   problems, such as
   rejection, depression,
   grief
Your life and faith: is there
   a God and a life after
   death?
Secular beliefs:
   Communism, socialism,
   capitalism
The ethics of peace,
   pacifism and
   disarmament
Structures of government,
   local and national
Party politics and using
   your right to vote
The law and the courts
The European scene: unity
   and diversity; the power
   of change 1945–92
The European
   Community: what it
   means to you
The Council of Europe:
   what it does for you
European unity after 1992

Figure 9 Social and political education: suggested summary of topics for years 1–5 of secondary school

mercial enterprises, took practical steps to keep women in the workforce by providing retraining schemes, maternity and paternity leave, nursery accommodation, child-care vouchers, and above all by exercising a genuine policy of equality of opportunity instead of paying lip-service to the ideal. For women with sound educational and professional qualifications and without children, the goal of true equality was achieved. For those whose education was limited by circumstance or who chose to have children, there is still a long way to go. The disparity of expectation between the sexes begins in the cradle but usually hardens as compulsory education draws to a close. The point was made in 1982, at the conclusion of the Preparation for Life project, that the general education of girls should be developed further to achieve parity of opportunity with that of boys. A similar concern was expressed in June 1985 by the Council of Ministers of Education of the European Communities. They adopted a resolution for an action programme on equal opportunities in education. Progress depends on whether official pressure on member states is sustained and attitudes towards the female sex are modified further at grass-roots level. At present certain migrant cultures and traditions make it difficult for girls in some areas of Europe to realize their potential or develop as individual personalities by establishing positive relationships outside the family circle. Democracy requires that they should do so, just as it requires greater attention to be paid to the needs of ethnic minorities, refugees, the handicapped and young people from less affluent areas of Europe. We will now look at what has been done to meet these requirements in the field of Intercultural Education.

EDUCATIONAL PREREQUISITES OF A DEMOCRATIC SOCIETY: INTERCULTURAL EDUCATION

In a continent characterized by diversity, geographical accident can determine youth opportunity. And it is not simply that differences exist between the Baltic and the Mediterranean or 'continental' and maritime regions: there is marked regional diversity, for instance, within Spain, Italy, Greece, Belgium and the United Kingdom. The differences can be ethnic, religious and economic (as in Northern Ireland) or take the form of a politico-cultural and linguistic divide (as between Catalan and Castilian). Preparation for life is thus a matter of preparation for diversity. Furthermore, in a democratic society, one of the underlying principles is that difference must not lead to discrimination; education must be open to all alike and children should be treated as autonomous and equal, whatever their colour, race or creed. The children of minorities, migrants and refugees are no exception to this dictum.

The linguistic and communication needs of the children of migrants and immigrants have been touched on in the previous chapter and undoubtedly the language policy of governments is one criterion for judging commitment to multiculturalism. However, what concerns us here is the broader socio-cultural implications of a multicultural society. The CDCC programme for the educational and cultural development of migrants and other minority groups made clear that they should not be regarded as problems thrust on European society, but as social assets and sources of cultural enrichment, which overarch their benefits to the service and industrial sectors of the European economy: for it must be recognized that 'if Europe is to compete successfully in world markets, its citizens will need . . . *sophisticated intercultural . . . skills*'.[18] However, the migration of peoples from other continents did create a cultural dichotomy between host and immigrant societies which could not be ignored. Even today the culture of second- and third-generation migrants, particularly adolescents, is neither entirely that of new arrivals nor that of the host country. 'Migrant culture' varies, depending on factors such as ethnic origin, the host traditions and present living circumstances (whether concentration in urban ghettoes or dispersal through the regions). The local situation may help second- and third-generation adolescents to assimilate the dominant culture or they may channel their energies into a subculture, as young West Indians in the UK espoused Rastafarianism in the 1980s (and the indigenous young took to punk). However, observers have noted that in multicultural societies the dominant culture often overrides the essential features of the minority cultures; and in the opinion of an independent expert, the balance of forces is such that only in a few areas (the use of leisure-time, consumer habits and clothing) do minority characteristics survive intact.[19]

In situations where minority cultures feel under threat, they tend to single out their values as being crucial to their cultural identity: in other words, family life, kinship patterns, male and female roles, traditions and expectations. But migrants are also subject to conflicting pressures. The social and economic pressure to communicate has produced the concept of assimilation; for example, in the UK there is a strong English-language compulsion to conform and become 'one of us'. Yet, for all that, assimilation as a solution finds diminishing favour and the Council of Europe has spoken out against it.[20] In fact, there are powerful counter-pressures against assimilation and towards separation (in effect a kind of apartheid), endorsed by 'ghetto' housing. It is manifested, for instance, in demands for separate schools. Yet the desire for separate education, enjoyed by white religious groups, is a logical extension of 'the right of withdrawal' in a country where Religious Education is predominantly Christian. Separation, however, pays a price: it is no use denying that culture clashes have occurred in Europe over matters such as dress, or that feelings have been inflamed by racism, anti-Semitism and the issue of 'blasphemy' *v.* freedom of speech and life in the Salman Rushdie case. So if assimilation and separation constitute antithetic solutions, a third response has been mooted, that of mixing the ethnic groups and cultures – *'métissage'* – leading to the undifferentiation or 'hybridization' of cultural norms, though this can only be contemplated as a very gradual process.[21] By a powerful consensus represented by the international organizations, the rational and humanitarian solution to multiculturalism is that Europe should continue along the path of education for mutual understanding to *pluralist integration*. This policy would seek to preserve a 'mosaic of cultures' and maintain the cultural identity of every cultural group on the basis of equal partnership.[22] Cultural pluralism and social integration require the practice of tolerance, open-mindedness and mutual respect, values inherent in the democratic concept of Intercultural Education, the Council of Europe's policy for the 1990s.[23]

What are the principal criteria for implementing an intercultural approach in a multicultural school? Council of Europe and EC experts have laid down certain priorities. First, there must be a constructive Modern Languages policy.[24] Secondly, the curriculum should reflect the concept of diversity in a positive way. According to a British educationalist, 'this means making *all* children more aware of the ethnic variety of modern Europe, more appreciative of the intrinsic worth of all cultures, more informed about the diverse origins of European society itself'.[25] It may be necessary (for example, in History, Geography, Music or Physical Education) to focus on topics or schemes that set out to explore the various cultural identities within one multicultural class. Differences are then more likely to be accepted and diversity seen to be mutually beneficial. With the self-esteem of Muslim pupils in mind, teachers have pressed frequently at Council of Europe seminars for the inclusion of the achievements of the Islamic civilization in the mainstream curriculum of History, Geography, and even Art, Science and Mathematics.[26] However, it is never easy to change attitudes or eradicate stereotypes. It takes an imaginative experiment of the kind held at the Tropenmuseum Junior, Amsterdam, to show the way. Since the Netherlands is a multiracial society and the creators of the Tropenmuseum programme were aware that most Western European children live with children from a range of cultures, their programme set out to familiarize 10–12 year olds with the background and problems of the various groups living in the Netherlands in the 1980s, under the charming title, 'There live a lot of people in the Netherlands: the story of the Turks, the Surinammers, the Gypsies and the Dutch'.[27] The same reasoning prompted teachers of a *Hauptschule* in the Black Forest to tackle openly the problems encountered by Turks in Germany through a multidisciplinary project called 'Turkey introduces itself'.[28] On a different level, it also motivated a journalist, Günter Wallraff, to disguise himself as a Turk for two years and recount his experiences in a book and a film.[29]

The third principle of CDCC policy stresses the importance of values and attitudes in framing teaching goals. Pupils should be encouraged to see that all people have their customs, faith and cultural traditions and these must be respected by everyone else. A German expert, speaking of his country, said:

> a first aim must be to give [German] children an idea of the importance of cultural and religious values in our traditions and in the traditions of other nations and parts of the world. Here learning and living should go together. It is important to look out for opportunities to meet people and especially children from another cultural background, to hear from them about their customs and to tell them about their own culture and religion. [Teachers should] be aware of the heritage of the Islamic culture of the Middle Ages and of the post-colonial situation in the Middle East, and not least of the reasons for the migration of labour in our own time. The foreign teacher needs a better knowledge of the history of Central Europe, the Muslim ones especially about the history and doctrines of Christianity, about the Enlightenment and the origins of the Industrial Revolution.[30]

These ideas lay behind the Kreuzberg Project, a scheme conducted in Berlin to bring together the German and Turkish communities.[31] While adjusting the particular cultural and historical topics, the same principles should be operative, for example, for French teachers with classes of Portuguese, Algerian and Moroccan migrants and English teachers with classes of Asians or West Indians.

In addition, schools should be able to make allowances for the special problems associated with social integration, such as dietary needs and religious holidays, as well as conflicting requirements over dress, role, co-education and sex education. Islamic ethics emphasize respect for and obedience to parents, cordial interpersonal relations, purity of thought and action, cleanliness and virtues such as generosity, honesty, mercy, charity, modesty and chastity, which, it could be argued, sit uneasily alongside the secular libertarianism of Europe today. For Muslim females especially, claims for equality of rights and opportunity and the ending of discriminatory practices may seem anomalous, although to deny these women basic human rights would be to exclude them unfairly from the processes of cultural integration into Europe.

Lastly, in a Council of Europe study of the education of children of migrant workers written a decade ago, Louis Porcher stressed the importance of teacher education in fulfilling intercultural objectives;[32] in particular, that initial and in-service education should include study of immigrant cultures, since only by being well-informed could the teacher set a convincing example of tolerance towards other values. European governments have understandably tailored their policies according to the political context of ethnic relationships. Porcher noted that the French government took the initiative in the field of teacher training as long ago as 1975 by establishing special Training and Information Centres for the Schooling of Migrant Children (CEFISEM), and study visits conducted in 1986–7 by a working group of the Association for Teacher Education in Europe (ATEE) confirmed that teacher training still holds the key to constructive teacher attitudes and expectations of ethnic minority pupils.[33] If teachers today know too little about ethnic minorities or reveal inappropriate attitudes, it suggests that teacher training could be improved further. To find a basis for international co-operation, a research project was initiated by the ATEE in 1988, with the support of the European Community, to develop a 'needs assessment instrument' based on the professional opinions of teachers on the concept and implementation of Intercultural Education.[34] Experts from four countries – France, the Federal Republic of Germany, the Netherlands and the United Kingdom – have been involved.

Interculturalism has a wider brief than concern for recent or second-generation migrant communities. In the 1980s educational provision was needed for long-standing minorities in danger of neglect, such as the Gypsies and the Lapps.[35] More recently, since the opening of frontiers between Eastern and Western Europe, the influx of new migrants into the more affluent West, particularly in Germany, creates a new social dimension. Consequently, there can be no moratorium on educational policies for intercultural understanding. Special programmes carried out in Finland and Sweden throughout the 1980s, to build up children's knowledge and awareness of other cultures, indicated the importance of suitable teaching materials and resources. A European teachers' seminar held in Sweden in 1987 singled out materials containing model case-studies of refugee children, produced by the United Nations Commission for Refugees (UNHCR), which projected a 'sensitive, positive image'.[36] At the same seminar, resources for promoting empathy were presented by experts from the Scandinavian countries, Greece and the Federal Republic of Germany, while the last of these disclosed pilot assessment procedures for identifying bias and gauging levels of prejudice among groups or in individual pupils. On a broader canvas, the changeover from a 'one nationality only' principle to that of 'multiple nationality' is seen as a step towards greater social harmonization in Europe.[37]

Intercultural education, like personal education, should be a socializing experience. It rests on the same axiom as CDCC policies on political education, that the future of European society depends on the ability and willingness of all its members to accept, preserve and promote human values, democracy and human rights.

HUMAN RIGHTS, DEMOCRACY AND MEDIA EDUCATION

The underlying violence in European society, epitomized by football hooliganism, terrorism and the growing incidence of sex- and drug-related crime, underlines the fragility of the human rights of individuals. Increasing violations put a premium on Human Rights Education in the 1980s and pinpointed the need for international action. To demonstrate its concern, the Council of Europe asked the Quaker Council for European Affairs in 1985 to undertake a study on the teaching of non-violent behaviour and co-operation in schools, and it also supported the teacher training programme of the International Institute of Human Rights in Strasbourg.[38]

The concept of human rights is rooted in European history, in the Declaration of American Independence (1776) from British rule and in the Declaration of Human and Citizens' Rights (1789) at the outset of the French Revolution, and European pupils need to be aware of that historical framework. Liberty, however, has a wide context of time and place and the massive convulsions of the first half of this century should never be forgotten. Students should leave school with clear knowledge of the legal instruments defining the human rights and freedoms which they enjoy.[39]

The twin pillars of contemporary civil and political liberty are the post-war United Nations Universal Declaration of Human Rights (1948) and the European Convention for the Protection of Human Rights and Fundamental Freedoms (1950). The social and economic rights of citizens are covered by the European Social Charter (1961), to which will be added the Social Charter of the European Communities on Workers' Rights after 1992, and ultimately perhaps – who knows? – the institutions of 'a European legal space', to which President Gorbachev referred in his address to the Parliamentary Assembly of the Council of Europe in July 1989. The first two spell out the quality and dignity of all people before the law, the need for effective political democracy to defend human rights and to inform people of their universal rights to life, liberty, security, justice and privacy. In addition, they set out the principal freedoms intrinsic to a just society, freedom from torture, slavery, retroactive criminal legislation, expulsion and discrimination in rights. The European Convention protects the citizens of its member states, all of which have ratified its guarantees. It operates through two institutions, the European Commission and the European Court of Human Rights. As membership of the Council of Europe grows, its competence will affect a growing number of young Europeans. As a matter of birthright, these young people ought to be conversant with the working of the Convention.

Considerable progress was made in the 1980s on Human Rights Education through the co-operative efforts of UNESCO, Amnesty International and the Council of Europe to advise and inform teachers. Many found UNESCO's publications, such as *Human Rights, Questions and Answers* and *Teaching for International Understanding, Peace and Human Rights*, immensely valuable, while the Associated Schools Project (ASPRO) treats respect for human rights as one of its main themes of study.[40] The first phase of the Council of Europe's programme on Human Rights Education, 1978–85, coincided with other important initiatives such as the work undertaken by the US National Council for the Social Studies, the Geneva Project, research at the University of York on Human Rights, the World Studies Project and the Jordanhill Project in the UK on International Understanding.[41] As a result, during the years 1980–5 much was done to clarify the methodology of Human Rights Education and surmount the criticism that it lacked intellectual rigour.

The 1985 Recommendation of the Committee of Ministers of the Council of Europe indicated that course planning should have both cognitive and affective aims.[42] Young people should have some knowledge of decisive events, key texts, institutions and legal suits and understand the concepts associated with Human Rights: the various categories, such as natural, human, civic, political, economic, welfare, minority and so on, and the procedural values involved, including justice, toleration, equality, discrimination, self-determination, genocide, oppression. By using case-studies of individual people wherever possible (campaigners like Andrei Sakharov or those who suffered the ultimate violation, such as Anne Frank or Dietrich Bonhoeffer) and themes like the treatment of prisoners of conscience in the First World War, abstract concepts and texts can be brought alive, indicating to pupils the importance of fair treatment and due process. Rights and infringements remain part of Human Rights Education but the affective area of learning depends on empathy, simulation and role-play, if not on actual involvement. As it happens, for many young Europeans the 1980s were marked by living experience of human rights issues, as they saw people's liberties endangered by the decisions of bureaucrats and technocrats, by state control masquerading as state security, by the effect of technology and the mass media on popular reaction and by threats to employment and health from a polluted environment. The stimulus to freedom stirred by events like the breaching of the Berlin Wall in 1989 was proof of the observation that 'Human Rights, more than any other subject, are inconceivable without enthusiasm and passion.'[43]

Public awareness of human rights violations in the 1980s was in no small measure due to the impact of the mass media. This points to another sensitive development of the last two decades which, like Human Rights Education, touches on the fundamentals of democracy. In 1981 the case for introducing Media Education was put forward by a group of English-speaking teachers:

> One of the hallmarks of a free society is the freedom of its public communication media. A free press, and the vesting of editorial freedom in the broadcasting media, are both indicators of, and safeguards for, the individual citizens of that society ... Add to this the extent of the consumption of the mass media by the young and the case for the inclusion of media studies in the school curriculum is overwhelming.[44]

The original aim of many media courses was paternalistic: as well as being an antidote to television, they set out to foster our cultural heritage and/or to encourage audiovisual awareness. But the use of the media before and during the Second World War gave intimations of the power which advanced communications would have, even in democracies, to filter information and mould public opinion in the guise of reporting news and providing entertainment. 'The media were not neutral carriers', observed the expert, Len Masterman, any more than the advertisers who made use of them; so pupils would have to approach them as critically as they were taught to approach advertisements.[45]

By the early 1980s, study of the media was included in the curricula of several European countries – the Federal Republic, Sweden, Switzerland, Norway and the United Kingdom, for instance – but there was little homogeneity. Sometimes Media Education was taught as a discrete subject, sometimes as an element in Social Studies or Social and Life Skills; frequently the media figured in language lessons of the mother tongue. In France, which was quick to perceive the relevance of the media to education, a novel approach was tried. Parents, other adults and teachers co-operated in what was called 'Educating the young in active viewing' (the Jeune Téléspectateur Actif Project, 1979–82) to develop the critical powers of lower secondary school pupils, relating television to other cultural influences.[46] In some European countries there was no formal provision a decade ago, but a number of these have since adopted Media Education policies.[47] New teaching styles have been involved, favouring dialogue and practical work. Pupils have opportunities to communicate through their own creative productions: newspapers, programmes, films, photomontages, posters, writing, interviewing, editing and experimenting. The media provide a lifelong and holistic educational process involving many categories of people, from journalists, broadcasters and researchers to parents, teachers and

children.[48] Certain criteria have been established as a result of these developments. First is the non-transparency of the media: they are engaged in representing (or re-representing) reality, not in merely reflecting it. Secondly, the
public is dealing with an 'intricate web of conflicting interests and pressures'
surrounding issues of ownership, control and influence, in which rhetoric and
ideology are powerful factors and media audiences have an increasing role to
play.[49] Lastly, to complicate matters further, today's world is swamped by the
sheer volume of information available, which circulates more widely and at
ever greater speed. So the media have a unique capacity to stimulate a critical
and informed understanding of contemporary events and controversial issues.
In other words, with the added sophistication of satellite technology, the mass
media are keyed into the functioning of democracy.

However, the mass media should not be regarded as automatic guarantors of
democracy. The wise point has been made that information 'is only of value to
an individual if he has learned to use it ... And it constitutes power only for
one who, having understood or interpreted it, has the means to take advantage
of it.'[50] The potential threat to democratic societies is ever-present, as was
intimated earlier in the context of Communication.[51] Europe cannot afford to
allow a gulf to grow 'between those who can speak about the world as they
understand and know it, and those whose experiences are inevitably formed
and interpreted for them by others – in short, between the media-rich and the
media-poor'.[52] Complacency is one of democracy's worst enemies, especially
in this age of informatics. Teachers have a responsibility through Media Education to devote time and attention to their pupils' skills of evaluation, their
capacity to identify bias and disinformation: in short, to the honing of their
critical faculties.

In conclusion, there are three priorities for the future. First, students should
be fully aware of sophisticated marketing philosophies aimed at manipulating
audiences. Secondly, the defence of public information systems which have
faithfully served democratic values should be an urgent consideration. Anyone
in doubt should question whether information should be treated as a commodity and source of profit, or whether it should serve social needs within the
public domain.[53] Thirdly, along with Human Rights, Media Education should
be construed as part of preparation for democracy. More emphasis should be
placed on action skills and experiential learning. One opinion to emerge from a
Council of Europe Symposium on The Secondary School and the Mass Media
was that:

> Media studies lay bare tacit assumptions about society, authority, value
> and truth ... it should be an activity which equips pupils with the means
> of making positive, autonomous personal judgements. A society is made
> stronger if it equips its citizens with the knowledge, skills and insights
> they need to undertake an informed and participatory role. Proper study
> of the media assists the realisation of this end.[54]

However, this kind of assertion has logical implications for the ethos and organizations of schools, which policy-makers and senior administrators may find unpalatable. According to some European teachers, by denying pupils numerous rights, the present hierarchical school structure creates a major obstacle to the education of pupils in democracy.[55] If pupils are not free to express their views – or if their views are totally ignored – teaching about human rights is pointless. In point of fact, progress towards democracy in schools was somewhat variable during the 1980s. The retrenchment which occurred in many countries, especially in the first half of the decade, was scarcely conducive to a liberalization of school structures. Some parents and teachers feared that democratization would undermine discipline, and the legitimate authority and rights of adults. However, the Council of Europe placed its faith in the importance of the democratic ethos: 'democracy is best learned in a democratic setting . . . where there is fairness and justice.'[56] Furthermore, the precedent set by the UNESCO and European Clubs supported the democratic process:

> Club activities provide a very real apprenticeship in democracy, provided of course that the pupils are free to organize themselves and to take initiatives for which they will assume responsibility . . . It is also within the club that the pupils will be able to express themselves, strengthen their reasoning powers, communicate. They must learn to listen to others, to tolerate their opinions, to recognize the differences and so enrich themselves.[57]

In 1985 the Committee of Ministers of the Council of Europe asked teachers to be positive towards the achievements of their students and urged parental and community involvement in support of pupil participation. Since that time the democratic tide has swept the European mainland. As educational changes follow (which they are likely to do) and political integration moves forward after 1992, the need for education for European citizenship becomes more pressing.

POLITICAL EDUCATION AND CITIZENSHIP

All the areas discussed in this chapter have a common denominator: they imply that living in Europe involves active citizenship in a pluralist society. As well as rights, young people have civic responsibilities. They need to know the extent of both, how they came about, how to exercise them effectively, how to participate in decision-making in trade union branches, professional bodies or pressure-groups, and the importance of taking up voting rights in local, national and international elections. Secondary schools constitute a type of political institution, in that they are places where power and authority are exercised: pupils can therefore reasonably expect to learn about political competence there. In particular, they ought to learn two lessons about democratic society. First of all, democracy brings diversity of opinion and disagreement, which has to be resolved by non-violent means and in a way that defends a person's or a group's rights to be different; secondly, in a democracy people have a right to discuss and to make choices rather than to have one policy or set of principles imposed on them.

Provision for education in civic matters is a well-established feature of European curricula, though different assumptions and approaches exist across the continent. The traditional form of education for citizenship in Western Europe has been the historical approach: the political development of Europe, concentrating on constitutions, laws and organizations, supplemented by political philosophy and international relations. This method set out to inform students. During the 1970s, under the influence of social science methodology, there was some rethinking of this approach and a shift of direction towards the consideration of concepts and processes, together with the attitudes and skills appropriate to active participation in a democratic system.

In fact, the clarification of the language of politics was necessary for the development of political education at school level. Political concepts, being analytical tools as well as technical terms, form an important link between political understanding and political knowledge. The latter is categorized into general concepts (like power, authority, liberty, rights); concepts which denote certain beliefs or ideologies (such as socialism, Communism, capitalism, liberalism, anarchism); concepts which are particularly applicable to democracy, since that is the prevailing political structure in Western Europe and increasingly in Central and Eastern Europe also (such as parliament, election, pressure group, free press); and concepts which relate to specific issues of concern in the twentieth century (women's rights, children's rights, abortion, free enterprise, privatization). Political understanding involves gaining insight into the structure and processes by which politics function: the machinery of government (local, regional, national and international structures, the contribution of political parties, pressure groups, interests, industrial relations, the educational system); the issues of greatest concern and disagreement (aims, priorities, values, means, outcomes); and the various groups involved in the political process (such as ministers, parties, trade unions, commercial and industrial interest groups, organizations with moral and social pressure like Greenpeace, CND – the Campaign for Nuclear Disarmament – or the churches). These suggestions are neither exclusive nor prescriptive and the concepts which teachers choose to employ will depend on their judgement of local or national situations.

As to the kinds of attitude which demonstrate political competence, they are in effect determined by the prerequisites of diversity and choice: the most desirable are toleration and the need for compromise and open-mindedness. That being said, often young people feel very strongly about issues and are the first to act from conviction. They should be reassured that the acceptance of compromise does not imply lack of commitment. On the contrary, life in a democratic society requires vigilance and judgement as to the limits of tolerance. Where do we draw the line? Certain concepts like totalitarianism, certain attitudes such as blatant prejudice, and certain ways of behaving – taking part in acts of terrorism, and even hooliganism and bullying – are antipathetic to democracy's survival, and it would be irrational and irresponsible if these were tolerated.[58] They run contrary to fundamental human rights – the natural rights of man – against which everyone should be protected by the rest of society. Political Education should, therefore, arm the young with the know-how to detect evidence of racism, sexual harassment, oppression, exploitation or religious intolerance, and thereby to identify the parameters of a democratic society in its and their own defence.

In the years 1980–2 the Council of Europe held three international conferences on the democratic theme, and the ideas put forward were received with varying degrees of enthusiasm. In Denmark, for instance, where the social and political sciences are held in high esteem, the situation favours the teaching of political education by well-qualified teachers who approach their task with conviction. The Council of Europe's southern member states took seriously the need for building up political literacy and Europe's wider democratic role. In the United Kingdom, where some valuable curriculum research was undertaken in the 1970s and early 1980s, a few experts voiced some serious questions about the democratic nature of the school system, and these may find echoes in numerous other educational systems:

> For example, do we train young people to live in a democracy by talking to them excessively rather than inviting their views? Does repeated copying from textbooks on worksheets produce autonomous citizens? Do such arrangements as a few prefects but many non–prefects, or the employment of corporal punishment, prepare for life in a democracy?[59]

In fact, until very recently in England, Political Education as a subject of the curriculum has been treated with a good deal of scepticism by pupils, teachers and parents.[60] It is an irony that, in a country which frequently boasts of its parliamentary tradition, there is a national tendency to be so coy about teaching and learning about citizenship and the politics of international co-operation. Only the prospect of 1992 has forced British educationists to bring 'citizenship' somewhat grudgingly into the new National Curriculum as a cross–curricular theme.[61] Though the British are not entirely alone in their reserve, they differ sharply on political education from their German counterparts. In the Federal Republic, European integration was a commitment enshrined in the *Grundgesetz* or Basic Law, and the obligations of schools are couched in terms of 'an educational mission' to instil in the young the importance of political co-operation and a sense of belonging to Europe. Since the adoption of the Resolution on Europe in the Classroom in 1978 (Table 7), which was confirmed and updated in a further resolution at the end of 1990 in the light of political events and the process of European integration, teachers have had the benefit of clear guidelines on areas of political knowledge and attitudes, providing an education 'designed to fit young people for their tasks as citizens of the European Community'. The revised version of this Resolution was adopted in

Table 7 Europe in the classroom

Resolution of Ministers of Education in the Länder of the Federal Republic of Germany, June 1978

The school should communicate knowledge and ideas on:

- the special character and diversity of Europe
- the principal historical forces at work in Europe
- social and economic structures in Europe
- the development of European legal and political thought and ideas of freedom
- the efforts to organize and integrate Europe since 1945
- the importance of joint action and supra-regional institutions to solve economic, social and political problems
- the need to achieve a fair balance of interests in Europe
- the importance of co-operation within the European Community
- the importance of co-operation between the member states of the European Community and other countries in the world
- the values and interests which govern decisions in Europe

The fundamental values . . . which inspire the school's educational aims must be set in the context of life within the European family of nations and states. This implies:

- a readiness to understand, to dismantle prejudices and to recognize what is held in common while at the same time appreciating European diversity;
- the development of European legal instruments on the basis of the principles and aims of the European Human Rights Convention and the Social Charter;
- good neighbourly co-operation and a willingness to compromise in order to do justice to the different interests in Europe;
- the realization of human rights, the desirability of equality of opportunity, and economic, social and legal security and freedom of movement.

This education is designed to fit young people for their tasks as citizens of the European Community.

December 1990 by the Ministers of Education of all the *Länder*, including the five of the former DDR (Table 8).

Progress towards European political unity took a step forward in 1986 with agreement on the Single European Act. The promise of 1993 in social terms is a society bound by faith in democratic values and by legislation designed to draw the citizens of member states together in a co-operative framework that should prove beneficial to all. *Perestroika* and *glasnost* in Eastern Europe leave open the possibility of a wider membership, but in a sense they have made Western Europeans more sophisticated in their expectations of democratic government.

Historical precedent suggests that while communities may co-exist, the forging of a nation-state – or an organization of nation-states, federal or otherwise – requires sustained, concerted action and common instruments of unity. The creation of a United States of Europe, based on one European society, may be some way off, but a number of steps have been taken in the 1980s to superimpose a new sense of identity that may in time subsume old loyalties to the nation-state. The appeal has been directed to Europeans themselves. The European Council paved the way by its Fontainebleau resolution of June 1984 that 'the Community should respond to the expectations of the people of Europe by adopting measures to strengthen and promote its identity and its image both for its citizens and for the rest of the world.' This was the origin of

Table 8 Europe in the classroom: European awareness

Resolution of Ministers of Education of the Länder of the Federal Republic of Germany, December 1990

The school has to convey knowledge and views on:

- the geographical diversity of the European region as a result of its natural, social and economic structures
- the political and social structures of Europe
- the formative historical forces in Europe, above all the development of European views on law, the state and freedom
- the patterns of development, features and evidence of what is despite its variety a common European culture
- the multilingual nature of Europe and its inherent cultural wealth
- the history of the European idea and the attempts at integration since 1945
- the harmonization of interests and joint action in Europe towards solving economic, ecological, social and political problems
- the tasks and working methods of European institutions

The basic values of state, social and individual life . . . must be seen in their relationship to life in the European community of peoples and states. This involves:

- the willingness to reach understanding so as to overcome prejudice and to be able to recognize mutual interests whilst at the same time affirming European diversity;
- an open-minded attitude to culture which transcends cultural borders yet preserves individual cultural identity;
- respect for the values of European legal commitments and the administration of justice within the framework of human rights recognized in Europe;
- the ability to co-exist as neighbours and a willingness to make compromises regarding the realization of the different interests in Europe, even when this involves sacrifice for the benefit of others;
- support for freedom, democracy, human rights, justice and economic security;
- the will to maintain peace in Europe and throughout the world.

---

the report on a People's Europe, adopted by the European Council of the European Communities at Milan in 1985 and reaffirmed in May 1988 in the educational programme for 1988–92. The member states of the Community were then urged to give a new stimulus in the perspective of 1992 to the strengthening of the image of Europe in education in the context of the People's Europe Report. Schools were asked to co-operate in initiatives to form European Clubs, intended to forge a truly European spirit among members of the community of European peoples and to promote activities which provide better information and contribute towards tolerance and an acceptance of pluralism, to promote awareness of European international interdependence and the need for co-operation, and to imbue pupils and young people with a sense of responsibility as European citizens for peace, human rights and the preservation of the environment and the cultural heritage.[62] Schools were also asked to participate in exchanges and special activities to mark Europe Day and to promote the European dimension in every possible way.

Meanwhile, the necessary symbols of supra-nationhood have appeared: a common passport for all citizens of the European Community, a European flag, a European anthem, and the prospect of a European coinage. All societies, it seems, have need of shibboleths and logos. For the first time in modern history, a substantial part of the European continent is acquiring the hallmarks of a single social identity. Personal, social and political education have to take this radical development on board.

NOTES

1 Some of these issues have already been discussed in Chapters 4, 5 and 6.

2 A summary of the influences on adolescents, based on the work of CDCC experts, is given in Blackledge, R. C. R. (1982), *Reflections and Observations on the CDCC Project No. 1 Preparation for Life*, Strasbourg: Council of Europe, pp. 19–21, 26.

3 (1982), *Final Meeting and Conclusions of the Special Project: Southern Europe, CDCC Project No. 1 Preparation for Life, Treviso, Italy, February 1982*, Strasbourg: Council of Europe, pp. 16–21.

4 Schleicher, K. (1980), *Report of the European Teachers' Seminar on Education for Parenthood and for Family Responsibilities*, cited in Blackledge, *Reflections and Observations*, p. 19.

5 Befring, E. (1980), *Preparation for Family Life and for Life in Society*, Strasbourg: CDCC.

6 Balle, Francis (1991), 'The information society, schools and the media' (Report of the Standing Conference of European Ministers of Education, 16th Session, Istanbul, 11–12 October, 1989), reprinted in Eraut, M. (ed.), *Education and the Information Society*, London: Cassell, p. 102.

7 *Ibid.*, pp. 102–3.

8 (1989), *Bulletin of the European Commission,* **6** (17), pt 1.1.9.

9 Blackledge, *Reflections and Observations*, pp. 16–17.

10 Befring, *Preparation for Family Life*, cited in Blackledge, *Reflections and Observations*, p. 20.

11 Recommendation No. R (87) 9 adopted 19 May 1987; (1988), *EUROFIT: Handbook for the EUROFIT Tests of Physical Fitness*, Rome: Council of Europe, pp. 6–7.

12 Starkey, Hugh (1982), *Report of the CDCC Symposium on Social Education for Teenagers: Aims, Issues and Problems, Solna, Sweden, September 1980*, Strasbourg: Council of Europe.

13 Deforge, Yves (1981), *Living Tomorrow: An Enquiry into the Preparation of Young People for Working Life in Europe*, trans. J. Barkas and N. Amphoux, 3rd edn, Strasbourg: Council of Europe.

14 Recommendation No. R (83) 13 of the Committee of Ministers to Member States, Appendix iv of *Principles for the Guidance of those Responsible for Programmes Concerned with Preparing Young People for Life*.

15 (1988), *Report of the Secretary General, M. Marcelino Oreja, to the Parliamentary Assembly on Problems of Education and Training in Europe, May*, Strasbourg: Council of Europe, p. 10.

16 Austin, Roger (1989), *The European Studies (Ireland and Great Britain) Project*, Strasbourg: Council of Europe. Dr Austin described how Catholic and Protestant students in Northern Ireland exchanged information with Walloon and Fleming

students in Belgium while investigating conflict and co-operation as part of their personal and social development programme.

17 *Report of the Teachers' Seminar at Honefoss, Norway, on Sex Stereotyping in Schools, 1981*, cited in Blackledge, *Reflections and Observations*, p. 15.

18 Stobart, Maitland (1988), 'The world in the European classroom, *Forum* (May).

19 Lanot, Jean-Raymond (1983), contribution in Rey, Micheline, *General Report on Migrant Culture in a Changing Society: Multicultural Europe by the Year 2000*, Strasbourg: Council of Europe, p. 11.

20 (1987), *Report on The Activities of the Council of Europe*, Strasbourg: Council of Europe, p. 83; also (1986), *Final Report on CDCC Project No. 7 on Education and Cultural Development of Migrants*, Strasbourg: Council of Europe.

21 I am grateful to Mr Ian Bliss of the Institute of European Education, Lancaster, UK, and a member of the ATEE Working Group Teacher Education and Intercultural Education, for drawing my attention to the typology of Professor C. Clanet of the University of Toulouse (1986), *L'intégration pluraliste des cultures minoritaires*, Toulouse: ERESI.

22 Bliss, I. (1990), 'Intercultural Education: a view from the United Kingdom, *European Curriculum Network,* **15**, pp. 10–18.

23 These ideas were discussed at the CDCC Seminars on Interculturalism and Education, Madrid, May 1987, and on Interculturalism: Theory and Practice, Limburg, Belgium, April 1987, the reports of which were published in Strasbourg as DECS/EGT (87) 26 and DECS/EGT (87) 22.

24 See Chapter 6; also Porcher, Louis (1981), *The Education of the Children of Migrant Workers in Europe: Interculturalism and Teacher Training*, Strasbourg: Council of Europe, pp. 81–8.

25 Craft, Maurice (1983), contribution in Rey, *General Report on Migrant Culture*, p. 9.

26 Nielsen, Jorgen S. (1981), *Report for the 13th European Teachers' Seminar on Cultural Values and Education in a Multicultural Society, Donaueschingen, October 1981, on the Training of Teachers of the Children of Migrant Workers*, Strasbourg: Council of Europe, pp. 17, 31. However, Bliss has warned that 'It is nonsense to suggest that you are giving children insights into other cultures simply by giving them odd examples of exotic things. It is sometimes suggested that by taking children to a concert of Indian music, or getting them to make a model of an Egyptian cat, or by referring to exercises in symmetry as Rangoli patterns, you are helping them towards an understanding of other cultures – and each of those examples is a real one. That understanding can only arise *if* you can help pupils to understand how Rangoli patterns relate to the Festival of Diwali and *if* you can present it in a way that children can relate to their own experience' ('Intercultural education', p. 16).

27 Gailly, A. F. (1982), *Report of the Case Study on the Tropenmuseum Junior* (in the CDCC's Project No. 7, *The Education and Cultural Development of Migrants*), Strasbourg: Council of Europe.

28 Trybus, Klaudia (1985), *Report of the 30th European Teachers' Seminar on Europe in Primary Schools, Donaueschingen, November 1985*, Strasbourg: Council of Europe, pp. 19–21.

29 (1986), *Report of the Study Session of Young People for Democratic Action in Europe*

(Jeunes pour une action démocratique en Europe – JADE) on Training for Europe, EYC, Strasbourg: Council for Europe, p. 17.

30 Lahnemann, Johannes (1981), 'The training of teachers of the children of migrant workers – experiences and perspectives in West Germany and West Berlin', in Nielsen, *Report on the 13th European Teachers' Seminar*, p. 12.

31 Lister, Ian (1984), *Teaching and Learning about Human Rights*, Strasbourg: CDCC, p. 33.

32 Porcher, *The Education of the Children of Migrant Workers*, pp. 67–99 *passim*.

33 Alkan, M. and de Vreede, E. (1989), *Education in a Plural Society: A Survey of the Professional Opinions of Teachers in Europe*, Brussels: ATEE/European Community, pp. 1–2.

34 *Ibid.*: Note that the subtitle is *Report of a Study for the Development of a Needs Assessment Instrument presented to the European Community*.

35 See Liegeois, J. P. (1987), *Gypsies and Travellers*, Strasbourg: Council of Europe; Lundmark, Bo (1987), 'The Lapps – an ethnic minority', in Pearse, Sanchia, *Report of the European Teachers' Seminar on Human Rights Education in a Global Perspective, Are, Sweden, August 1987*, Strasbourg: Council of Europe, pp. 13–14; also for a summary of current trends and future needs, see Garbett, J. (1990), 'On the way towards multi-ethnic societies in Europe?' (Anglo-German Seminar, Berlin (30 October–4 November 1989), on Intercultural Education in Europe), *European Curriculum Network*, **15**, pp. 20–8.

36 Pearse, *Report on Human Rights Education*, p. 13.

37 Sarlis, Paul (1989), 'Nationality and mixed marriages in Europe', *Forum* (January).

38 *Report on The Activities of the Council of Europe*, p. 84.

39 For a list of materials and CDCC publications on Human Rights Education in schools, see Starkey, Hugh (1984), *Report of the CDCC Symposium on Human Rights Education in Schools in Western Europe, Vienna, May 1983*, Strasbourg: Council of Europe, Selective Bibliography, Appendix 1, p. 23; Heater, Derek (1984), *Human Rights Education in Schools: Concepts, Attitudes and Skills*, Strasbourg: Council of Europe; Lister, *Teaching and Learning about Human Rights*; Pearse, *Report on Human Rights Education*.

40 (n.d.), *Practical Manual: Partners in Promoting Education for International Understanding: For Participation in the UNESCO Associated Schools Project*, Paris: UNESCO.

41 Lister, *Teaching and Learning about Human Rights*, pp. 2–5, 33.

42 Recommendation No. R (85) 7 of the Committee of Ministers to Member States on Teaching and Learning about Human Rights in Schools.

43 Mariet, François (1980), *Report of the 8th European Teachers' Seminar on The Teaching of Human Rights in Upper Secondary Education, Donaueschingen, May 1980*, Strasbourg: Council of Europe, p. 4.

44 Corset, Pierre (1981), *Report for the Symposium on The Secondary School and the Mass Media, Grenoble, France, June–July 1981*, Strasbourg: Council of Europe, p. 20.

45 *Ibid.*, p. 9. The same view is expressed in Balle, Francis (1991), 'The information society, schools and the media' (Report for the 16th session of the Standing Conference of European Ministers of Education, Istanbul, October 1989), in Eraut, M. (ed.), *Education and the Information Society*, London: Cassell, pp. 94–5.

46 *Report of France to the 16th session of the Standing Conference of European Ministers of Education, Istanbul, October 1989 on the Information Society – A Challenge for Education Policies?*, Strasbourg: Council of Europe, pp. 51–2.

47 See *ibid.* for all the National Reports, which survey individual government policies. In Denmark, for example, instruction in mass media has been obligatory for all upper secondary school pupils since 1 August 1988.

48 Masterman, Len (1988), *The Development of Media Education in Europe in the 1980s*, Strasbourg: Council of Europe, p. 11.

49 *Ibid.*, p. 16.

50 Balle, 'The information society', p. 106.

51 See Chapter 6, p. 115.

52 Masterman, *The Development of Media Education in Europe in the 1980s*, p. 10.

53 *Ibid.*, pp. 23–5.

54 Corset, *Report on the Mass Media*, p. 22.

55 Mariet, *Report on Human Rights*, p. 24; for a discussion of democracy in schools, see Lister, *Teaching and Learning about Human Rights*, pp. 27–9.

56 Starkey, *Report on Human Rights Education in Schools*, p. 16.

57 Mariet, *Report on Human Rights*, p. 17.

58 Slater, J. G., and Hennessey, R. A. S. (1977), 'Political competence' unpublished paper, p. 3; (1988), *Report of the European Teachers' Seminar on Bullying in Schools, Stavanger, Norway, August 1987*, Strasbourg: Council of Europe.

59 Slater and Hennessey, 'Political competence', p. 4.

60 Before 1939 political education and civics were linked to Great Britain's imperial and world role. From 1945 citizenship or civics courses were linked to studies of the Commonwealth and international relations, when they were often taught at 16–19 years in grammar and public schools. But for some thirty years from the late 1950s or early 1960s, citizenship slipped out of the public sector curriculum in favour of other social science approaches, except for minority options in European Studies (13–16 years) or Government/International Affairs at 16+.

61 The National Curriculum Council refers to citizenship in terms of individual, family, community, national, European and international dimensions (1990), *Curriculum Guidance Document Three: The Whole Curriculum*, Gateshead: NCC, p. 5.

62. (1988), *Official Journal of the European Communities*, **31** (C177).

CHAPTER 8

Education beyond the Classroom

LEARNING OUTSIDE THE CLASSROOM

Learning about Europe can never take place exclusively inside the classroom. In the first place, the educative potential of school is limited by its inevitable timelag in relation to real life. A great deal of valuable education is experiential and comes, not from textbooks and teacher-talk, but from encountering people and places. Furthermore, learning is a process that continues throughout active adulthood. There is nothing novel in any of these statements. The Grand Tour was the time-honoured system of further education for Europe's aristocracies and well-to-do bourgeois families. From the eighteenth century to the eve of the Second World War, the privileged discovered their cultural heritage in the course of foreign travel. However, when travelling for pleasure was resumed again in Europe in the late 1940s relatively small numbers of children were able to benefit.

Another generation passed before the dramatic expansion of travel facilities enabled people of average means to seek new horizons at relatively low cost. This new freedom of movement affected perceptions of education as much as other aspects of life. What happened was that secondary schooling took to the high street, the workplace, the study centre and holiday work camp, to the family homes of 'foreigners' and the historic sights of Europe's most famous capital cities, battlefields and shrines. So a whole range of opportunities, venues and activities opened up, to be welcomed by those who knew that the classroom has its limitations as a place of effective learning.

This is particularly true of the arts and human sciences in which the educational goals are, to a degree, affective. Every teacher knows that there is a certain credibility gap between the reality of first-hand knowledge and the vicarious experience conveyed by audiovisual technology, despite the increasing sophistication of resources and equipment supplied to schools. The official documentation of the Council of Europe and the European Commission concerning the promotion of an awareness of Europe admits to the need to supplement school learning in a number of ways. Key recommendations of the 1980s stressed the importance of provision ۱۰r young people to travel, take part in exchanges and make direct contact with their European contemporaries: a senior administrator argued in 1986 that it is impossible to build Europe without these youth exchanges.

Some educational authorities in the United Kingdom are invoking the principle of 'European Entitlement' by which all young people should experience living, studying and working in another European country during the years of compulsory education.[1] And to these formal statements should be added the weight of Europe's changing social climate – the egalitarianism and evident gregariousness of youth culture, as well as the more genuine democratization of society – which lends support to the idea that extra-curricular opportunities are a highly desirable part of education.

THE DEVELOPMENT OF EXCHANGE SCHEMES IN EUROPEAN EDUCATION

In secondary schools today exchanges have become a valuable resource. The word 'exchange' is used here as a useful shorthand term for a wide range of activities. It amounts to any form of direct cultural experience arising from personal contact with people of a different community or country and their way of life. Contacts can be of varying and unspecified length, and exchanges include group and individual visits for study purposes, formal exchanges between the pupils, teachers or educational administrators of any two countries, joint projects, school-linking partnerships between countries, cultural trips, events arising from town twinning arrangements and the exchange of correspondence, audio-video cassettes, satellite links and live conferencing.

In the last decade, the number of European and international exchanges has increased steadily. Statistics are not easy to come by, but one striking outcome of the Franco-German treaty of 1963 was the massive interflow of young people between France and the Federal Republic, facilitated by the Office Franco-Allemand de la Jeunesse, which has transformed the historic relationship between these two countries over the past twenty-five years. In contrast, the UK's youth links with neighbouring countries have been more modest, though the trend is encouraging; and it should be noted that a government agency, the Central Bureau, was established as early as 1948 with sole responsibility for educational visits, exchanges, conferences, correspondence and other schemes linking educational institutions, and that more recently it has taken on the administration of several European Community exchange programmes. In 1981 the Central Bureau was able to report encouragingly to the Neusiedl Symposium that some 5000 schools had been linked to partner schools, giving rise annually to some 70,000 home-to-home exchanges between France and the United Kingdom, 12,000 between the Federal Republic of Germany and the

UK and proportionately large numbers with Denmark, the Netherlands, Spain, Italy and other states.[2]

France is England's leading exchange partner, followed by Germany, Spain and Italy with the USSR a strong newcomer. The exchange scene is generally buoyant.[3] Thousands of school classes have partner classes. A project of Social and Economic Competence (SEC) involves classes in Greece, Italy, Portugal and the UK; European Work Experience (EWE) involves 17 year olds in the UK, Belgium, Italy, Spain and Germany. There are special exchanges for music, history, sport and environmental education. Artistic activities, such as concert tours of county and national youth orchestras and smaller groups of instrumentalists, make a profound contribution to international understanding; or, as a French Inspector put it, 'they bear a message of freedom; they transcend the divisions between men and peoples and thus constitute an incomparable means of communication.'[4] School visits to Europe's military battlefields provide a reminder of European diversity in its most uncompromising form; those to the great monuments of classical Greece and Rome explain in visual terms the origins of European culture. Trips to the ski centres of France, Austria and Italy cater for some 40,000 pupils each winter from the UK alone, not to mention from other countries; and subject studies are enriched by joint learning, as the Anglo-French 'Our Europe' environmental project has shown.

However, the commonest type of exchange is still that of correspondence by letter and cassette. To deal with them there is a network under the auspices of the International Federation of School Correspondence and Exchange (FIOCES), funded partly by UNESCO and administered with the help of the French Ministry of Education.

Within Europe the provision for school travel and youth opportunities varies from one country to another. In Germany the *Länder* have their own *Auslandsämter* (international offices), and their role in facilitating and helping to finance school exchange programmes has been very fruitful. Since the foundation of its Youth Exchange Office in 1963, the Federal Republic has signed exchange agreements with a number of European countries, including Denmark, Belgium, the Netherlands, the United Kingdom and also some East European states, in addition to the French treaty mentioned above. France, with its own office for youth exchanges, shares this positive approach to youth programmes and has some 200 non-profit making educational organizations offering a wide range of activities to young people. Encouraged by the European Community's commitment to the promotion of mobility through its own Youth Exchange Bureau (ECYEB, founded 1987), the Italian Ministry of Education also increased its provision for international exchanges. In addition, there are fifteen National Centres for European Education (CEEs) in Western Europe, twelve from the European Community states, together with Austria, Sweden and Switzerland; they are linked through an International Centre for European Education, funded by the European Commission and currently located with the Portuguese Centre in Lisbon.

In Scandinavia there is a tradition of school travel – mostly to the UK, France and the Federal German Republic – for modern language courses. The Danish national agency, the Information Centre for International Study and Exchanges in Copenhagen, handles links and exchanges between Danish and other European institutions. However, for European students who wish to study in Scandinavia, institutions like the International Education Centre (IUC, founded in 1985) in Svendborg, Denmark, offer a range of programmes. The IUC has mounted residential courses using the new information and communication technology for language learning, courses on aspects of Danish culture, fieldwork and practical work in connection with scientific, historical and industrial studies. Recently, however, the chief emphasis has been on international and environmental issues and Europe's common future.[5]

In 1987–8 the British Central Bureau and the Youth Exchange Centre were involved in negotiated agreements for youth exchanges between the United Kingdom and the USSR, Portugal and Bulgaria (the latter seeking thematic exchange projects, based on sports, drama, archaeology, caving and youth choirs). Older secondary students have taken part in Language Camp projects in Poland, Hungary and Turkey, acting as language assistants in return for a month's working holiday. The Central Bureau also supports the Project Europe 16–19 Bursary Scheme, enabling young British students to make intensive study visits of between ten days and three months to another EC country, and it runs a School Links Service to help schools and individual classes establish bilateral exchanges and visits. For instance, through the mechanism of the Central Bureau, primary and secondary schools in Austria, Belgium, Czechoslovakia, Denmark, the Federal Republic of Germany, France, Hungary, Italy, Norway, Poland, Spain and Sweden were seeking links with British partner school in the spring of 1990. Since the signing of the Protocol on School Exchanges and Links between the USSR and the UK in 1988, over fifty exchanges have taken place in an expanding programme of school exchanges. In addition, there has been a rapid increase in the number of private educational agencies set up to arrange visits, penfriend links and exchanges between individual students and institutions, while many reciprocal arrangements between schools are organized by individual Modern Language teachers themselves, since they are often in a position to exploit personal contacts with European colleagues elsewhere.

Opportunities for teacher exchange are also expanding. For instance, in 1989 the Central Bureau offered British teachers 'job swaps' during 1990 with teachers in Austria, Belgium, Denmark, France, the Federal Republic of Germany, Italy, Spain, Switzerland or the USSR. The high profile given to both teacher and student exchanges by the Commission of the European Communities since the first action programme of 1976 has completely altered educational priorities. In particular, the resolution of the European Council in May 1988, instigating the new action programme for 1988–92, gave enormous publicity to school exchanges. As a central feature of their policy of heightening European awareness, member states were invited to introduce a comprehensive range of contacts, including long-term stays, involving teachers, pupils and parents. The effectiveness of this strategy should be apparent from the Education Committee of the EC's report on the measures taken by member states for strengthening the European dimension in schools, due in June 1991. Furthermore, the extent and pattern of educational exchange schemes in the EC should be evident by that time.

Pioneering initiatives are under way complementing established linking arrangements. In the UK, where a European Awareness Pilot Project involving twelve local educational authorities was started in June 1988, a *mélange* of interesting enterprises is now emerging.[6] Within the framework of this project, three secondary schools under one English local authority have organized exchange visits for their 14–17 year-old pupils studying Economics and Business Studies with their peers in northern France, a scheme which includes a joint problem-solving exercise with industrial experience. This is only one of many initiatives to develop Business Studies links for school students. In another authority a small secondary school exchanges a whole year group with a school in Normandy with which it is partnered. Visits to Brussels, Strasbourg and Luxembourg serve as useful back-ups to learning about the machinery of European government in courses of social and political education. A European Studies (Anglo-Irish) Project has taken sixth-formers from Northern Ireland to the Irish Studies Centre in Belgium to meet young people who share the experience of living in countries with traditional religious and cultural divisions. Another authority has plans to send pupils to Bolzano, capital of the Alto Adige, which lies at a historic intersection of political, cultural and linguistic influences. Besides the pilot project, the Central Bureau supported sixteen other European Awareness Development Projects in 1989–90 and a further sixteen in 1990–1. One of these was a in-depth evaluation of the intercultural learning outcomes derived from student exchanges (excluding language objectives) based on the strong links already existing between Leicestershire (UK), the Saarland (FGR) and Seine Maritime (France).

While most of the exchange arrangements operate between pupils, classes and schools, since the 1960s there have, of course, been many educational linking schemes in operation between the cities and towns of Europe, such as that between Bordeaux and Bristol. In 1981 there were over forty links between British local education authorities (LEAs) and their French counterparts, the *départements*. Since 1976 the English LEA of Bedfordshire has participated in a home-to-home exchange with L'Oise, which currently involves twenty-five schools, in addition to a sixth-form exchange. Bedfordshire also uses study facilities in Calvados and has exchange links with a *liceo scientifico statale* in Arezzo near Florence, and more recently has established one in Pomezio near Rome. The Strathclyde authority in Scotland has its own International Exchange Unit and has arranged exchange links with Poland, Yugoslavia, Spain, and Calabria in southern Italy. To enable more ambitious programmes to take place, there are now links on a regional level, involving consortia of education authorities. In the present climate a great many contacts between European schools, East and West, are being explored.[7]

THE VALUE OF EXCHANGE EXPERIENCE TO PUPILS

The traditional purpose of pupil exchanges has been the improvement of language skills. This remains an important element in most schemes, but experience of another country should also lead to empathetic understanding of different environments and lifestyles, and for that reason a call went out to European teachers of Geography from the Utrecht Symposium of 1989 to 'encourage . . . European exchanges and field-trips for students, teachers and others involved in geographical education'.[8] Even so, the educational benefit to individual pupils, whose horizons may be totally different from their hosts', is impossible to quantify and will depend on a number of factors.[9]

If teachers are agreed on one matter, it is the need for careful planning and preparation and the avoidance of *ad hoc* arrangements, while clear and realistic objectives are also necessary. The time spent in another country should include a range of activities, and follow-up work should be planned in advance. Although home-to-home exchanges are generally thought to be the most valuable, they are seldom successful without the full co-operation of parents and teachers. Preliminary communications and/or visits by teachers should obviate any financial, linguistic or personal difficulties. If proper preparations are made and the exchange is seen as a constructive learning experience, the gains will be invaluable. Pupils can observe the attitudes and values of others of their age group. They will be aware of environmental differences and should understand the effects on ways of life. And this learning will be free of the constraints of traditional modes of study.

As if to illustrate the point, some pupils from a school in Venice, who went for the first time on a Parisian exchange, were reported as having found their 'experiences had them stepping out of their classes and approaching directly historical, geographical, social, religious, economic realities without the help of books . . . The study subject is the journey itself; all preceding and successive moments swivel around it in a natural interdisciplinary way.'[10] In other words, these Italian pupils were able to overstep the rigid boundaries of school disciplines, gain new insights, and develop a sense of achievement and confidence in their skills of communication. In a healthy way the experience enabled them to correct their assumptions and prejudices and it opened up the chance of lasting friendships, enriching their personal and social education. The teacher involved in the three-week Venice–Paris exchange summed up the benefits for his pupils with enthusiasm: 'One learns to know each other and to overcome the mistakes created by clichés, distrust, gossip, suspicion, fear and hatred. Maybe one could learn to be happy in this century and in this society of violence and selfishness.'[11]

THE CONTRIBUTION OF THE COUNCIL OF EUROPE TO EXTRA-CURRICULAR ACTIVITIES

For many years the Council of Europe has been responsible for organizing opportunities and special events for bringing together young people from different European member states. It also liaises extensively with other organizations such as the European Community and facilitates school-based and extra-curricular activities involving secondary students and teachers.

One of the exciting new developments is the constructive exploitation of information technology and data communication. Of the new media it appears that the range of computer tools – word processors, automatic data search programmes, computerized dictionaries and writing monitoring programmes – is likely to be most helpful to schools in the first instance. For many years pupils have corresponded with their contemporaries in other European countries by letter, or more recently by audio- and video-cassette. Since most schools of the member states now possess computers, in the autumn of 1988 a Council of Europe Colloquy was held in Exeter, UK, to discuss how these can be best used to link schools in new ways, such as through the preparation of databases, electronic mailing and satellite link-ups.[12] The European Studies Project, involving Irish, Belgian and British pupils, was one of the first schemes to use E-mail, but a growing number of schools are now exploiting the potential of NICT. Mention has been made earlier of the Anglo-Dutch electronic mail links sponsored by Shell UK in 1989.[13] An E-mail network has been established between schools in the three European cities of Bremen (Germany), Ambérieu (France) and Dudley (UK). In Wales, the Mid-Glamorgan authority is developing a 'whole school' project in cross-curricular European Awareness using E-mail or video exchange with partner schools on mainland Europe, and the Devon authority in England has pioneered the use of E-mail facilities with its primary and secondary schools. In the near future, a substantial European network of computerized school links could be functioning, and the situation is ripe for further development towards a worldwide network. In this respect the determination of teachers with expertise (such as the Gateway group, who first came together in Exeter in 1988 to take the lead in exploiting E-mail links) is crucial to the success of the new technology.

However, direct personal contact can still be the most satisfying way of bringing young people together. Large groups of secondary school children have enjoyed visits which the Council of Europe sponsored between 1978 and 1985. In these years Greece, Italy, the Federal Republic of Germany and the United Kingdom acted as host countries to young Europeans from other countries. A recent innovation has been the four Children's Theatre Encounters held in Belgium, Switzerland, Denmark, Austria and Luxembourg respectively between 1982 and 1990, and the first European Youth Theatre Encounter for 200 young people aged 16–25 years from some twenty European countries, held at Stratford-upon-Avon, England, home of the Royal

Shakespeare Company. One promising aspect of the enterprise was the interest shown by the three Eastern European countries of Bulgaria, Czechoslovakia and Hungary at the discussion and planning stage. This first Youth Encounter (which was followed by a second in the Federal Republic in 1989) was both a practical experience in drama and an opportunity for getting to know other Europeans. Spain, for example, sent regional representatives who included young people from the Canary Islands, the Balearics, Catalonia and the Basque region; Denmark sent five from the Faroe Islands.[14] The event was described in glowing terms by the educational press: 'a new *lingua franca* was fashioned out of a pool of theatrical skills that came from all corners of Europe. With the clarity, energy and frankness that only the young seem capable of generating, language barriers were transcended.'[15]

The policy of 'town twinning' supported by the Council of Europe has also brought about closer links between secondary school age children. While individual twinning arrangements vary in detail, it is common for mayoral visits to take place, accompanied by civic receptions, organized entertainments, cultural visits, and events involving youth participation, and private hospitality is generally offered by the citizens of the communities involved. To see how the scheme can operate successfully, let us take the examples of two historic English cities of Roman origin, often 'paired' as the seats of the Yorkist White Rose and the Lancastrian Red Rose in English medieval history. Today the archiepiscopal city of York is twinned with Dijon, provincial capital of the medieval Duchy of Burgundy, and with Münster in Germany, once the seat of a Carolingian bishopric and an old commercial centre involved during the thirteenth and fourteenth centuries in the English wool trade as a leading member of the Hanseatic League. Lancaster, with half the population of and less grand than York, is in fact a European 'quadruplet'. Its three municipal partners under the town twinning scheme are Perpignan, near the Franco-Spanish frontier and once the fortified capital of the province of Roussillon and the Aragonese Kings of Majorca; Rendsburg, formerly a fortress town astride the Eider, on the Schleswig–Holstein border; and Ålborg in northern Jutland, site of one of the oldest settlements in Denmark. In addition, Lancaster has an unofficial youth link with Almere in the Netherlands which grew out of the official Ålborg arrangement. But in a display of phenomenal European commitment to peace and goodwill, the civic authorities of Ålborg had (at the last count) established twinning links with twenty-one towns and cities. In addition to Lancaster, Ålborg's 'twins' are Almere, Antibes, Edinburgh, Gdynia, Fredrikstad, Fuglefjord, Haifa, Husavik, Innsbruck, Karlskoga, Leningrad, Racine, Rapperswill, Rendsburg, Riihimaki, Scoresbysund, Solvang, Tulcea, Varna and Wismar.

For Lancaster, town twinning provides two major youth activities. The principal event is the annual Youth Games (inspired by the Olympic Games and sponsored by local authorities and businesspeople) which have been held on a rotating basis since 1974. Accompanied by civic delegations and a team of 'leaders', usually sports teachers and coaches, some 400 pupils of 14–16 years, from Perpignan, Rendsburg, Ålborg and Almere, compete in sixteen different classes of event with 150 Lancastrian secondary school students. Staying in the homes of local residents, the visitors learn something of family life in another country. Regular school exchanges for language learning have also grown out of the town twinning links; two-fifths of Lancaster's secondary schools have operated links with Rendsburg and three currently do so, involving over fifty 13–15 year olds.

The educational links between York and Dijon began in the early 1950s when a York grammar school was paired with a Dijon *lycée*. By *c.*1970 the scheme had been extended to all secondary schools in York, and the LEA took over the travel arrangements, giving moral and some financial support. About a hundred York pupils of 13+ visit their host families during the Easter holidays and receive the Dijon pupils in July–August. Similarly, some seventy or eighty York pupils whose main foreign language is German visit Münster and the Nordrhein-Westfalen Land annually, and there is a sixth-form college exchange for about twenty-five students a year. While there is no equivalent of the Youth Games, York has musical links with its 'twins'. From the mid-1950s the York Youth Operatic and Choral Society had contacts with Dijon, Münster and West Berlin, and in 1989 exchange visits took place between groups of young musicians from York and Münster.

Town twinning links are merely one means of entry into the 'European experience'. Europe at School – European Schools Day Competition, which grew from an initiative in 1953 by the European Youth Campaign in France, set out to encourage awareness of Europe and its cultural heritage among school children and to reinforce the European dimension in education. The Council of Europe, together with the European Cultural Foundation and the Commission of the European Communities, supports the European Schools Day Competition, which is open to all pupils and students of member states. The national Committees organize events on a national level but the European Committee selects the subjects for this annual competition. Entries by individual students, small groups or class groups are organized in three categories: 17–21 years, 14–16 years and 10–13 years; and audiovisual presentations are acceptable in addition to essays and art work, so enabling the contestants to demonstrate a range of skills. In 1988–9 the two designated themes were History and Today's Importance of Human Rights, and The Third Election for the European Parliament. In 1989–90 the main topic was Tourism as a Resource for the Development of European Citizenship, with alternative themes based on art work or the contribution of the Council of Europe to the idea of European unity. In 1990–91 the focus has been on Europe of Tomorrow.

The National Juries are empowered to award certificates for effort or cash prizes of commendation, but entrants whose work is forwarded to the International Jury are awarded commemorative silver medals and a variety of prizes. Some twenty Youth Gatherings are held each year and are attended by over 500 young Europeans. The prize winners in the senior category receive travel bursaries, enabling them to attend these civic gatherings, which represent a unique experience and one that gives meaning to the underlying concept of the Competition. The success of Europe at School – European Schools Day Competition can be measured by the fact that in recent years over 1 million entries have been received annually, and these have come from no less than nineteen member states.[16] However, the organizers hope that eventually young people from all European countries will take part and that this forum will be extended in view of the new East–West dialogue.

The Prize Winners' Conventions constitute one aspect of the concern for youth which the Council of Europe has demonstrated during the past twenty years. The European Youth Centre (EYC) in Strasbourg and the European Youth Foundation (EYF, founded 1973) provide the framework for the Council's Youth programme, while the EYF subsidizes international youth activities for some 5000 young people a year. The People's Colloquy on 'Parliamentary democracy – rejection, indifference or participation?', held in Strasbourg in May 1984 to mark the thirty-fifth anniversary of the founding of the Council, and involving 350 secondary students and thirty teachers from fifteen member states, served as a precedent for the 1985 European Youth Week, a successful part of the celebrations for International Youth Year and the Second European Youth Week in May 1989, marking the fortieth anniversary of the Council of Europe.[17]

Since young people are now acknowledged as a pressure group in European society, both political and non–political organizations and lobbies use the European Youth Centre as an international forum for colloquies and study sessions on issues within the mandate of the Council of Europe. In recent years, the EYF has been the venue for the Young Farmers' and 4H Clubs, for Young People for Democratic Europe (JADE), the International Union of Socialist Youth (IUSY), the World Federation of Democratic Youth (WFDY), the International Federation of Liberal and Radical Youth (IFLRY), the European Union of Jewish Students (EUJS) and the Framework for All European Youth and Student Cooperation. In 1988 new ground was broken when representatives of the latter came together for a Youth Peace Seminar: Helsinki and Beyond.[18] In the same year young people from Eastern and Western Europe also met for the first time with members of the Parliamentary Assembly of the Council of Europe. These gatherings of young Europeans from East and West have demonstrated the extent of mutual problems and concerns (from personal freedoms, drugs, mobility and the environment to peace and security); but not least, they have shown the keen interest of young people in East–West cooperation, the North–South dialogue and the dichotomy between the Europe of the Twelve and the Europe of the Twenty-four.[19] However, the Council of Europe aims to increase participation, believing that large-scale involvement in pan-European events is the key to empathy and international understanding.

For young people of secondary school age (11–19) the purpose of extra-curricular activity is to reinforce teaching and learning in school. But all learning depends on the expertise and enthusiasm of teachers, and it is particularly important that those who teach in secondary schools have sufficient breadth of experience and vision to help their students to develop into informed and clear-sighted citizens. The Council of Europe has long been aware of this need, and for some years it has operated a European Teacher Bursaries Scheme to enable over 500 teachers a year to attend short in-service courses in other member states. So far, some 15,000 European teachers have made use of this scheme. The Donaueschingen Academy for the In-Service Training of Teachers in the Federal Republic of Germany has served as the venue for many teachers' seminars, and the proposal of the Columbo Commission that a residential European Teachers' Centre should be established as a focal point for the Council of Europe's education programme for teachers and teacher trainers has been strongly supported by successive Secretaries General.

OTHER EUROPEAN INITIATIVES TO PROMOTE EXCHANGES, VISITS AND YOUTH LINKS

The number of schemes and organizations for bringing Europeans closer together has proliferated in the 1980s. There are now major programmes for young people over secondary school age, for the needs of special groups of young people, and projects for primary, higher, technical and vocational education, such as ERASMUS, COMETT, EVE and PETRA. Strictly speaking, these programmes lie outside the scope of this study, and among the welter of organizations, large and small, international and local, contributing to secondary school exchanges, it is only possible to make a few cursory observations. The Council of European National Youth Committees (CENYC) is one such Brussels-based body; it represents the interests of national youth councils to intergovernmental organizations such as the Council of Europe. However, mention must be made of the UNESCO Clubs, the first of which was set up in 1947: the idea has borne fruit in the establishment of European Clubs (which include among their functions the organization of Europe Week and Member State Weeks and of visits to national and similar clubs or schools of the European Community and Council of Europe countries). But more particularly, UNESCO's Associated Schools Project (ASPRO), an educational programme for International Understanding and Co-operation, which began in 1953, provided a model for many subsequent initiatives.[20]

Extra-curricular activities including school exchanges were a feature of many of the ASPRO schemes, but these were always linked to specific learning objectives. Among the early participants, a group of young people from a Danish school visited southern Italy to study the economic rehabilitation of isolated villages, while some Swiss pupils reinforced their project on Greece with a visit to that country. The Associated Schools Project has continuously demonstrated that education for international understanding depends on positive attitudes, tolerance and humility. By 1974, another milestone year, since it marked the founding of the Centre for European Education in Brussels, the

UNESCO project involved 1000 educational institutions in sixty-one member states. Between 1974 and 1986 the number of institutions doubled to involve ninety-three countries. For instance, mention has been made of the fifteen National Centres for European Education.

To take a random sample of other schemes, CloseUp Europe extended its exchange programme for 1989–90 with Danish government support. The French government offered bursaries in 1989 to enable selected students to participate in cultural festivals and Youth Encounters at Bourges, Avignon and Pau. In 1990 the Wolfson Foundation offered prize money of £10,000 to the best group initiatives on the theme of Cultural Links with Europe. The Young Historians scheme in the United Kingdom, which is financed by the Leverhulme and Boyle Trusts, is supporting a network of schools working on a project to explore the cultural legacy of the Roman Empire throughout Europe. The schools involved are in Oldham, in the north of England, and they are linked with schools in Beaune in France, Legre in Denmark and Bislupin in Poland.

A word might also be added here about the recent experiments in work shadowing, where pupils learn and work closely together on practical projects. An increasing number of school courses (such as the British TVEI – Technical and Vocational Education Initiative) recognize the importance of helping students to develop skills and appropriate attitudes to work, but in 1986 teachers saw the advantages of extending work experience from the locality to give students vocational experience in business and organizations in other European states. By 1989 work shadowing exchanges between some sixteen British schools and further education colleges had been set up in conjunction with similar institutions in Spain, Italy, the Federal Republic of Germany and France. One pilot scheme linked a Berkshire (UK) secondary school with a Technical Institute in Milan; twelve 17 year old English students were provided with work shadowing placements in local manufacturing, industrial, power, transport, commercial and local government institutions and a 40-hour study module of the social, economic and political situation of the Milan area as part of their A-level Urban Geography course. In return, the study specialisms of twelve Italian students – in Science, Information Technology, Electronics, Social and Business Studies, Language and Arts – were matched by work shadowing placement in English industrial, educational, publishing and theatrical establishments. Reciprocal hospitality gave the students the opportunity to experience family life and tourist attractions in the partner country.[21] The idea has steadily gained ground and further work shadowing schemes with Denmark, Greece and Sicily are planned. The TVEI consortium of one LEA in the UK European Awareness Project is exploring ways of extending the experience of all young people of 14–18 years through work shadowing or work experience on mainland Europe. Finally, mention should be made of professional bodies committed in principle to European co-operation and exchange programmes. The Association for Teacher Education in Europe (ATEE) and the European Association of Teachers (EAT) have worked assiduously to this end. The European Secondary Heads' Association (ESHA), a new organization, now lends its weight to the pressure for links between all European Community schools to promote language learning and cultural perspectives.

The European Community's involvement in the field of education has made it the major partner of the Council of Europe. In 1977 the Commission of the European Communities organized a conference in Venice to examine the matter of pupil exchanges, and subsequently the Council of Ministers confirmed that the encouragement of contacts between pupils was one of the three practicable facets of a European dimension in education. This was reiterated by Jacques Delors, President of the Commission, in a speech of 17 January 1989 to the European Parliament.

However, the launching of a Task Force and the Youth for Europe programme marks a new stage in EC policy for the young. Youth for Europe (YFE), scheduled to run to the end of 1992, is co-ordinated by the European Community Youth Exchange Bureau (ECYEB) in Brussels. Its purpose is to promote two-way, trilateral and multilateral exchanges of young people from different social, economic and cultural backgrounds and to foster awareness of common European issues. ECYEB is particularly concerned for disadvantaged students such as those from the less accessible regions of the Community. Grants are available for groups of young people aged 15–25 years to make visits from one to three weeks, and priority is given to 16–20 year olds. In addition to YFE, the first phase of the LINGUA programme (1990–4) includes proposals for school exchanges to enhance provision for language learning. Another aspect of the European Community's action programme for 1988–92 has been its proposals for dealing with the transition from education to adult and working life. One British educational authority has established a Transition to Adult Life Project (TAL) in response to the EC initiative, involving students aged 14–18 years in three secondary schools within a deprived catchment area. This TAL programme has established links with projects in Valencia in Spain, Lot in France and Shannon in Ireland, which have already provided twenty-eight young people with the chance to take part in two weeks' work experience in those countries. To date there are a total of eight TAL projects, operating in Denmark, Germany, the Netherlands, the Republic of Ireland, Scotland and England, which have established links with each other.[22]

The fact that exchanges should not be limited to certain curricular areas, such as Languages or the Humanities, is now firmly established. European awareness, which is the end product of all the activities we have been describing, should be viewed in cross-curricular terms. For this reason the links between the Science departments of two secondary schools, one in France and the other in the UK, is particularly interesting. We are told that both sets of students explored the chemical composition and creation of glass and its use throughout the ages. They learned about medieval glass, glass for domestic purposes such as glazing, and glass for glass fibre optics in the medical and telecommunication industries. Much of the work was undertaken successfully through small group study visits to institutions and sites where the uses of glass was in evidence: that is to say, to glass factories, hospitals and a medieval cathedral where a restoration programme was under way.[23]

Challenging schemes such as this particular one depend for success on the apacity of teachers to respond to the demands which exchanges make on their time, energy and expertise. The EC scheme for Short Study Visits for Education Specialists provides opportunities to observe particular aspects of educational practice, such as work with handicapped children. In this respect the European Community works both as a prime mover and as a body that subsidizes and co-operates with national agencies.

LEISURE, TRAVEL AND TOURISM

Speaking of the difficulties of enlivening formal classroom lessons on post-war Europe, one teacher admitted that for the pupils, 'It's only interesting if they've been to Spain or Italy or Greece on holiday. It needs a great deal of impact in the way it's put across.'[29] There is a certain irony in these words, for it is unusual for children to associate holidays with education or vice versa. Indeed, holiday experiences can reinforce popular prejudices about other nationalities. Sometimes the child's impressions of other countries become distorted by unavoidable circumstances, like those of an 11 year old whose mental picture of the physical map of Europe was formed by repeated holiday charter flights from Heathrow, England, across the mainland to Majorca. None the less, more leisure-time and the expansion of the tourist, transport and leisure industries have made regular school trips possible, while millions of families have followed 'abroad'. As these growing numbers of Europeans take holidays outside their own country, crossing frontiers by car, train, plane or boat, significant numbers of children and adolescents experience the rich variety of sights and sounds of Europe. Those opportunities have changed the eating habits and the vocabulary of school children, modified their tastes and encouraged them to believe that things can be different without being alien. The often inchoate assimilation of Europe's diversity has proved the first step towards awareness and understanding.

As they outgrow family holidays with parents, an increasing number of older secondary students are drawn to the idea of working holidays and language-study holidays, such as those at the Pädagogischer Austauschdienst in Bonn, FRG, or the English Language Summer Camps held in Eastern Europe. Some of the work-experience schemes, like the GAP Activity Projects, apply only to young people over the age of 18 or are linked with vocational and training programmes, but there are over 600 organizations offering European language courses in twenty-five countries, and the UK Central Bureau has published a guide on these Study Holidays to assure young people that they can be as enjoyable as they are instructive:

many courses teach more than just languages; for example, in Spain, one of the many things that can be done in addition to studying Spanish, Basque or Catalan is to study Flamenco guitar and dance; in France you can take part in French wine and cookery workshops; and in Italy you can study Italian art, ceramics and sculpture.[25]

Young Visitors' guides to Britain, Spain, Belgium, the Netherlands, Germany and Denmark give comprehensive and supportive information about living, studying and holidaying in those countries. For secondary students over 18 the Go Europe Club in the Netherlands aims to link young people (15–18) interested in taking part in activities as varied as adventure holidays, grape-picking or computing.[26] So although language learning was often the prime reason for study courses abroad, it has become clear that travel, work experience, study holidays and exchanges have considerable potential in supplementing other areas of the curriculum.

One of the new concerns of the 1980s, as we have seen, was Environmental Education. Although the links between tourism, education and the environment may appear tenuous at first sight, their mutual dependence is accepted by many teachers and by organizations concerned with nature conservation and the protection of the environment. The young child's instinctive curiosity about the natural world is well documented. Europe's flora and fauna can provide interest and even fascination to children on holiday as well as being the subject of school field studies. In different ways, leisure and learning are brought together in nature reserves, parks, countryside residential centres, farm schools and conservation information centres. For older secondary students, the growth of outdoor pursuits – walking, rock climbing, caving and orienteering – offers the prospect of continuing holiday interests in adulthood. However, the impact of tourism on the environment can be devastating, and the leisure industry has awakened the need for active responsibility. The Mediterranean resorts, for instance, receive some 100 million tourists a year, and the strains on the infrastructure and the environment compelled the introduction of the Mediterranean Action Plan in 1975. Similarly Europe's Alpine regions have been threatened by mass tourism and it is now realized that Europeans must consider a viable alternative in 'gentle' or 'alternative' tourism, involving ecologically sensitive management, with greener cities and smaller-scale enterprises which respect the host society.[27]

The educational implications of these ideas are still being worked out. 'Tourism' is an established topic of Geography syllabuses, but until school-based learning is linked to leisure or an exchange scheme giving practical experience, the full significance cannot be appreciated by secondary school students. However, there are now changes on the horizon. A UK GCSE (General Certificate of Secondary Education) course on Travel and Tourism, sponsored by major business groups, involves 15 year olds in work experience in hotels, restaurants and tourist-related businesses in France. An Anglo-Spanish school project on Tourism involved the recording of a series of TV programmes by British students, which were broadcast by satellite to Spain and included an interview with the new Minister for Tourism. Schleswig-Holstein is another area where local pressure groups have tried to change attitudes through special tourist campaigns, while taking account of the recreational needs of the young.[28]

Another strategy, which has been promoted by the Council of Europe, is the leisure concept of cultural tourism. This came out of the move to protect many of the neglected areas of European culture – the physical evidence of the commercial, artistic and spiritual activities of Europeans in the past – by linking them to the expanding leisure and tourist industries. The growth of adult education through summer schools and the popularity of activity holidays provided an additional incentive. The value of cultural tourism is supported by the European Community and by UNESCO, and the Council of Europe's initiative on one cultural route – the so-called Silk Road – is part of UNESCO's world-wide project. The Council of Europe's development of the old travellers' routes across Europe, the architectural and industrial heritage of rural society and inter-regional artistic influences (discussed in Chapter 5) has immense potential for interdisciplinary learning outside the classroom. The concept of a 'cultural route' opens up possibilities for activity projects such as a Roman trail or the study of packhorse routes (the medieval equivalent of the motorway or the *autoroute*) along which wool merchants and clothiers passed on their way to the great markets and fairs of Europe. Other ideas already under consideration by the Young Historians Scheme in the UK is a study of the battlefields of northern Europe, from Waterloo to the Normandy beaches, and a comparative cultural study of the impact of the Renaissance and the Reformation on the cities and communities of Prague, Budapest and Berlin. The exploitation of cultural routes is in its infancy but the potential is now clear, and the fact that 1990 was the European Year of Tourism acted as a spur to schools to devise some innovative projects.

All the initiatives and trends discussed here suggest that organized youth mobility will be one of the growth areas of the 1990s. Freedom of movement is one of the valued rights of a democratic society. There is no denying that there have been barriers to youth mobility, but these are diminishing.[29] Since the liberalization of Poland's passport policy, for example, its people are free to leave the country, and 1 million Poles travel abroad annually.[30] So although most of the examples on which I have drawn relate to Western Europe, already the freedom of young East Europeans to travel to the West is adding a new dimension to the picture of a mobile European society which has emerged with the expansion of the European Community.

This grass-roots development is reinforced by intergovernmental initiatives at the commercial, scientific and technological levels, and all reflect the Council of Europe's principal goal of drawing Europeans closer together in a spirit of co-operation. That, in turn, depends on getting rid of stereotyped thinking, learning to respect differences and appreciate the common bonds of culture, history and the environment. These goals are much easier to achieve through direct experience of other European countries than they are in the isolation of

EUROPEAN CITIZENSHIP

PUPIL ACTIVITIES
Short 1–7 day trips
Extended visits – 3 weeks–3 months
Home-to-home exchanges
Activity holidays and leisure activities
Cultural tours
Whole school links
Class/group partnerships
Town twinning events
Working holidays
Short study visits
Study holidays
Summer schools
Summer language camps
Competitions, such as European Schools Day Competition/Schools and Colleges Competition
Youth colloquia and workshops
Arts encounters – theatre/music
Work experience (EWE, TAL)
Work shadowing
Special European events, such as European Year of Tourism 1990, Mozart Year
Communication exchanges, such as audio- and video-cassettes, E-mail, satellite TV, live conferencing, penfriends

EXCHANGES · LEARNING · WORK EXPERIENCE · VISITS · LEISURE AND "LIFE-SEEING" · LINKS

INTERNATIONAL ORGANIZATIONS
The United Nations Educational, Scientific and Cultural Organization (UNESCO)
The European Community
The Council of Europe
The European Cultural Foundation

PROJECTS AND SCHEMES
Youth for Europe
European Town Twinning Scheme
Council of Europe Teacher Bursaries Scheme
EC European Awareness Projects
LINGUA
European Studies Project
Project Europe 16–19 Bursary Scheme
Our Europe – Anglo-French
Closeup Europe
Associated Schools Project

EUROPEAN CO-OPERATION

SOME KEY AGENCIES
European Community Youth Exchange Bureau (ECYEB)
European Youth Foundation (EYF)
European Youth Centre, Strasbourg (EYC)
International Federation of School Correspondence and Exchange (FIOCES)
Bilateral Youth Exchange Offices, such as Office franco-allemand pour la jeunesse, Deutsch-Französisches Jugendwerk
National Youth Exchange Centres or Offices, such as Central Bureau for Educational Visits and Exchanges
Fifteen National Centres for European Education
International Centre for European Education, Lisbon
The European Association of International Christian Youth Exchanges (ICYE)
Other non-governmental organizations

SOME ADDITIONAL ORGANIZATIONS
Council of European National Youth Committees (CENYC)
European Confederation of Youth Club Organizations (ECYC)
International Federation of Europe Houses (FIME)
Association for Teacher Education in Europe (ATEE)
European Association of Teachers (EAT)
European Secondary Heads Association (ESHA)

EUROPEAN UNDERSTANDING

INTERNATIONAL UNDERSTANDING

Figure 10 Summary of education beyond the classroom

the classroom. Furthermore, they are important goals because learning to understand one's fellow Europeans is a necessary preliminary to world-wide international understanding. The Italian teacher from Venice understood this European priority and expressed it eloquently:

> One does not build Europe with books but in travelling, in cancelling political borders; the young want to educate themselves that way, as soon as they can do it . . . It is indeed in our hearts that Europe is built and one reaches this heart through experience, human contacts, the real knowledge of daily life and the interests of young people of the same age.[31]

There was a time when these words might have been dismissed as pious idealism, but, in fact, teachers today have to be hard-headed realists. What this teacher observed as the hopes and expectations of a class of Italian pupils can be replicated in a great many European schools.

NOTES

1 *Report on the UK European Awareness Pilot Project 1988–89*, p. 7. London: Central Bureau for Educational Visits and Exchanges.
2 Platt, James (1981) 'The role of educational visits and exchanges and school correspondence' (paper for the Symposium on Europe in Secondary School Curricula: Aims, Approaches and Problems, Neusiedl-am-See, April 1981), Strasbourg: Council of Europe.
3 (1988–9), *Annual Report 1988–89 Statistics*, London: Central Bureau for Educational Visits and Exchanges; also Willcocks, John (1985), *Fair Exchange: An Examination of Recent Figures on School Visits Abroad* (Occasional paper based on a survey by the Language Teaching Centre, University of York), London: Central Bureau for Educational Visits and Exchanges.
4 Zweyacker, A. (1980), 'The contribution made by extra-curricular activities to education in human rights', in Mariet, F., *Report of the 8th European Teachers' Seminar on The Teaching of Human Rights in Upper Secondary Education, Donaueschingen, May 1980*, Strasbourg: Council of Europe, p. 18.
5 (1989, 1990, 1991), *Introduction to the International Education Centre, Svendborg, Denmark: Course Overview*.
6 *Report on the UK European Awareness Pilot Project 1988–89*.
7 (1987–8), *Annual Reports of the Central Bureau for Educational Visits and Exchanges 1986–7, 1987–8*, London: Central Bureau for Educational Visits and Exchanges; (1989), *EUROEDNEWS*, **27/28**.
8 Graves, Norman (forthcoming), *Report of the Symposium on Geographical Information and Documentation on European countries, Utrecht, September 1989*, Strasbourg: Council of Europe, p. 32.
9 *Report of the Conference on Exchange as a Resource*, arranged by the UK Centre for European Education, the Central Bureau for Educational Visits and Exchanges, the

Centre for Information on Language Teaching and Research and the Modern Languages Association, UK CEE, March 1981.

10 Serra, Michele (1989), 'The educational usefulness of international exchanges', cited in *EUROEDNEWS*, **27/28**, p. 77.

11 *Ibid.*

12 Carpenter, J. P. (1989), *Report of the Colloquy on Computerised School Links, on Using the New Technologies to Create Links between Schools throughout the World, Crossmead Conference Centre, Exeter, Devon, UK, October 1988*, Strasbourg: Council of Europe.

13 See Chapter 6, p. 117.

14 Lovegrove, Hugh, *Final Report of The First European Youth Theatre Encounter, Stratford-upon-Avon, UK, July–August 1987*, Strasbourg: Council of Europe.

15 (1987), *The Times Educational Supplement*, 14 August, cited in *ibid.*, p. 16.

16 (1989, 1990), *Reports of the Europe at School – European Schools Day Competition, 1988–9, 1989–90*, Bonn: Europe at School Co-ordinating Unit.

17 Roy, Alain (1989), *Final Report of the Youth Event for the 40th Anniversary of the Council of Europe, EYC, Strasbourg, 1989*, Strasbourg: Council of Europe.

18 (1988), *Final Report of the Seminar and Working Materials of the Youth Peace Seminar: Helsinki and Beyond, EYC, Strasbourg, June 1988*, Strasbourg: Council of Europe.

19 Roy, *Final Report of the Youth Event.*

20 UNESCO (1987), *Yes, We Can . . . Together!* UNESCO Clubs and Associations, Paris: UNESCO; (1987), *UNESCO Associated Schools Project*, Paris: UNESCO; (n.d.), UNESCO, *Practical Manual for Participation in the UNESCO Associated Schools Project*, Paris: UNESCO.

21 (1989), 'Work experience and work shadowing', *School Unit News* (Central Bureau, Autumn), pp. 9–10.

22 *Draft Report of the European Awareness Pilot Project 1988–89.*

23 *Ibid.*

24 Goodson, I. F., and McGivney, V. (1985), *European Dimensions and the Secondary School Curriculum*, Lewes: The Falmer Press, p. 75.

25 (1989), *Schools Unit News*, (Central Bureau, Autumn), p. 4.

26 *Ibid.*, p. 5.

27 Travis, Anthony S. (1988), 'Alternative tourism'; Krippendorf, Jost (1988), 'A responsibility to be shared'; both in *Naturopa*, **59**, pp. 25–9.

28 (1989), *Schools Unit News* (Central Bureau, Autumn), p. 8; *Report of the European Awareness Pilot Project 1988–89*; Kramer, Gerd (1988), 'It's nature we want', *Naturopa*, **59**, pp. 8–9.

29 Dannemann, Gerhard (1988), 'Barriers to youth mobility', *Youth of the 22* (Bulletin of the European Youth Centre and European Youth Foundation), **1**, p. 9.

30 (1988), *Summary Report of the Round Table on The Contribution of Young People to Furthering East–West Co-operation in Europe, Strasbourg, October 1988*, Strasbourg: Council of Europe, p. 4.

31 (1989), 'European education in Italy's secondary schools', *EUROEDNEWS*, March, p. 75.

CHAPTER 9

Europe and the Wider World

THE DEVELOPMENT OF AN INTERNATIONAL PERSPECTIVE

The spread of teaching and learning from the classroom to the outside world is simply one indication of the expanding horizons of education. Through the movement of peoples from the 1960s and the revolution in telecommunications, the concept of the world as a 'global village' has acquired greater reality. As a result, experts have questioned assumptions about the way young Europeans should be prepared for life and citizenship, especially the view that 'education for Europe' is solely a matter of *national* ends and means. In the light of his experience in the Netherlands, the Director of the Centrum voor europese vorming in het Nederlandse orderwijs (CEVNO), Henk Oonk, recommended that 'First and foremost it is essential to develop a concept of "international education"', confirming the policy statements of the Council of Europe and UNESCO, which call upon European society to 'display a sense of solidarity with the rest of the world'. They also assert that education should reflect 'understanding and respect for all peoples, their cultures, civilisations, values and ways of life' and that students should experience 'an international dimension and a global perspective in education at all levels and in all its forms'.[1]

There have been many advocates of international education in the twentieth century. After 1945 the United Nations agencies pressed for education for international understanding. Through its Associated Schools Project (ASPRO) UNESCO provided a mechanism for practical co-operation between school pupils of different nations, and from the 1970s the United Nations International Children's Emergency Fund (UNICEF) contributed to the production of teaching materials with a global dimension. On a national level the UK Centre for Education in World Citizenship encouraged the study of world issues from its foundation in 1939, while in the 1970s the UK Centre for World Development Education (CWDE) made advances through its curriculum research programme. Meanwhile the Nordic states led the way in implementing a global perspective, and their reformed secondary curricula reflect the humanitarian goals of post-war Scandinavian society. In this respect they were followed closely by the Netherlands, where for thirty years CEVNO has provided a focal point for international education. Other countries also modified their curricula to include world problems in Geography and History syllabuses; the Austrian general educational aim (*Algemeine Bildungsziel*) lays down that children should share in the 'life of Austria, Europe and the world' and elaborates on this principle in the guidelines for teaching History and Geography to the young.[2] In a number of state systems global issues are raised in inter- or multidisciplinary studies, using social science concepts: among these are the Scottish Modern Studies or Contemporary Social Studies and the German *Gemeinschaftskunde*.

However, from 1979 the Council for Cultural Co-operation (CDCC) broke new ground with its campaign for an educational dialogue with non-European countries. Aware that teaching exclusively about Europe left educators open to charges of Eurocentricity, the CDCC took an increasing interest in curriculum programmes of World Studies and Development Education. None the less, its experts were conscious of the problems involved. Courses designed specifically to counter Eurocentrism can produce other forms of ethnocentricity such as 'Black History';[3] and unless international education has a clear rationale, it invites a tendency to incoherence and sentimentality.

THE RATIONALE FOR A GLOBAL DIMENSION IN EDUCATION

The principal justifications for bringing the world into European curricula have been widely publicized by the United Nations and other organizations. The statute of UNESCO advised that 'Since wars begin in the minds of men, it is in the minds of men that the defences of peace must be constructed.' Article 26 of the Universal Declaration of Human Rights states that 'Education ... shall promote understanding, tolerance and friendship among all nations, racial and religious groups.' So the rationale of international education was founded firmly on the belief that it would raise future generations of Europeans to promote world peace. Out of that philosophy grew the movement for Peace Education in Scandinavia and for Peace Studies in the University of Bradford, England, and at the Atlantic College, Wales. A product of the Nordic genius, Peace Education was pioneered at the research level by Johan Galtung and Magnus Haavelsrud, and developed in secondary schools with the support of the Finnish and Swedish national authorities. Progress has been made in working out relevant concepts, including the important idea of 'positive peace', and teaching strategies that draw on emotional commitment and desire for action.[4] The peace motive has also proved a strong incentive for international education in Austria. Here the regulations laid down in 1962 by the Ministry of Education and Culture state that one of the aims of secondary education is 'to enable young people . . . to contribute towards the common tasks of mankind through their devotion to freedom and peace'.

A peaceful world signifies the acceptance of co-existence and interdependence. The 1974 UNESCO recommendation on Education for International Understanding required those in charge of educational policies to stimulate 'awareness of the increasing global interdependence between peoples and nations', by a combination of learning, training, information and action. Countries responded variously to this UN appeal, and again Austria provides a good example of a constructive state response. The curriculum for 6–10 year olds lays the foundation for 'an open attitude to the world at large' (in the context of *Heimat- und Lebensnähe*) while in class 3 (8 years) special priority is given to meeting people from foreign countries. This approach is taken further at secondary school level, demonstrating that Austrian educators take their international responsibilities seriously.[5] Yet all educational policy-makers have to take account of the new preconditions of world power. A demographic revolution has produced a young and increasingly urban workforce in southern Asia and Indonesia, which forms more than half the Earth's population; and a complex pattern of economic and political structures now prevails. Despite the approach of the Single European Market, Europe still depends upon other areas of the globe for raw materials, energy and commercial outlets. If Europe's young are to prosper, they cannot afford to ignore the realities of interdependence. On the contrary, they must be aware of their competitors and their economic systems and cultures. The explosive pace of change puts a premium on a 'world-view', enabling students to exercise intelligent and responsible judgements as citizens of Europe and of a wider world.

So far the rationale for setting European education in a global context has been expressed in broad brushstrokes, but there is a sense in which a world dimension was introduced into the curriculum for specific and pragmatic reasons. Faced with multicultural classes, teachers found their first priority was to bridge the gap of cultural understanding between children of different ethnic communities. It was essential to counter ignorance and suspicion on all sides, to deal with the ingrained parochialism and intolerance of strangers which surfaced intermittently among pupils and parents. One solution lay in the structure of the curriculum, in circumventing the conventional constraints of syllabuses in order to range more widely in terms of subject matter and strategies. The objectives were to give pupils greater insight into the immense variety of the world's cultures, thereby breaking down their sense of isolation or exclusivity, which is frequently the cause of prejudice and stereotyped thinking.

One function of a global dimension, then, is the elimination of undesirable attitudes in the young, whether they originate in regionalism, national xenophobia, Eurocentrism or any form of discrimination. On the positive side, a global dimension should stimulate the development of awareness and empathy towards people of all cultural affinities. Some readers may notice an anomaly in this assertion: the same claim was made earlier for a European dimension in education. I would argue, however, that if European studies are planned in such a way as to make students aware of the positive interaction between Europe and other civilizations, there should be no conflict of interest. On the contrary, the global and European approaches should be mutually reinforcing, particularly in the area of attitudes and attributes, if teachers see it as one of their goals 'to develop global empathy . . . [tapping] a person's perceptions and the cognitive representations of that person's emotions, beliefs, values, desires and of the relevant portions of the world around them'.[6] By learning to empathize with the situations facing adolescents in Japan or Brazil or North Africa, young Europeans should find it easier to comprehend the individuality of their own culture, as well as its changing relationship to others:

> The study of world issues, problems and cultures can also sharpen our understanding of our own societies by putting them into wider perspective. In the process, it is possible to come to a greater awareness not only of those things we have in common and to a clearer perception of universal human needs and rights but also of those which are distinctive. In doing so, we secure rather than subvert the basis of our social identity which is properly the concern of the schools.[7]

There is another curricular argument, one relating to knowledge and syllabus content. In the human sciences the importance of balance and perspective is acknowledged: balance in time, space and social experience, balance between the immediate and familiar and the uncharted and remote. From an adolescent standpoint, the divisions between these perspectives have become increasingly blurred. Thanks to communication technology, events at a distance can seem as commonplace as those happening on the doorstep. So scenes in Kabul or Tiananmen Square, Johannesburg, Cape Town or Beirut, Berlin, Prague or Vilnius, assume a familiarity – as images on the television screen – which falsifies the distinction between 'local' and 'international', particularly for the young. Clearly the international order is far from homogeneous or stable, but it would be unwise, not to say counterproductive, to place geographical or cultural prescriptions on the education of Europe's youth. On the contrary, as the Elsinor Symposium on History teaching advocated in 1965, the national and European horizons should be broadened to a world perspective whenever the opportunity presents itself. But the American National Council for the Social Studies was adamant that global education should not be limited to History and Social Science curricula; it should permeate the whole curriculum. Indeed, in 1975 the eminent space scientist, Bruce Murray, warned that 'we must recognize that we live at a unique point in the history of the world . . . We are all desperately in need of a new world view, consistent with the facts of science, but much broader and more encompassing.'[8] His opinion was later confirmed by three Austrian *Gymnasium* students, who told a Council of Europe conference that, in learning about certain issues of international significance, they had gained valuable insights from their lessons in Biology, Chemistry, Physics, Politics, Music and Art.[9]

Clearly there is a strong case for exploiting curricular links between Europe and other world cultures (see the summaries on p. 191). However, in justifying it we have to be sure of the parameters of the exercise. There are two aspects to be considered. The first is a practical point affecting syllabuses and timetables: how can other areas of the globe be accommodated into the process of teaching and learning *about Europe*? The second is a matter of the efficacy and suitability of world studies for the preparation of students *for life in Europe*: how can a global dimension assist them in their future role as adults, parents and citizens?

EUROPE AND THE WIDER WORLD: STRATEGIES AND APPROACHES

These questions formed the kernel of wide-ranging discussions in CDCC symposia and seminars during the 1980s, where a great deal of thought was given to teaching and learning goals, the selection of appropriate subject matter, strategies, approaches and teaching materials.[10] It is difficult to distil the conclusions of so many specialists and teachers who contributed informed opinions to the dialogue, based on their varied experiences. The spirit of their intentions is presented in the summary of goals for teaching and learning about other cultures and societies (p. 191). These are couched as broad aims to be interpreted by teachers according to the specific circumstances of their schools. In practice, the majority probably accept the principles underlying education for international understanding and global interdependence, but many different viewpoints have been expressed on the matter of strategies and approaches.

Broadly, these fell into three categories. First, there were the exponents of traditional subjects, who argued for the infusion of the new material on other cultures into the formal curriculum of discrete subjects. In defence of this point of view, a large number of subjects lend themselves in varying degrees to an international dimension. Secondly, since the multi- or interdisciplinary approach is already established in some countries, this is another option, and it is likely to provide a flexible vehicle for teaching about the complexities of another civilization. In addition, there is a third option, a development of the second. If curriculum time and space allow for the introduction of specially designed units of Area Studies (either as free-standing modules or as part of an existing interdisciplinary course), these can prove the most appropriate vehicle, because by definition Area Studies have a natural cohesion and lend themselves to the concept-values approach implicit in the goals and in the rationale presented here (Table 9). The most comprehensive solution might be the inclusion of a different Area Module into each year of the secondary school curriculum, alongside the provision for European studies.

As to the question of suitability, Council of Europe experts repeatedly put forward powerful arguments for the inclusion of specific cultures within the

Table 9 Teaching and learning for international understanding

Disciplinary approach: single subjects	Specialist approach: Area Studies	Multi- or inter- disciplinary approach
Geography	American Studies	World Studies
History	Canadian Studies	Development Education
Economics	South-East Asian Studies	Environmental Education
Sociology	Chinese Studies	Peace Education
Civics	Japanese Studies	Intercultural Education
Religious Studies	Asian Studies	Political Education
Art	African Studies (North and	Modern Studies
Music	South)	Human Rights Education
Language/Literature	Latin American Studies	Media Education
Biology	North–South Issues	Social Education
Home Economics		

learning experience of European students, particularly for the age group 16–19 years. The justifications most commonly used were the *distinctiveness* of those cultures, their *enduring importance* in the world scene and/or their *significance* in political, economic or cultural terms to Europe's past and present, as their likely relevance in the future. In addition to these criteria, it was felt that they would enliven the imaginations of pupils, add focus to their study of Europe and provide fresh opportunities for them to exercise a range of skills. All these arguments have been taken into consideration in the summary of goals (p. 191). So with these observations in mind, it is time to look more closely at the implications of teaching about the cultures and countries which were examined under the Council of Europe's programme of the last decade.

UNDERSTANDING OTHER PARTS OF THE WORLD

North America

It is hardly surprising that the Council of Europe's programme of colloquies gave high priority to teaching about the United States and Canada and that the programme linked teachers from those countries with European teachers so that they could pool their expertise and examine problems together. Given the superpower status of the USA and the special relationship between the two continents in the twentieth century, the decision had a great deal to commend it. Even President Gorbachev acknowledged this crucial interdependence. 'The realities of today and the prospects for the foreseeable future,' he said, 'are obvious: the Soviet Union and the United States are a natural part of the European international and political structure.'[11] In addition, the long-standing presence of Canadian and US NATO forces and their families on European soil, and the historic European roots of many North American communities, making them part of the Atlantic 'circle of influence', added weight to these arguments. And there was a final consideration in the influence of American popular culture on European youth. Consequently, in the years 1982–4 two Council of Europe teachers' seminars and a major conference were held for American and European teachers and academic experts, to discuss the key issues involved in Teaching about the United States of America, to be followed in 1984–6 by two on the subject of Teaching about Canada in Secondary Schools in Western Europe.

The European participants at the first of these four seminars revealed the power of the hidden curriculum in schools, which probably ran counter to the aims and substance of their teaching about America. This force was the mass media, with its phantasma of beguiling images and limitless capacity for myth creation. The effect was to give European pupils a partial and fragmented vision of the USA. However, teaching and learning about another culture could not ignore the impressions, absorbed during pupils' early years, which they brought to school, for these were the basis of much stereotyped thinking. In European schools, teaching about America usually occurred in History, Geography, some form of Social Studies and in English as a foreign language (the last of these being the principal vehicle, except where English was the national tongue). Other problems acknowledged by several teachers were the complexity and diversity of the subject matter and lack of a cross- or total curriculum approach, as well as the difficulty of keeping abreast with recent publications on the USA, both for classroom use and for their own information.

One useful outcome of the first seminar at Donaueschingen was the production in 1984 of an annotated bibliography on recent works on American society, commissioned by the Atlantic Council of the US (ACUS). In addition, the European teachers agreed that it was imperative to identify clear goals and discriminatory criteria for selecting what pupils should learn about the USA. Many of the ideas debated there emerged again during a second seminar at Tallberg in Sweden and at the major conference held in Washington DC at the end of 1984, sponsored jointly by the CDCC, ACUS and the US National Council for the Social Studies (NCSS). Covering a vast range of issues under the designation Teaching and Learning about Each Other: the USA and Western Europe, this symposium resulted in the presentation of six outlines of courses for teaching about the USA to European secondary school pupils. The proposals illustrated different approaches drawn from the experience of experts in Denmark, Norway, Portugal and the United Kingdom: learning through topics, broad themes, key concepts, child–centred learning, the use of discrete subjects and the multidisciplinary mode. Progress was also made on defining goals for teaching about the USA in Europe, notably in the paper by Frank Fitz-Gibbon, 'Reflections on European perspectives on teaching about the United States', which argued strongly for a bifocal values model, built around the affective goal of empathy and the procedural concepts of distinctiveness, similarity and difference.[12]

Some of the key differences between American and European cultures have been highlighted in Council of Europe publications. It was Henri Janne's opinion that for Europeans liberty had to provide real protection of their freedoms, that is to say, effective security rather than legal guarantees. The reason is that the European has 'a deeply felt, ancestral, psychological dread of the state' but a kind of schizoid need for authority and unfettered freedom, the product of centuries of struggle. The American, on the other hand, having broken away from these traditions, has become in sociological terms 'an eternal emigrant' and therefore tends to approve of the state which bestows on him or her personal and constitutional guarantees. Europeans, again as the victims of history, separate their spirituality from their society and seek ideological utopias, sometimes Christian, sometimes socialist or liberal or philosophical, but Americans, nurtured on the idea that they have a role in building their society, identify their utopia with it. This explains the significance of notions like the American Dream, the New Frontier, the New Deal, the myth of the American Way of Life. Lastly, there is a difference between the European and American concepts of pluralism. European pluralism, which came about after centuries of strife, culminating in twentieth-century political and ideological divergence, is essentially socio-political; Europe's democratic parties offer the electorate a choice of political society. American pluralism is based on socio-political consensus, the choice being between religion and personal ethics.[13] The dominant values of American society are achievement/success; activity/work; humanitarianism; moral orientation; efficiency/practicality; progress/material comfort; external conformity; scientific rationality; patriotism/nationalism; democracy and individuality.[14] While these values can be traced to their European origins, they have been modified by the American environment and people to acquire new meaning.

Teachers need to know how the various differences as well as the common values of the Atlantic Community can be translated into manageable themes, topics and activities of the kind that will develop desirable skills and attitudes. The priority, as Fitz-Gibbon indicated, is

> the capacity to appreciate why Americans may be more or less likely to view a given circumstance in the same way as a European; why Americans are more likely to attach importance to some things rather than to others, and how these priorities differ from those of many Europeans. What is important is to appreciate how Americans see the world and themselves. It is this which makes them distinctively, uniquely American.[15]

Similar views were expressed by Dr Carole Hahn, who advocated an approach based on value-centrality and stressed diversity, similarity and the development of empathy. 'It is the ability to take on the perspective of another that is crucial to international understanding,' she concluded, 'regardless of whether we agree with the other's position.' This values approach had been discussed at the first teachers' seminar on American Studies in 1982, where a working group of teachers produced a module for 14–17 year olds on the concept of Empathy. This could serve as a useful model for achieving enlightened attitudes because it highlights the way images and stereotypes affect teaching about 'foreigners' and 'foreign places'.[16] The proposals were as follows:

A *Identification* of European images/stereotypes about the USA, e.g.
- the USA is a violent society;
- the USA is a male-dominated society;
- the peoples of the USA are uniformly rich;
- the USA is a mobile society wedded to change;
- Americans are worshippers of technology;
- Americans are addicted to size and the belief that 'bigger is better';
- Americans are highly individualist;
- Americans are highly achievement-oriented;
- Americans are arrogant with regard to capabilities and achievements of the USA;
- Americans have a naive view of the world as a result of the superficiality of their culture;
- American women are either spoiled by affluence and/or ardent feminists;
- Americans believe strongly in their political system and their Constitution.

B *Consideration* of the degree to which the USA and Western Europe can be said to have a common culture, and to be an 'Atlantic community'.

C *Analysis* of attitudes in Western Europe and the USA to key ideals, institutions and phenomena, e.g. progress, equality, patriotism, materialism, the impact of technology on society, legitimate national interest.

D *Discussion* of paradox of the diversity yet unity of cultural values in the USA in the light of the disparity in the conditions of rich and poor in the USA and also bearing in mind the changing ethnic balance of American society. Thus, are the notions of the 'Melting Pot' and *'E pluribus unum'* still appropriate designations for contemporary US society?

E *Identification* of actual American values which may well be taken to be:
- achievement and success;
- moral orientation/humanitarianism;
- progress/material comfort;
- freedom/democracy;
- science;
- individual personality;
- activity and work;
- efficiency and practicality;
- equality;
- external conformity;
- nationalism/patriotism;
- racism and group superiority.

Enquiry-based project to implement the Empathy Module, studying in depth

Puritan New England	1690;
The Sioux Nation	1870;
Italian Immigrants	1900;
Mid-West Suburbia	1950;
Ghetto Blacks	1965.

Methods: group/class discussion of sources prior to project; simulation and role play; active groups work; short visit/exchange/encounter; class assignment to assess changes in perspective as result of enquiry.

In the 1980s, teaching about Canada was less well-developed in European schools, so there was less awareness among European pupils of Canada's distinctiveness. This was partly because Canadian studies were overshadowed by American studies, but also because of a lack of teaching materials. The greatest interest seemed to be in Finland, Norway and the UK, although the fact that 25 per cent of Canadians speak French and cherish both a French and a bilingual cultural tradition suggests that it offers unusual potential to Europe's French-speaking nations. Indeed, Canada offers all European students a good model for comparison, for it is a multicultural country, governed by the quest for unity and national identity in the face of strong regional diversity and conflicting loyalties. Additionally, Canada has a long-standing role as a world peacekeeping power and as an active participant in movements and organizations for international co-operation. Another lesson to be learned is that Canada's history should not be approached (as it has customarily been) from a Eurocentric standpoint. Although 'Canada is dominated by its geography' (as a vast, northern and regionally divided country it bears some comparison with the USSR), experts believe that the most effective way of studying Canada in the European curriculum is through the interdisciplinary approach, making use of case studies illustrating concepts drawn from Canadian experience, such as Communication, Regionalism or Federal–Centre tensions.[17]

The cultures of Asia

So much for the familiar cultures of the North American continent with their Anglo-Saxon, Hispanic and Gallic roots. Meanwhile, the Council of Europe was engaged in exploring possibilities of dialogue with very different parts of the world in pursuit of mutual understanding. Indeed, CDCC experts looked first in the direction of the Pacific and as a preliminary they were asked to analyse the kind of press which these so-called 'other parts of the world' received in European secondary curricula. A series of teachers' seminars followed, starting in 1981, the first of which looked at Teaching about Japan.

Discussions revealed that most young Europeans acquired little knowledge of Japanese society and culture in the course of their secondary education, despite Japan's pre-eminence as a Pacific and global power, the fact that it is one of the world's few distinctive monocultural societies (in contrast to Europe) and that it is among the ten most populated nations on earth. Learning about Japanese history seemed to hinge on five dates with international implications: 1905, 1931, 1937, 1941 and 1945. Young Europeans harbour stereotyped mental images of Japanese people, though racist attitudes have diminished since the 1960s when British comics still sustained images of Britain's former enemies as 'fanatical', 'slit-eyed killers', as 'slippery as snakes'. Some countries, notably France, Portugal and the Netherlands, established post-war cultural links with Japan and many Japanese brand names were (and are increasingly) familiar to European pupils. Yet even in the early 1980s secondary curricula took little account of Japanese economic supremacy, especially in the field of high technology. Syllabuses failed to indicate Japan's role today as the principal 'Western' influence in East and South-East Asia. History teaching was insufficiently concerned with Japanese success in repulsing Western influences in the sixteenth and seventeenth centuries at the height of Europe's first age of colonization, and with Japan's achievement in being the only non-Western nation to embrace modern industrialization in the nineteenth and twentieth centuries.

The invitation extended in 1983 to a group of influential European educators by the International Society for Educational Information (ISEI) in Tokyo was therefore a welcome initiative. That study tour has resulted in the production of teaching materials and in-service courses for teachers wanting to bring Japan and the Pacific Rim into their programmes. However, difficulties remain in sustaining a Japanese dimension in secondary teaching. The main problems are twofold: the lack of teacher confidence and knowledge of Japan's history, language, religion, social values and traditional culture, and the inadequate range of resources available. (Good-quality media material, like the BBC Schools Television series *The Crowded Islands*, should be more widely disseminated.) So although many European teachers acknowledge that their pupils should learn about traditional Japanese society in order to understand Japan, in practice there is a temptation to limit teaching to the context of World History since 1939 or of Economics or contemporary International Relations.[18]

In 1983 the Council of Europe also turned its attention to teaching about China. The contemporary relevance of China needs no emphasis here, except to say that experts believe in time to come its political impact will overshadow the power of the USA and the USSR, while its economic potential makes it likely that it will outstrip Japan. Yet the educational justification for studying China also rests on its ancient and distinctive culture, which has made it a 'mirror-image' of Europe. Learning something of the essential difference between the two is, in the opinion of sinologists, a good antidote to Eurocentrism. An international teachers' seminar was followed by the publication of a trenchant report on Teaching about China in Secondary Schools in Western Europe. This set out frankly the problems and curricular constraints but suggested what young Europeans might reasonably be expected to learn about China before leaving school. Experts also analysed the Chinese identity, explaining Chinese social values and providing information on essential areas and knowledge, potential teaching sources and alternative approaches.[19] They appreciated that the curriculum cannot easily absorb new subjects, but China's early scientific and technical discoveries deserve far more attention than they usually receive in History syllabuses – inventions such as gunpowder, the harness, the magnetic compass, the mechanical clock, printing, the gimbal suspension and the seismograph. Texts are available through which young Europeans can learn about Chinese perceptions of the European, and about European attitudes towards China and its people. This kind of material can help to counter negative stereotypes, which can sometimes be reinforced by the use of case-studies. In addition, Chinese art and literature (such as the great vernacular novels in translation) have great potential, particularly for older students.

In the opinion of the Council of Europe's experts, there ought to be a place for both China and Japan in the first years of European secondary education, and further in-depth study is desirable at the 16–19 stage. But there are cogent reasons for extending these studies to the rest of Asia, so that proper recognition is given to the importance of those states of South-East Asia and the Pacific Rim which have great concentrations of population and are among the world's most dynamic economies. Asia is a continent of historic civilizations and the home of several world religions. It includes the subcontinent of India and multicultural societies that look with pride to the past and with confidence to the future. Asia has great potential in terms of human and natural resources, which cannot help but affect the future of Europe in an age of increasing interdependence. More particularly, in view of the various Asian minorities in Europe's school population, intercultural programmes would benefit from the inclusion of Asia in international studies, while the self-development of European students in general should be taken into consideration. As those teachers involved in American Studies confirmed, pupils whose horizons are broadened, even through vicarious experience, who can learn to respect contemporaries of a different culture, are themselves enriched in terms of their personal values. The eminent Asian scholar, William Theodore de Bary, wrote: 'Today no people can "find" themselves or discover their real identity, except in relation to others.'[20]

There is no general strategy for dealing with Asia in European curricula. Many factors influence the criteria for selecting content, not least the centuries-old links between European nations and their former colonies. For instance, the Moluccas figure in both History and Geography syllabuses in the Netherlands – a typical history theme being From Dutch East Indies to Indonesia – but India rarely so. In the UK the reverse is true, while geographers involved in Development Education often take examples from Pakistan, Bangladesh or India. Japanese haiku have been successfully introduced into literature lessons in Belgian schools. Indian authors or works about India are sometimes found in English literature syllabuses in the UK, Denmark and the Federal Republic. On the other hand, India's image has sometimes suffered from being used as a case-study of a Third World country with serious problems, whereas China is taken to show how Communism works in a relatively poor and highly populated country. China most commonly appears in History, Geography or Religious Education syllabuses, but its modern political history overshadows its ancient culture.

The final impression is that 'pupils are exposed to Asia in a fragmented way. To understand any Asian society, the pupils must see how geography, politics, economics, religion and culture intersect and influence each other.'[21] This is a plea for the kind of interdisciplinary approach advocated at the Lisbon seminar in 1983. Yet in practice a variety of less ambitious strategies prevails. Case-studies which figure in Development Education, History and Geography need to be used carefully for the reasons indicated. It would be beneficial if European Art teachers could take a leaf out of Portugal's book, where the ancient art forms of the Orient and Asia Minor, such as Indian and Chinese decorative art and their influence on European art, are to be found in visual arts syllabuses. Music and literature perhaps deserve a more secure place in secondary schools if justice is to be done to the Asian dimension.

The Islamic world

The political revival of Islam in the world has not only challenged the superiority of the superpowers and the European nation-states but has drawn attention to the need for Europeans to learn more about Islamic civilization. France has already made a symbolic cultural gesture with the new Institut du Monde Arabe in Paris, a light-filled tribute to Arabian style in a European setting. However, in the educational field the situation calls for an extension of Intercultural Education to ensure that provision for well-structured courses about Muslim societies and cultures are part of European school curricula and available to all pupils, not simply those living in racially mixed areas. For the issue here is not strictly one of multiculturalism or the relationships between migrants, immigrants and indigenous Europeans, even though the number of citizens of Muslim stock in individual European countries is quite significant – over 1 million in the UK, 4½ million in France, some 50 million in the USSR. It is about the kinds of Muslim society and culture which exist *outside* Europe, about which many in the West hold dangerously simplistic views that have been exacerbated by the much-publicized incidents of hijacking and hostage-taking. Dr Jorgen Nielsen's work on cultural values and education in a multi-cultural society (see below) shows that for some time there have been differences between rank-and-file Muslims and their leaders: in Germany, for instance, the aspirations of most Turkish Muslims diverged noticeably from the segregationist right-wing politics of their Qur'an school leaders, and it may be assumed from the range of reactions to Salman Rushdie's book *The Satanic Verses* that the attitudes and customs of the immigrant communities in Europe have become different (sometimes radically so) from those of the fundamentalist leadership in Iran. The lack of homogeneity in Muslim habits, customs, practices (including religious practices) and spoken languages means that it is inaccurate to generalize about many matters. It is also important to remember the geographical extent of the Islamic world as well as its proselytizing power: the saga of Muslim influence and control which overflowed from its original heartland into Africa, India, Malaysia, Indonesia, Central Asia and, nearer home, across the Mediterranean to the Iberian peninsula and the Balkans. This simple fact alone, of Islamic territorial expansion, makes it imperative to bring Islam into European secondary curricula.

The problem for many teachers, however, is the one we have noted before, namely a lack of specialist knowledge of the history, culture or social structure of Islamic communities *outside* Europe. The academic training of teachers can leave many of them ill-equipped. How many degree courses in the Humanities and Social Sciences include studies of Islam? Whenever teachers are asked to take on other area studies they also face difficulties in securing information and resources. Yet it is vital that they are fully informed and appreciate Islamic viewpoints if in turn they are to encourage pupil understanding and empathy. So it is valuable to know what teachers from other parts of the world recommend as priorities; Europeans certainly benefited from their American colleagues' suggestions for teaching about the USA. Equally important are the insights Muslim teachers give on their own culture. The theologian Imam Mehdi Razvi summarizes the

four distinct yet completely interrelated and inseparable meanings implicit in Islam: 1. Revelation of God through the Prophet Mohammed in the form of the Holy Qur'an and the Sunna (model) of the Prophet. 2. Immediate, existential experience of the individual believer. 3. The socio-political reality of the Islamic community. 4. A historical vision of a better, more just and harmonious world.

It is also immensely salutary for teachers throughout Europe to learn the Imam's view of Islamic relations with Europe and European culture. He said:

It is the third time we Muslims have appeared on the map of Europe, this time, though, not as invaders but as average human beings looking for better economic opportunities. Our people have come mostly from poor areas of the third world which have been thoroughly exploited, their economies shattered, their population uprooted, their intellectuals alienated, their political development arrested and their original culture fragmented and destroyed . . .

Western powers have exploited our resources, destroyed our traditional structures, and have condemned our population to live a life of abject poverty . . . The fight against the colonial and post-colonial exploitation is far from over, and in this long conflict religion has become for the Muslim masses a rallying point of progressive and genuinely revolutionary elements. Because the subjugation of Muslim countries has been carried out by governments who have called themselves liberal, secular, progressive, socialist and democratic, these words have become meaningless for most of our people . . .

Only when this essential difference in our respective historical experiences is fully understood, can we start to discover points of convergence. Islamic culture cannot be separated from the historical, psychological and religious experience of the Islamic community. It is a religious culture in the broadest sense of the term. A culture which has grown out of so many ancient traditions – Semitic, Hellenic, Iranian and Indian, just to mention a few – is not only very rich in its content and value, but has been able to bring forth an impressive crop of local and regional varieties . . .

Islam is for us both a faith and a way of life, regulating not only individual and personal lives, but the whole of society.[22]

This is a powerful statement of the difference between modern Europe and Islam. We are reminded that in Europe the union of faith and social organization, inherent in early Christianity and the ideal of Christendom, was eroded by secularization, by the eighteenth-century Enlightenment and finally in the nineteenth and twentieth centuries by political ideology. Islam, on the other hand, today rejects both capitalistic liberalism and Marxist totalitarianism. It is the teacher's task to explain this fundamental difference, while standing back from value judgements. Similarly, it falls to teachers to inform young Europeans of the contribution of medieval Islam to philosophy, the arts, pure science and technology. In the course of four centuries, Islamic scholarship produced polymaths like Omar Khayyam and Ibn Sina (known also as Avicenna), author of the *Canon of Medicine*, one of the world's most famous medical encyclopaedias; the Iberian Ibn Rushd (or Averroës), philosopher, physician and chief judge of Cordoba; and Ibn Tibbon, born in Marseilles of a famous academic family, regent of the Faculty of Medicine at the University of Montpellier, translator of Ptolemy's *Almagest* and inventor of a quadrant adapted by European mariners. To these we might add the names of Alhazen for his work on optics, Ibn an-Nafio, who anticipated by 350 years William Harvey's discovery of the circulation of the blood, Al-Battani for his study of astronomy, Al-Razi, whose *Kitab al filahah* was the outstanding medieval work on agriculture, Ibn Zuhr of Seville, whose clinical methods profoundly influenced medical practice throughout Christian Europe, and lastly, Ibn Battuta, the Marco Polo of Morocco, who travelled to Ceylon, the Maldive Islands, Sumatra and China. The genius of these men and their influence on medieval European thought is probably still underrated in European schools.[23]

Educators attending the 1983–4 Council of Europe gatherings on the Renaissance Voyages of Exploration did their best to warn fellow teachers that 'care should be taken to do justice to the considerable achievements of contemporary civilisations in other parts of the world', notably in Africa, India, China and Japan.[24] Participants expressed their concern that it was common practice to teach the voyages as a celebration of European success, despite the precedent of a major UNESCO project in the 1960s on The Mutual Appreciation of Eastern

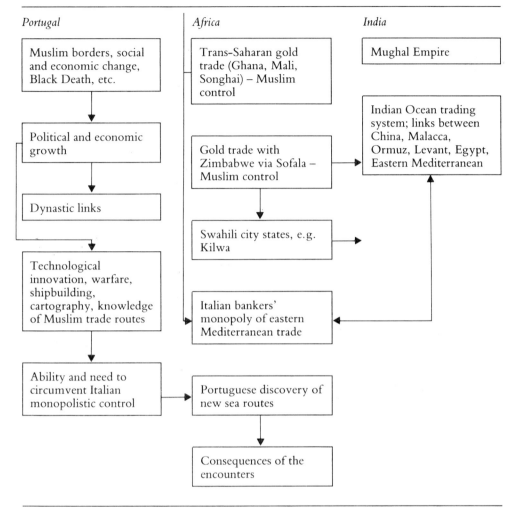

Figure 11 The age of encounter or of discovery?

Source: Bahree, Patricia (1986), *Asia in the European Classroom*, Strasbourg: Council of Europe, p. 46.

and Western Cultural Values. Yet it should be possible to interpret particular episodes of history, such as the exploration of the world's sea routes by European seamen, as examples of cultural interaction, and so that they legitimately serve the cause of international education (Figure 11).

Brazil

Mention has been made of the Council of Europe symposium in 1983 on the Portuguese Voyages and of the Evora workshop in 1984 on Teaching about the Portuguese Expansion in the 15th and 16th centuries and the World Encounter of Cultures. In the same spirit the Parliamentary Assembly of the Council of Europe passed a resolution on cultural relations between Europe and Latin America, while it was decided to pursue this subject with a seminar on the relationship between colonizers and colonized peoples in a major Latin American country.

Brazil was chosen for the case-study because it has a cultural mosaic of great diversity, the result of the ethnic encounter of Europeans (first and foremost the Portuguese, but some Dutch, French, English, Swiss, Germans, Italians and Poles) with African slaves, who were mostly Sudanese and Bantus, and the indigenous Amerindians. The purpose of the seminar was to identify the roots of Brazilian multiculturalism and to analyse from a multidisciplinary standpoint both the process of encounter and the syntheses which resulted. Although economic and technological factors explain the domination of European culture (especially through language and religion) in the colonial period, the effect of miscegenation and acculturation produced a distinct society in Brazil. It became clear that the development of Brazil and other Latin American countries opened up the pedagogical dimension of multiculturalism so that there was a strong case for including it in the Social Science and/or History curricula of European schools.[25] The educational dialogue established between Europe and Latin America was taken further in 1986 when another theme – Democracy and Democratisation – was the subject of a colloquy organized jointly by the Council of Europe and the Institute for European–Latin American Relations.

Africa south of the Sahara

This survey of the Council of Europe's educational dialogue with other parts of the world would not be complete without some reference to the continent of Africa, which was the subject of a European teachers' seminar at Lahti, Finland, in 1984. The 500-year history of relations between Africa and Europe, involving, on the European side, the Portuguese, Dutch, British, Spanish and French, has been described as one of 'dependency and exploitation'; as a consequence, History curricula have tended to ignore the indigenous history of the African peoples, an omission which gave rise to stereotyped views and perpetuated inaccuracies and prejudices in school textbooks into the 1980s.[26] And yet the fact remains that 'Africa is a continent with much to offer the rest of mankind through the riches of its manifold art forms and its deeply humane social philosophy.'[27]

In studying the history, ecology and cultures of Africa south of the Sahara (subjects synonymous with the concepts of time, place and society), it is evident that the continent reveals stimulating contrasts with European experience. Differences are more pronounced than similarities: the urban culture of industrialized Europe is the antithesis of the largely rural or village culture of most regions of Africa. Yet there are paradoxes, too: in its way southern

Europe also has a rural socio-economic structure,[28] and the apartheid system is the creation of Afrikaners of European descent. However, Europeans should resist blanket interpretations of Africa as an 'underdeveloped' continent and focus on the interdependencies between nations and the importance of the self-help movement in sub-Saharan Africa. Students should learn that Africa's future depends on a balance being struck between consumer demands for Africa's resources and the development needs of the African countries themselves.

GLOBAL DEVELOPMENT AND NORTH–SOUTH ISSUES

Education in the problems of global development and the North–South divide was an initiative of the 1980s. From 1979, when the CDCC held a seminal conference at Lillehammer, Norway, to review topics of international significance, one fundamental issue remained on the agenda: how to reconcile the *de jure* equality of cultures, implicit in the universal statements of Human Rights, with the *de facto* existence of dominant and dominated cultures. This is much more than a European question, though the subject of intolerance, prejudice and violation of human rights has been a feature of European history. This is a global issue with many dimensions, cultural, social, religious, economic and geo-political. The Council of Europe responded with a programme of curriculum innovation through a new interdisciplinary study called Development Education. This was defined as 'education for global consciousness, for an awareness – as well as an understanding – of the problems facing us and of all that is at stake, for the desire in every individual to share responsibility and work in a co-operative spirit at the most appropriate levels – local, national and international.'[29]

The definition goes on to list eleven aims for Development Education which are couched in terms of attributes and skills that pupils could be expected to acquire. Michael Williams produced further guidance in the form of a grid describing Development Education in operation, which was submitted to the Haikko symposium on The World in the European Classroom.[30]

As part of the Council of Europe's programme of global awareness, the work started at Lillehammer was continued at a conference held in Lahti, Finland, in 1981, where four aspects of global development and conflict, namely energy, urbanization, population and disarmament, were examined in depth. After consultation with other international bodies in 1980–2 the CDCC recommended that whenever possible Development Education should be supplemented by direct intercultural experience outside the formal curriculum. In addition, some European teachers felt they should be widening the scope of their teaching, hence the CDCC seminars on sub-Saharan Africa, Brazil and the literature of Spanish America. From the recommendations of a teachers' seminar in 1985 on Geography for International Understanding in the Primary

School came the promotion of school networks between countries both in and outside Europe. But the Haikko symposium of 1986 made it clear that there was still a formidable variety of world-wide issues, from race, hunger, human needs, human rights and poverty, to new technology, energy, space, war and peace, which should be taught with an international perspective. Of these, Human Rights and Peace Education were again the focus of a CDCC seminar at Are, Sweden, in the summer of 1987, and problem issues, such as motivation, the difficulty of promoting 'worthy causes' and the implications for methodology, were discussed.[31]

However, if there was one aspect of international education which emerged as the major priority it was concern for the global division between the 'haves' and the 'have-nots', the North–South Issue. The Brandt Report ('North–South, a Programme for Survival') made specific reference to the role of schools and of all those responsible for education in widening people's views and focusing attention on the escalation of world problems. The Lisbon Declaration of April 1984 on Europe's role and responsibility to the Third World was followed by further Resolutions of the Parliamentary Assembly of the Council of Europe in 1985–6. At Lisbon a call had been issued for a European-wide initiative. This came to fruition in January 1988 with the launching of the European Public Campaign on North/South Interdependence and Solidarity, through co-operation between the Council of Europe and the Commission of the European Communities. The campaign's Organizing Committee was presided over by King Juan Carlos I of Spain and included three heads of state representing southern continents – President Alfonsín of Argentina, President Aquino of the Philippines and President Diouf of Senegal – and the prime ministers of Norway and India. Their purpose was to raise public awareness of the complex relationships between Europe and the Third World and to prevail on Europeans to accept their moral obligations as citizens of the world. A series of ministerial round tables was held in European capitals and a major colloquy under the auspices of the Secretary General of the Council of Europe took place in Lisbon, where a permanent North–South Centre has been established. A subsidiary educational outcome was the publication of a teaching pack for use in European secondary schools. Finally, at the close of the campaign in June 1988, Madrid was the venue of a European conference of parliamentarians and representatives of non-governmental bodies. They issued the Madrid Declaration that 'European governments and non-governmental organisations should promote Development Education – both at national and European level – so that the European public opinion will become aware of the growing interdependence between Europe and the developing countries and of the need for solidarity.'

The importance attached by the Council of Europe to International Education is borne out by the fact that a total of twenty-four teachers' seminars involving 1200 participants were held in the decade of 1978–88 to examine global issues. The seminars were also facilitated by the Council of Europe's co-operation with UNICEF and other international non-governmental organizations, as well as numerous national societies and agencies. Now there remains the challenge of maintaining the momentum created by the North–South campaign, a task which will be carried out by the Lisbon Centre. And against this backcloth International Education continues to present teachers with a demanding curricular task, for as the Director of CEVNO pointed out, 'international education' is a multifaceted concept. In addition to extending pupils' skills and their knowledge and understanding of other cultures and regions of the world, it ought to ensure that 'European co-operation, development co-operation, peace and security, human rights and the environment are accorded due respect.'[32]

SUMMARY OF THE RATIONALE FOR GIVING EUROPEAN CURRICULA A GLOBAL DIMENSION

European curricula should incorporate a global dimension in order to:

1 promote international understanding, peace and co-operation between nations;

2 respond to the realities of global political and economic interdependence and the need for mechanisms of co-existence;

3 counter ethnocentricity in all its forms and assist in creating a responsible and tolerant intercultural ethos in European society;

4 enrich pupil understanding of Europe by undertaking comparative studies which promote balance and perspective in pupils' learning.

SUMMARY OF GOALS FOR TEACHING AND LEARNING ABOUT OTHER CULTURES AND SOCIETIES

1 To identify in terms of knowledge the distinctiveness of other cultures and societies and to appreciate their contribution to human creativity.

2 To understand the similarities and differences and the areas of interaction between other world cultures and European civilization, and so to develop a balanced awareness of Europe's distinct identity.

3 To induce empathetic attitudes and human responses to the peoples of other cultures, which will be reflected in the personal value systems and actions of young Europeans.

4 To extend pupils' cognitive and aesthetic skills and stimulate their imaginations by using geographical, historical and sociological evidence, audiovisual media, and literary and art forms illustrating the distinctive achievements of other cultures.

NOTES

1 Henk Oonk, 'Europe in Dutch primary schools', in Trybus, Klaudia (1986), *Report on the 30th European Teachers' Seminar on Europe in Primary Schools, Donaueschingen,*

November 1985, Strasbourg: Council of Europe, p. 26; Council of Europe Recommendations No. R (83) 13 and (83) 4; UNESCO Recommendation concerning Education for International Understanding, Co-operation and Peace, 19 November 1974.

2 Halbritter, Hermann (1986), in Trybus, *Report on Europe in Primary Schools*, p. 13.

3 O'Connor, Edmund (1980), *World Studies in the European Classroom*, Strasbourg: Council of Europe, pp. 11–12.

4 See *ibid.* for a succinct discussion of alternative approaches to International Education.

5 'European aspects of the curriculum', in Trybus, *Report on Europe in Primary Schools* (Austria), p. 36.

6 Branson, Margaret Stimmann (1984), discussion paper on 'What do Americans think that the average European should know about the USA?' in Williams, Roy, *Report of the European Teachers' Seminar on Teaching about the USA in Secondary Schools in Western Europe, Donaueschingen, October 1982*, Strasbourg: Council of Europe, p. 50.

7 O'Connor, *World Studies*, p. 15.

8 Murray, Bruce C. (1975), *Navigating the Future*, New York: Harper and Row, p. 210.

9 Peacock, David (1981), *Report of the CDCC Symposium on Europe in Secondary School Curricula: Aims, Approaches and Problems, Neusiedl-am-See, Austria, April 1981*, Strasbourg: Council of Europe, p. 14.

10 For example: European Teachers' Seminar on Development Education in Secondary Schools, Donaueschingen, Federal Republic of Germany, 1980; CDCC Symposium on Europe in Secondary School Curricula, Neusiedl-am-See, Austria, 1981; European Teachers' Seminar on Europe and Asia, London, 1982; European Teachers' Seminar on Teaching about China in Secondary Schools in Western Europe, 1983; European Workshop for History Teachers on Portuguese Expansion in the 15th and 16th Centuries and the World Encounter of Cultures, Evora, Portugal, 1984; CDCC Symposium on The World in the European Classroom, Haikko, Finland, 1986. A bibliography of the reports on the eighteen CDCC Teachers' Seminars of 1979–86 is printed in (1986), *Education for Life in an Interdependent World*, Strasbourg: Council of Europe (doc. DECS/EGT (86) 41).

11 Speech to the Parliamentary Assembly of the Council of Europe, July 1989.

12 Fitz-Gibbon, J. Frank (1984), 'Reflections on European perspectives on teaching about the United States', discussion paper for joint conference on Teaching and Learning about Each Other: The USA and Western Europe, Washington, DC, November 1984.

13 Janne, Henri (1981), 'Europe's cultural identity' (paper for the Symposium on Europe in Secondary School Curricula: Aims, Approaches and Problems, Neusiedl-am-See, April 1981), Strasbourg: Council of Europe, pp. 9–12.

14 In the view of the American Teachers' Panel at the European Teachers' Seminar on Teaching about the USA in Secondary Schools in Western Europe, Donaueschingen, October 1982, in Williams, *Report on Teaching about the USA*, pp. 17, 36.

15 Fitz-Gibbon, 'Reflections on European perspectives', p. 10.

16 This model drew on the ideas put forward by Dr Carole Hahn at the European Teachers' Seminar on Teaching about the USA in Secondary Schools in Western Europe, Donaueschingen, October 1982, and was worked out by a group of teachers there (Williams, *Report on Teaching about the USA*, pp. 35–7).

17 Galvao, Maria Emilia (1985), *Report of the European Teachers' Seminar on Teaching about Canada in Secondary Schools in Western Europe, Donaueschingen, October 1984*, Strasbourg: Council of Europe.

18 Tames, Richard (1981), *Report for the 11th European Teachers' Seminar on Education for International Understanding – Teaching about a Non-European Culture: The Case of Japan, Donaueschingen, May 1981*, Strasbourg: Council of Europe. A teaching model for linking Japan and Europe using the theme Continuity and Change is printed in O'Connor, *World Studies*, pp. 18, 49–50.

19 Thomas, Graham (1984), *Report of the 22nd European Teachers' Seminar on Teaching about China in Secondary Schools in Western Europe, Donaueschingen, November 1983*, Strasbourg: Council of Europe.

20 de Bary, William Theodore (1972), 'The liberal arts amid a culture in crisis', *Liberal Education*, **LVIII** (1), quoted in Bahree, Patricia (1986), *Asia in the European Classroom*, Strasbourg: Council of Europe, p. 9.

21 *Ibid.*, p. 28.

22 Razvi, Imam Mehdi (1981), 'Cultural values and education in a multicultural society – a Muslim view', in Nielsen, Jorgen S., *Report for the 13th European Teachers' Seminar on Cultural Values and Education in a Multi-cultural Society, Donaueschingen, October 1981, on The Training of Teachers of the Children of Migrant Workers*, Strasbourg: Council of Europe, pp. 6–9.

23 The Committee on Education and Culture of the Council of Europe's Parliamentary Assembly is scheduled to organize a major colloquy in Paris in May 1991 on The Contribution of Islamic Civilization to European Culture.

24 Symposium on Teaching about the Portuguese Discoveries in Secondary Schools in Western Europe, Lisbon 1983, reported in (1986), *Against Bias and Prejudice: The Council of Europe's Work on History Teaching and History Textbooks*, Strasbourg: Council of Europe, p. 47. See Figure 11, p. 187, for a teaching model linking Europe, Africa and India.

25 Caldeira, Arlindo Manuel (1986), *Report of the European Teachers' Seminar on The Birth of Brazil: Roots of a Multicultural Society, Lisbon, Portugal, December 1985*, Strasbourg: Council of Europe.

26 Gunner, Elizabeth (1985), *Report of the European Teachers' Seminar on Teaching about Africa South of the Sahara, Lahti, Finland, August 1984*, Strasbourg: Council of Europe, pp. 3–6.

27 *Ibid.*, p. 1.

28 (1982), *Final Meeting and Conclusions of the Special Project: Southern Europe, CDCC Project No. 1, Preparation for Life, Treviso, Italy, February 1982*, Strasbourg: Council of Europe, p. 27.

29 Williams, Michael (1986), 'The world in the European classroom' (discussion paper for the CDCC Symposium at Haikko Congress Centre, near Porvoo, Finland, September 1986), Strasbourg: Council of Europe, p. 10.

30 *Ibid.*, p. 17.
31 Pearse, Sanchia (1987), *Report of the European Teachers' Seminar on Human Rights Education in a Global Perspective, Are, Sweden, August 1987*, Strasbourg: Council of Europe.
32 Oonk, 'Europe in Dutch primary schools', p. 26.

PART 4

STRUCTURES AND AGENTS FOR CHANGE

CHAPTER 10

Towards an Effective Education for Europe

THE CONTINUING BACKCLOTH OF CHANGE AND DIVERSITY

This study began with a discussion of the outstanding changes affecting Europe in the present century. Now, in trying to draw together the various strands of that and subsequent discussions, and in assessing the curricular developments in train or under consideration, we return to that original theme of *change*. There is a certain irony in this intention, for while the project was under way, Europe entered on a radical political and social transformation, as if to underline the argument and also to challenge some of the initial assumptions and propositions. In self-defence, the words of Professor Maurice Craft come to mind, when he was giving an overview of the needs of multicultural education in Europe by the year 2000: 'No intelligent observer will regard the analysis of challenges and opportunities presented by . . . Europe at the end of the 20th century as other than highly speculative. The social processes involved at both the macro and micro levels are extremely complex and only too easy to over-simplify.'[1] If we agree with him that nothing is certain, there is still perhaps an obligation to reflect very briefly on the kind of European society for which teachers are preparing the young and the kinds of assumption which must be in their minds, as well as the vision of Europe which young people uphold themselves. At a Youth Peace Seminar representing opinion from both Eastern and Western Europe, held on the eve of the European Revolutions of 1989, participants spoke of their aspirations for the future.[2] Prominent among their hopes were:

- the ending of divisions in Europe;
- a peaceful Europe;
- free exchange of people and ideas;
- a common European home;
- the right to live where one pleases;

- the right to use the mother tongue;
- justice;
- protection for smaller countries and cultures;
- the involvement of citizens;
- a common language;
- one currency.

In the short interval between the seminar and the present day these 'hopes for the future' have by and large been achieved or can be regarded as realistic goals. So what assumptions should Europeans now make about the future of European society as they face the watershed of 1992, followed by the psychological challenge of a new century? Taking an earlier CDCC prediction of social characteristics as a guideline,[3] European society may well follow this pattern in the 1990s:

1 The whole of Europe will be based on, or aspire to, the political principles of democracy and human rights, though the former may be embodied in various forms.

2 There will be an increasing trend towards decentralization and regionalization, counterbalanced by greater direction from the centre – from Brussels? Strasbourg? Berlin? – and by certain frictions over the role of the nation-state.

3 The general movement towards participation at school, at work and in public life will continue, and grass-roots activities will be an accepted feature of 'The People's Europe'.

4 European society will continue to be multicultural and will respond with a broad policy of cultural pluralism and social integration in which the rights of all minority groups will be recognized and protected.

5 Changes in family structure and the increase in one-parent families are likely to continue: in some parts as many as half the next generation of young Europeans will never know traditional family life. These changes will affect relationships between teachers and pupils in school.[4]

6 Sexual stereotyping and discrimination will be eliminated in principle (if not universally in practice) by legal process.

7 Europe will continue to develop as an urban society but there will be a strong trend to protect the environment against uncontrolled industrialization and exploitation, and alternative forms of tourism and agriculture will be developed to meet the growth of leisure and the need for conservation.

8 Regional variations in employment patterns will continue, as those heartland regions with modern communication networks prosper at the expense of more marginal areas and of the European periphery.

9 The influence of the new information and communication technology will have a profound effect on commerce, industry, bureaucratic and governmental processes, education, life-opportunities and working patterns.

10 Society will become increasingly mobile, and working outside one's

country of birth will be the norm for a growing percentage of the skilled and professional population.

11 The general demographic trend will be towards a continuing decrease in the birth rate and an ageing population.

12 There is likely to be increasing divergence and tension between the values of the conventional family, the school system, the media, the Christian Churches and other mass religions, and society as a whole.

13 Social pressures will force governments to take national and international action against the pollution of the environment, ecological damage and global warming.

14 From the 1990s the spirit of an international European community will evolve on a broad front. There will be an expanding Single European Market with accompanying social and economic developments, a general commitment to the notion of 'The People's Europe', a widespread awareness of European identity, formalized by passports, youth and pensioners' concessionary cards etc., and unrestricted mobility.[5]

15 In a world where human contacts are accelerated by the communications revolution, where fundamental issues of ecological welfare are seen to be world-wide in their cause and effect, and finally, where the deep economic disparity between the developed and developing worlds is considered unacceptable by a majority of people, greater respect will be paid in public life, education and the media to the notion of 'Europe in a global context'.

A European Forum at Lyon in 1989 emphasized three of these trends in particular. Coining the formula, 'Mobility, openness and solidarity', the participants underlined the importance to Europeans of freedom of movement, pluralism and democracy.[6] However, if these are the general conditions in which the education systems of Europe are to operate in the coming decade, the same systems may still be affected by national government policies which are governed by *national* interests and traditions, or in some instances by regional ones. At the same time, national authorities and policy-makers should take account of the recommendations of the major international organizations, in addition to the concerns of non-governmental organizations which represent grass-roots opinion, and other support agencies and audiences. The point has been made elsewhere, but bears repeating, that supranational educational initiatives such as the introduction of a European dimension into secondary education can only be achieved with the accumulative consent of many groups and individuals acting as facilitators, and within the particular framework of national systems.[7]

The divergent nature of national traditions is one of the inhibiting factors in 'Europeanizing' the curriculum. The dichotomy between elitism and comprehension, the duration of school attendance, the age structures for entry, selection, transfer and school leaving, instruction time and learning-related activities such as homework are all variables, together with school subjects and syllabuses. In some countries general education is provided by a fixed syllabus, 'whilst in others it is possible to describe general education as a department store shopping spree'.[8] Despite measures to achieve the recognition of vocational and professional qualifications in European Community Member States, greater individualization of education systems and increasing diversity in the classroom have been observed.[9] Yet this situation has been accompanied by other general developments. The extension of the formal curriculum to take account of new priorities for preparation for life in Europe (such as Environmental and Development Education, Personal, Social and Health Education, Computer Science and Citizenship, discussed in Chapters 4, 5, 6, 7 and 9) is one discernible European trend. Another is the targeting of attainment standards to ensure pupil potential is fulfilled. In France, for instance, a national target of 80 per cent exists for the secondary level certificate. Moreover, there has been a move towards closer contact with the outside world and linking education to training. In Belgium compulsory education can be completed on a part-time basis; in Austria and the Federal Republic of Germany training can be alternated with school attendance.[10]

THE NEXT STEP FORWARD...

Attention has been drawn to these educational diversities because they indicate that uniformity in European educational systems is neither a realistic nor a desirable goal.[11] However, that does not discount the need for, or the possibility of, a fundamental, sustained and collaborative campaign on the part of European national governments, with the encouragements and help of those supranational bodies with a concern for European co-operation. It has been suggested that it would be profitable to establish an intermediary body, linking the primary and secondary institutions of the European Community Member States, which would provide an overview between the Council of Ministers and the Community on matters such as harmonizing the educational systems.[12] Certainly, there has to be some consensus at the highest levels on a common philosophy and framework of curricular principles for Education for Europe, including goals for teacher education, teacher training and a radical concept of 'exchange' in line with post-1992 mobility and the new information and communication technology (NICT).

An alternative way of initiating such a major campaign with international public support may be via the public and democratic forum of Europe's parliamentary machinery, namely in the European Parliament and the Council of Europe's Parliamentary Assembly. What is beyond dispute is that a concept of European Education cannot be built on token gestures and improvised strategies designed to 'bolt on' Europe to existing syllabuses as an ill-fitting addition to already overcrowded curricula. That would be futile and it would be to fly in the face of social, political and economic reality. In point of fact, after twenty years of gestation, European Education is ready to emerge as a robust issue that cannot be brushed aside.

Certain governments anticipated this development some while ago and laid down their own criteria for European Education. The most explicit and complete statements of European 'intent' appear in the Basic Law (1949) of the Federal Republic of Germany and the Resolutions of the Ministers of Education of 1978 and 1990 (Tables 7 and 8):

> The school has the task of making the European peoples and countries aware of the integration process and the realignment of their relations. It is intended to make a contribution towards developing awareness of European identity and fostering understanding of the fact that in many spheres of our lives European terms of reference apply and that European decisions are necessary.[13]

In so far as they are carrying out this clear mission statement, which was confirmed in 1990, German schools (and particularly the *Gymnasien* with bilingual sections) are already contributing towards the development in the rising generation of a consciousness of European unity. Furthermore, the 1990 Resolution makes specific recommendations for further development of 'Europe as a part of the curriculum'. At a time when other European governments are engaged in national evaluation and restructuring exercises, they have an unparalleled opportunity to place their commitment to European Education on a similar footing. In the UK national European Awareness Project the notion of 'European Entitlement' floated by some education authorities – one LEA makes 'a pyramid of entitlement' central to its policy statement – could go half way towards this goal.[14]

Meanwhile, support agencies such as the National Centres for European Education have proliferated in the past decade, together with bodies serving more specialized needs, such as the National Information Technology in Education Centre (NITEC) in Ireland, the Computer-Assisted Learning Centre in Geneva or the Centre de Liaison de l'Enseignement et des Moyens d'Information (CLEMI) in France, in addition to those mentioned earlier which have distinguished records in serving European Education. Taking account of all these matters, together with the researches and recommendations flowing to and from the CDCC and the EC with regard to the European dimension, it is now time for us to take stock. The European Ministries of Education of member states of the EC will have been examining their provision for a European dimension since 1988, but if there is to be compatibility between European education systems, *all* states should be ready to conduct national audits to review their machinery for planning, financing, implementing, controlling and assessing that dimension. However, these reviews cannot afford to be in isolation of each other, for comparability and cross-fertilization of ideas are essential ingredients in compatibility. The capacity of the Council of Europe to bridge relationships within a wide catchment area – as between Eastern and Western European states – could prove crucial in this context. In addition, there may be benefit from extending the practice of bilateral and trilateral activities.

TOWARDS THE 'EUROPEAN SECONDARY SCHOOL'

In this study our intention has been to focus on secondary schools. In drawing the discussion to a close, it may be useful to attempt a summary of the main issues to emerge and the main priorities which are the concern of teachers, parents and the pupils or students themselves. To do this is a matter of homing in on specific points of argument and, above all, questions which need to be asked and answered.

It should be said that in any number of European countries there are schools which could serve as models for developing the prototype of the 'European secondary school' for the twenty-first century, though equally, it should be admitted that many of these excellent institutions serve the special needs of a particular group of children rather than the broad-based requirements of a national system. Many of them place a heavy emphasis on bilingual competence, knowledge of additional foreign languages and literature in translation as the hallmarks of a European Education. The European Schools in Luxembourg, Belgium, the Netherlands, Italy, England and the Federal Republic of Germany, for example, were established in the 1950s to educate the children of officials employed by the member states of the burgeoning European Community. Theirs is a multinational student body, who are offered an academic curriculum leading to the European Baccalaureate; foreign languages are used as instruments of communication and teaching other disciplines, and from the fourth year it is possible to study three foreign languages. The 115 schools of the International Baccalaureate Organization (IBO) and the 150 European institutions of the European Council of International Schools (ECIS) also provide an explicitly international education for their pupils.

On a national plane, schools with international and bilingual sections, such as Alberdingk Thijm College, Hilversum, in the Netherlands, or Kungsholmen's *Gymnasium* in Stockholm, Sweden, represent the minority of schools with advanced foreign language learning programmes. A different 'model' emerged in the UK at the time of its entry into the European Community. An English comprehensive school established itself as a prototype of 'European Education in action' by pioneering (within the English system) annual pupil experience of living in mainland Europe, in a controlled and defined scholastic setting, such as in *centres de vacances*, and through exchanges with a German *Gymnasium* and a carefully planned programme of interdisciplinary European studies directed to environmental learning, supported by languages and the human sciences. It established a minority tradition that has inspired other schools.[15]

All these are exemplars of the kind of educational provision to which Europe is beginning to move. But we need to look more closely at some of the particular issues to be settled. These are treated under five heads: the school infrastructure; the school curriculum; the pupils or students; teachers and teacher training; and relations between the school and the outside world. And all the while there are some fundamental questions raised by the European dimension which everyone involved in education may (and, hopefully, will) reflect upon in the near future.

Checklist

- How far does the European dimension offer an acceptable new style of 'General Education' meeting the requirements of preparation for life, work and citizenship in Europe in the twenty-first century?

- How can/should we marry the European dimension to technical and vocational education in the informatics society?

- What might we reasonably look for in 'the European School' which aims to serve all pupils of a range of abilities in the 1990s and beyond?

- Does the European dimension make such demands upon secondary curricula that European states should consider a multilateral extension of compulsory education to the age of 18 years?

Checklist for effective European teaching and learning

- Do pupils need to be grouped according to age for effective learning to occur?

- Do teachers need to ask for permission to experiment with new practices?

- Is individual responsibility and status based on subject specialism or the execution of administrative function? Does that produce the best response in teachers? What part do creativity and flair play?

- Why is much time and effort devoted to supervision and control of pupils instead of promoting pupil learning?

- Does the school management *delegate* rather than *devolve* responsibility?

- Is there easy access to the head teacher?

- What kinds of consultation process exist between:
  (a) the head teacher and the teaching staff?
  (b) the teachers and pupils or students?
  (c) the non-teaching staff and other members of the school?

- What matters are referred to consultation: academic? curricular? pedagogical? disciplinary? pastoral/counselling? careers guidance? financial/budgetary? international/public relations/school image?

- What kind of decision-making machinery exists (for the same matters)?

- What opportunities are there for direct pupil participation in aspects of school management, and which aspects?

- Does the school organization reflect the teaching styles prevalent in the school?

- What are the organizational implications of the new technologies in establishing links with schools in other countries?

The school infrastructure

There are three facets to infrastructure: the organization, management and control of the school; the ethos or attitudinal infrastructure; and the physical school – the buildings, grounds and environment. Arguably 'the European school' would profit from having a flexible pattern of management, not over-burdened by administration. The two may even be better separated. It has been known for organizational efficiency and routine administration to substitute for effective curriculum delivery. In fact, good management practice in schools lies in the direct facilitation and the enhancement of the learning process.[16] This needs endorsing at a time when the school faces unusual pressure, as it does during a major curriculum innovation exercise. Management, too, should take account of the fact that democracy is the norm in most of Europe, and perhaps they ought to be reminded that

> the school is the first real community with which the child has any contact . . . where he develops an awareness of power and social relationships. If it is organized on authoritarian lines, the child will tend to accept this as customary in human organization: equally, if it is organized democrati-cally and he is encouraged to participate, he will develop an ability to take part in democratic society . . . We believe the concepts of real democratic control are best learnt through practice.[17]

So from the standpoint of 'role model' and teaching effectiveness, it is widely claimed that the school should have an open and democratic structure. In this climate it is healthy to reconsider the hierarchical organizational practices and the assumptions which still dominate in schools in some parts of Europe.

It would be surprising if the organization and management of schools did not undergo modification by the year 2000 in response to democratic devices of consultation, negotiation, self-instruction and collaboration. The full impact of the informatics and telematics revolution has yet to be absorbed by educational administrators and teachers, although perhaps the 'Peace Dividend' could ulti-mately finance the information and communication technology needed to carry out a radical transformation of Europe's schools for the twenty-first century. Certainly, changes are likely to affect:

- the traditional function of the secondary school;
- the formal and traditional curriculum;
- the relationship between teachers and pupils and the teacher's role;
- the organizational device of the single age-group classroom;
- the possibility of autonomous, auto-directed learning leading to self-education;
- the nature and organization of resources;
- the duration of state-sponsored education and training.

The management structure relates directly to the attitudinal infrastructure, or what may be called the 'school ethos'. Though it is impossible to quantify the impact of the structure and ethos of school on personal and social development, they undoubtedly influence pupil attitudes. In 'the European school' there should be an ethos of 'European consciousness', reinforced by a mission to encourage pupils to be 'good Europeans'. It should be apparent from the behaviour and responses of the teachers, pupils and other staff whether Europe constitutes 'their common home', how sincerely they are committed to European values and citizenship, to Europe's responsibilities in the world and its heritage. The school ethos should reflect the capacity of members to be flexible, to accept that 'Within our changing society, the fundamental values of the European civilisation persist – and will continue to be cherished – while "new" values in respect of inter-cultural understanding and appreciation must be enunciated and disseminated.'[18] Those new values would be upheld by school 'policies to eradicate sexism and racism and to promote human rights. There should be clear responsibilities for the implementation of such policies.'[19] They would of course also underline the democratic impulse of the school as a place where 'pupils should be encouraged to participate freely in class discussions on a variety of issues, to ask questions and to work together with their teachers towards discovering answers.' Finally, democracy implies a spirit of egalitarianism: 'schools should recognize that not only intellectual but also artistic, musical, physical and practical achievements are important.'[20] There should be recognition of individual gifts and skills and communal effort such as taking part in school orchestras, theatre productions or team sports. So we should ask the following questions:

Checklist

- Does the school have a clear educational mission related to Europe?

- Does it impart a sense of belonging to a European community of nations?

- Does the school ethos exemplify democracy, tolerance, open-mindedness, and the upholding of human rights?

- Does the school ethos support and value the contribution of all its pupils, whatever their particular talents?

- Does the school offer the kind of environment for its pupils which matches what is taught in the formal curriculum?

This leads us straight to another important point. Despite what some people claim, good facilities and resources are important to education and pupil progress. Democracy can only be learned in a democratic setting and a 'European mentality' ought to be nurtured in civilized surroundings. In 'the European school' the quality of life should be a priority for which the school accepts responsibility.

There should be clean indoor areas where pupils can meet in their spare time;

visible examples (such as photographs, collages, reproductions, artefacts) of European painting, drawing, sculpture, ceramics and folk art, for all to enjoy; there should be areas set aside for information and communications about/with other European countries. As a matter of course the school library and gymnasium should be focal points for European displays and the former should contain a section on European Literature in translation. There could be facilities for watching features, news or films in European languages during recreational time rather than confining such activities to formal classes.

All signs, notices and instructions throughout the school should be in three European languages as part of normal procedure. Where there are school canteens or other eating facilities, menus could be trilingual. Special weeks highlighting the food of one country could be organized on a rotating basis. 'Foreign' visitors should always be welcome guests of the school. To sum up, the school authorities should be asked to consider the following question:

Checklist

- What facilities, systems, resources and opportunities exist which are helping to create a European atmosphere inside the school?

The school curriculum

'The school curriculum' is an umbrella term which requires qualification. The terms 'informal curriculum' or 'hidden curriculum', referring to those attitudes and values covered by 'the ethos', require no further comment. 'The parallel curriculum' is often used to describe those messages and standards emanating from the external world, notably the press, radio, television and film media, though in some parts of Europe we should need to include the voice of the Church in addition. The main focus of this study, however, is 'the formal curriculum', the regimen of subjects taught in the classroom or outside in a formal sense. In the vast majority of schools Europe already figures in the formal curriculum; in some there is a conscious policy on the basis of a mission statement.

How can we judge whether a coherent European programme is being implemented, and how can the formal curriculum serve the European dimension?

1 The starting point is full consultation with all members of the school, including parents and pupils. Everyone in the community has the right to know why change may be necessary and should be fully informed about the resolutions and recommendations of the Council of Europe and the Council of

the European Community concerning the introduction of a European dimension (a prerequisite for member states).

2 Head teachers and senior staff should also ensure that the school community understands the implications of change: the rationale for a European Dimension implicit in the Council of Europe/ European Community resolutions, the definition of Europe implied in official statements, the goals to be achieved (summed up, for example, in the twenty goals on pp. 36–7). When all parties are informed, a declaration of intent can be agreed.

3 A curriculum audit is held to review and assess (using appropriate discriminatory criteria) by what means (subjects, approaches, staffing and material resources) Europe is being presented in the existing curriculum:

Checklist

- Is Europe taught in a disciplinary and/or an interdisciplinary structure?

- Which aspects of European history are covered in the History syllabus?

- How far do History/Social Science syllabuses deal with Europe's cultural heritage, the importance of science, religions, Human Rights issues?

- Which aspects of European geography are covered in the Geography/Social Science syllabuses? In what other ways does Geography teaching currently contribute to the understanding of Europe?

- How far does the Modern Language teaching cater for the skills needed in present-day Europe? Is the school involved in the LINGUA programme?

- What provision is made for Cultural, Aesthetic and/or Media Education?

- What contribution is made/could be made by the Natural Sciences?

- What provision is there for promoting international understanding?

- Which subjects of the existing curriculum contribute to preparation for life in Europe in respect to personal, social and political competence?

- What provision is made in the formal curriculum for exchange/contacts by pupils with other European or non-European pupils/countries?

- What provision exists for cross-curricular linkages between subjects?

- What proportion of staffing/resources currently contributes to provision of European teaching/experience?

---

4 As the result of the audit and assuming that it indicates a need for a more structured approach to the European dimension, *consultation* follows on a range of curricular matters, such as:

(a) the methodology of 'Europeanizing' the curriculum: teaching and learning approaches; disciplinary/interdisciplinary/cross-curricular strategies; blending and balancing the curriculum;

(b) Europe in the traditional subjects: input of knowledge/content, skills, attitudes;

(c) Modern Language policy;

(d) personal and social development strategies;

(e) Political Education/Citizenship policy;

(f) Cultural Education strategies;

(g) the integration of NICT into the curriculum;

(h) strategies for International and Intercultural Education: Development Education, Environmental Education, Science Education.

5 Curriculum innovation may have to be agreed on:

(a) *additional knowledge input* into traditional syllabuses, such as History, Geography/Environmental Education, Art, Literature, Science;

(b) *updating* existing subject provision, such as Modern Language teaching, to increase general language competence in at least one foreign language; language awareness programmes, such as non-examination modules providing 'taster' courses in several European languages; provision of minority language courses (European and non-European); programmes for inducing high-level language skills: foreign languages for teaching other subjects, formation of bilingual classes;

(c) *a major communication drive* to develop linguistic skills: exchange programme, networking, use of E-mail, teleconferencing, etc.;

(d) *a skills policy:* arising from the need for greater flexibility and transferable, interpersonal and technological skills, a cross-curricular grid of skills for life and work in Europe should be agreed (cf. Modern Language and Citizenship policies);

(e) *disciplinary and interdisciplinary arrangements* to implement (c) and (d), especially a cross-curricular programme to suffuse the formal curriculum, using key-value concepts such as unity/integration; liberty/democracy/individuality; interdependence/pluralism;

(f) *a support programme* of extra-curricular activities relating to Europe, emphasizing active learning, personal involvement, direct experience, such as involvement in sports events, youth debates, home-to-home exchanges, study visits, language and music festivals, European Clubs, competitions, media projects, town twinning events, tourism, political lobbies, work experience, work shadowing, holiday camps;

(g) *organization and management* of the European dimension: to provide greater flexibility of staffing (through clusters, teams) and extension of teacher expertise through school-based INSET programmes. Teaching strategies have to deliver on:

- a clear disciplinary base;
- subject correlation by inter-/multi-/cross-disciplinary modes;
- a policy of consistency and compatibility; avoidance of repetition, duplication, omission across subjects;
- a clear definition of teacher responsibilities;
- balance produced by sharing in implementation responsibility;

- progression of learning (cf. the Brunerian 'spiral') and sensitivity to pupils' learning styles;[21]
- high teacher skill in using audiovisual media and NICT;

(h) *delivery mechanisms:* budgeting and staff management of resources, NICT hardware, software, conventional printed materials; greater use of research findings, especially materials produced by INSET collaborative ventures, samples of good practice, Action Inquiry projects;[22] use of databanks, CDCC publications, the European Documentation and Information for Education (EUDISED), Education Information Network in the European Community (EURYDICE); unidimensional Media productions (see (c));

(i) *pedagogical implications:* to supplement conventional classroom methods, a planned programme of:
- active learning and participation techniques;
- foreign language usage for teaching other subjects, such as History;
- communication and autodidactic experience through NICT;
- visual education to stimulate cultural and environmental perceptions;
- exchange and direct personal contact for study, work and leisure to stimulate international and intercultural awareness;

(j) *assessment procedures:* provision will vary according to national systems, but procedures should seek to establish:
- progression of subject content to give knowledge about Europe;
- progressive attainment of measurable skills, such as linguistic;
- eradication of bias, stereotyped thinking, racist and sexist attitudes;
- evidence of more positive perceptions, co-operative responses, levels of European and international consciousness.

6 An internal evaluation of the European curricular initiative should be held after the agreed policies have been implemented and all those involved in the original consultation process should be asked to contribute. The primary aim of the evaluation is to establish:
- to what extent the original goals have been achieved;
- what further measures should be taken to implement them;
- whether the initiative has been a valid instrument of change in response to the changing nature of Europe.

The pupils or students

In implementing and evaluating the European dimension in the secondary curriculum, we should never overlook the fact that the underlying goal is to improve the quality of experience that it provides for young people of *c.*11–19 years of age. They can expect to gain:

- *entitlement:* assurance of their entitlement to the education which will best prepare them for life, work and active citizenship in Europe; entitlement to equality of opportunity as a human right. In due course entitlement may also extend to personal experience of at least one other European country during secondary education.

- *autonomy:* the fostering of a sense of personal identity and worth in all students so that they develop initiative, creativity and self-direction for adulthood.
- *motivation:* students should develop a positive attitude to Europe, to training and work, to the European cultural heritage and environment and to their citizenship role, as well as to their individual selves.
- *access:* training in the means of communication, particularly in study skills and in telecommunications, enabling students to access information and knowledge as they require it.
- *awareness:* greater awareness and understanding of political, social, economic, environmental and cultural issues, through being better informed about Europe in a global context.
- *empathy:* the capacity for social awareness or to empathize with the situations and responses of others, to avoid bias and stereotyped thinking – a key to interpersonal skill in a multicultural society.
- *competences:* by acquiring knowledge, increasing areas of understanding and developing skills, competence in interpersonal relations, work opportunities and personal development should be achieved.

As a corollary to these rights, it has been suggested to Europe's adolescents that they should respond by showing their willingness to:

   i. be inquisitive about society, its functions and procedures, its institutions and organizations, its norms and values;
  ii. think and reflect on all facets of life in society and on (your) personal part in it;
 iii. be aware of yourself and your capabilities;
 iv. take part in life and society wherever it is possible, and be ready to accept responsibilities;
  v. be personally and compassionately committed to the pursuit of values and norms which will contribute towards the realization of human rights and human dignity.[23]

Teachers and teacher training

All discussion of Europe in the curriculum emphasizes that 'the quality and success of Europe's education system depend on the skills and commitment of our teachers, and in turn, these depend on the quality and relevance of their training.'[24] However, a distinction is usefully made between initial teacher education (ITE), initial teacher training (ITT) and in-service training (INSET); and collectively, these constitute a major study in their own right.

Teacher education involves imparting understanding of Europe and skills relevant to work and citizenship, and arousing awareness of Europe and attitudes conducive to co-operation in a pluralist society. The subject-based academic education of secondary teachers is outside the scope of this study, although it is clearly desirable that student teachers should acquire an adequate foundation of knowledge about European subjects through their chosen discipline(s). There is also strong pressure (expressed in a series of Council of Europe and European Community recommendations and resolutions) for all trainee teachers to have first-hand experience of another European country so that their knowledge of European History or Geography, for example, is firmly based on experience and reinforced by fieldwork, exchanges and study visits. Nor should the desirability of experience outside Europe be overlooked. Although the European teacher should study Europe, Europe should always be seen in the global context, and schools require teachers with that wider vision and a first-hand knowledge of other parts of the world. Equally, it is widely accepted that the knowledge of one European language other than the mother tongue should be required of teachers if they are to be receptive to intercultural perspectives. Language competence is also a matter of linguistic *skill*, but as practising teachers know, they need a range of pedagogical skills to manage the complex curricular demands of European education.

Lastly, knowledge is arguably one of the elements that shape our attitudes, the other two being values/emotion and response/behaviour. Effective teaching about Europe requires a high degree of motivation. This is a matter for all teachers who are involved in teaching, school policy-making and management. However, a special responsibility for leadership falls on the head and senior teachers to manage staff development and act as 'multipliers' of the innovative ideas needed to implement a coherent European dimension.[25] In the changing patterns of teacher training, the involvement of heads and experienced teachers is most important. While INSET programmes may constitute one of the growth areas for action on the part of the EC and the CDCC, 'research on educational innovation has confirmed that the role of the head teacher is crucial, even in a centralised system where he or she is given relatively little devolved authority.'[26] Moreover, the aims of European Education present all governments with the imminent prospect of massive in-service initiatives. Although many will call for external staffing (by teacher training institutions and central research institutes), ongoing programmes are likely to be an internal school responsibility, and these will have budgetary and resource as well as attitudinal implications. Yet, in the last analysis, what is needed is a European teaching force committed to overcoming institutional inertia, believing passionately in the European dimension, and able to activate it in schools.

To sum up, initial teacher education and training should provide student teachers with:

- substantive knowledge about Europe through academic courses;
- understanding of subject methodology and its pedagogical implications, including active and self-directed modes of learning;
- first-hand experience of the external world, including Europe, through living, working or studying in at least one other country, giving encouragement to take an interest in European and world affairs;
- knowledge of at least one foreign language and culture;
- linguistic competence enabling the teacher to communicate his or her academic subject in a foreign language if required;
- training in interdisciplinary approaches to subjects and to teaching – involvement in team/cluster planning, devising courses and programmes with more than one subject dimension; participation in cross-curricular strategies; encouragement to experiment and develop teaching materials for interdisciplinary teaching;
- training in the use of new information and communication technology;
- training in mixing with communities and organizations outside school – involvement with parents, the media, public and teachers' associations;
- a common core of values appropriate to a democratic, intercultural society, including respect for a code of professional practice based on the principles of pluralism, objectivity and neutrality;
- encouragement to play an active role in organizations and in democratic processes and be sensitive to intercultural situations;
- the motivation to undertake curriculum innovation to stimulate European awareness and contribute to the implementation of a European dimension by diverse means throughout the school.

In addition, INSET should:

- create fresh attitudes and new responses in head teachers and teachers;
- provide the methodological, scientific and technological training to meet the new, practical demands of contemporary society.

In particular, INSET should provide teachers with opportunities to:

- study change and development in practical settings;
- take part in collaborative investigations in which theory is grounded and tested in research-based teaching and the outcome is the development of improved teaching materials and resources;
- enlarge and deepen their knowledge-base of Europe, both in practical and in academic terms.

It is recognized that these are ambitious and comprehensive goals. In the realities of school, how can they be achieved? How can we be sure that new entrants into the teaching profession will meet these onerous demands? No system is foolproof, but at interview it may be possible to gauge the degree of motivation and insight of a newly qualified teacher by asking for a positive response to the following questions:

Checklist

- Have you had first-hand experience of living, working or studying in another country?

- What have you learned from this experience?

- How will you contribute to the development of the European dimension in this school?

Relations between the school and the outside world

Education for Europe postulates an outward-looking approach to learning and to life. Involvement in the locality or region, awareness of the national contribution to Europe and a perception of Europe in its global context are essential to European Education. Implicit, too, is the understanding that 'the European school' is a fully fledged community in itself, which has learned to accept other people's differences and wants to establish communications with them. The European school would therefore pay particular attention to:

- the relationship with the primary school(s) in its catchment area, because:
  (a) liaison with primary schools will assist curricular progression and continuity in implementing a European dimension;
  (b) the primary school lays the groundwork for social skills and the development of European awareness and understanding;
  (c) language skills and 'language awareness' are readily acquired at this level;
  (d) problems of individual pupils can be allayed by routine communication;
- the relationship with technical, further and higher education institutions (as appropriate), because it is recognized that the European dimension carries over to other levels of education and is part of the continuing education of adult citizens;
- the disadvantaged and handicapped, in both the local and national communities, but especially in the less developed regions of the world;
- representatives of the media, local business and industry, politicians and local community leaders;
- all Europeans, but especially the pupils' contemporaries in other states.

Checklist

- What procedures exist to establish a rapport with the local primary schools? What further steps could be taken?

- Is there any liaison over language awareness and language learning initiatives between primary schools and 'the European secondary school'?

- Is there voluntary pooling of resources between schools in the area?

- Does the school promote a 'European entitlement' policy or equivalent?

- Does the school have a European Club?

- How is the school involved in town twinning schemes?

- What kinds of active exchange scheme are there with other European institutions?

- What range of contacts does the school have with other European institutions/individuals? What range of activities is involved?

- What percentage of the pupils have direct experience of another European country:
  (a) annually?
  (b) in the course of their secondary education?

- What percentage of teaching staff are involved in European/world initiatives?

- What activities does the school promote for handicapped young people?

- Does the school have ongoing activities in connection with UNESCO's Associated Schools programme and/or the European Schools Day Competition?

- Have telecommunication or other links been established with schools in other countries? If so, which and for what purpose?

- What links has the school established with media/business personnel?

- What steps has the school taken to develop a sense of European identity and citizenship in its pupils?

Finally, the implications of these questions were encapsulated by a German expert in a request to everyone involved in the educative process.[27] Addressing head teachers and staff of secondary schools first, he said:

Please
- never forget that the school is always related to its surroundings, environment and community;
- open up schools to the outside world;
- go into the community and its organizations and bring them into the school;
- develop procedures for better understanding and collaboration.

Then, speaking 'To the parents, representatives of institutions and organizations and of the community, and to journalists', he asked:

Please

- do not oppose the school which has its own responsibilities and educational tasks;
- accept school as a chance to aid you in social education;
- encourage and support the school, go into it and take part in its community life;
- help the teenager to discover and enter the adult world.

In these pleas for co-operation between the parties involved in education, we are reminded of the fact that schools and teachers are increasingly subject to public accountability, while parents and public constantly conduct a personal evaluation of a school's goals and achievements.

CONCLUSION

All educational institutions exercise a certain formative influence. They contribute to the shaping of young people's aspirations and abilities, their thought processes and patterns of behaviour and, more obliquely, their personalities. In this respect schools have a stake in the kind of society which evolves during the next generation. If European society is to emerge again as a powerhouse of ideas and technological achievement and if it is to play a constructive and humanitarian role in world affairs, much depends on the quality of education experienced by Europe's children in the 1990s. That education must prepare the young for life in a democratic, multicultural, multilingual Europe. It must inform them about their past and present, about their culture and environment, so that the knowledge gained gives them understanding, empathy and insight for the future. It must develop their aptitudes and skills, enabling them to take part in an active process of communication and interaction with people of other cultures, while seeing their lives in the social context of a single, democratic Europe.

This is neither rhetoric in praise of a spurious form of internationalism, nor a eulogy for a revitalized civilization. Nor, indeed, is it a political message, masked as an exhortation to Eurocentricity. Education should rise above propaganda. The teacher is concerned with all the different expectations youth brings to the Europe of tomorrow, and in truth cannot afford to be either a Europhobe or a hypernationalist. Europe is not something to be idealized. It will continue to confuse, irritate and defy the hopes of people, including teachers and students, who are aware that all too often 'Europe melts away as soon as you want to think of [her] in a clear and distinct fashion; she falls to pieces as soon as you want to recognize her unity.'[28] However, that unity was not always a civilizing force, and in equity young Europeans should never forget the inhumanities perpetrated in the name of universal Christendom and the potent secularism of the European nation-states. At the same time they ought to be aware that diversity can also be divisive and debilitating, just as sectional and national interests can undermine common goals. What is beyond dispute is that the rising generation will need to respond positively in their lifetime to the demographic superiority of Asia, Africa and the Americas and the economic competition of the Pacific Rim. Those formidable challenges cannot be met in a spirit of confrontation, by nation-states acting in collusion, much less in isolation; they require collective initiatives and international dialogue.

The process of preparation for dealing with those world issues starts in school. It is a complex learning process, which begins with the understanding of self and expands through progressive layers of perception to an appreciation of 'being a European'. In this way a 'European dimension' in the curriculum activates the dynamics of education. No one has ever suggested that a responsible and self-critical – that is to say, a *mature* – level of 'European consciousness' can be easily conveyed to pupils or that it can be readily acquired by them, for the very reason that 'the difficulty of thinking of Europe is at first the difficulty of thinking *one among many and many among one.*'[29] But to this there is a simple yet gnomic answer: nothing worthwhile in education is imparted without skill and dedication nor assimilated without a degree of effort.

NOTES

1 Craft, Maurice (1983), contribution in Rey, M., *General Report on Migrant Culture in a Changing Society: Multicultural Europe by the Year 2000*, Strasbourg: Council of Europe, p. 9.

2 (1988), *Final Report of the Seminar and Working Materials of the Youth Peace Seminar: Helsinki and Beyond, EYC, Strasbourg, June 1988*, Strasbourg: Council of Europe, B18.

3 Blackledge, R. C. R. (1982), *Reflections and Observations on the CDCC Project No. 1 Preparation for Life*, Strasbourg: Council of Europe, p. 23

4 (1990), *Family Change and Future Policy*, London: Family Policy Studies Centre.

5 In the not too distant future informed opinion expects the European Community of the Twelve to expand to include the EFTA countries, neutral Switzerland and Austria and some former COMECON states.

6 *Rapport General du Forum européen organisé à Lyon par Europe Education, 20–1 janvier 1989*, Lyon: Europe Education.

7 For an analysis of principal audiences and participants in an analogous field of education, see Williams, Michael (1986), 'The world in the European classroom' (discussion paper for the CDCC Symposium at Haikko Congress Centre near Porvoo, Finland, September 1986, Strasbourg: Council of Europe: pp. 3–5.

8 Doebrick, Peter (1989), 'Trends in Education', in *Report of the EYC/EFIL Study Session on Understanding and Working with European Systems, Strasbourg, 1989*, Strasbourg: Council of Europe, p. 6.

9 Newman, Simon (1989), 'A European view of education systems', in *EYC/EFL Report on Understanding and Working with European Systems*, Strasbourg: Council of Europe, p. 8.

10 *Ibid.*

11 There are still a great many factors inhibiting the growth of European awareness and the integration of European curricula, but the intention of this study is to be as positive as possible; a catalogue of contentious issues would scarcely be helpful at this stage (cf. Slater, John (1990), *Report on the UK European Awareness Pilot Project 1988–90*, London: Central Bureau for Educational Visits and Exchanges, pp. 13, 22–3).

12 *Rapport General du Forum européen.*

13 Resolution on Europe in the Classroom, 8 June 1978, adopted by the Standing Conference of Ministers of Education and Cultural Affairs of the *Länder* in the Federal Republic of Germany, in (1981), *Selection of Texts on Education for International Understanding and Teaching about Europe*, Strasbourg: CDCC, p. 21.

14 Slater, *Report on the UK European Awareness Pilot Project, 1988–90*, p. 7.

15 (Forthcoming) *Papers relating to the CDCC/EC Conference on International Secondary Education, Namur, Belgium, May 1990*, Strasbourg: Council of Europe; Ingatestone School, Essex, UK.

16 Fitz–Gibbon, F. (1989), *Towards Self-Enablement in the Managing of Schools: A Discussion Paper*, Kirkby: Ruffwood School.

17 NUT (n.d.), 'Democracy in schools', cited in Lister, Ian (1989), *Teaching and Learning about Human Rights*, Strasbourg: Council of Europe, p. 27.

18 Cotsapas, Phoebus (Athens College, Athens, Greece), contribution to Rey, *General Report on Migrant Culture*, p. 25.

19 Starkey, Hugh (1984), *Report of the CDCC Symposium on Human Rights Education in Schools in Western Europe, Vienna, May 1983*, Strasbourg: Council of Europe, p. 17.

20 *Ibid.*

21 For example, some children learn more readily through the ear, others through the eye; visual education has also created a tension 'which pits the civilization of the written word against the civilization of the image' – Salter, M. (1989), *Languages for Communication: The Next Stage*, London: CILT, p. 8; Balle, Francis (1991), 'The information society, schools and the media' (Report for the 16th session of the Standing Conference of European Ministers of Education, Istanbul, October 1989), in Eraut, M. (ed.), *Education and the Information Society*, London: Cassell.

22 For example, the teaching materials and strategies emanating from the Action Research Units of the EC Teaching about Europe in the Primary School Project: see Bell, Gordon, H. (1989), 'Europe in the primary school: a collaborative venture between schools and teacher trainers', *British Journal of In-Service Education*, **15** (2), pp. 87–95.

23 Zöllner, C. (1982), 'Social education for teenagers: 10 points for consideration', in Starkey, H., *Report of the CDCC Symposium on Social Education for Teenagers: Aims, Issues and Problems, Solna, Sweden, September 1980*, Strasbourg: Council of Europe, p. 33.

24 (1988), *Report of the Secretary General, M. Marcelino Oreja, to the Parliamentary*

Assembly on Problems of Education and Training in Europe, May 1988, Strasbourg: Council of Europe, p. 8.

25 Peacock, D. (1982), *Report of the CDCC Symposium on Europe in Secondary School Curricula: Aims, Approaches and Problems, Neusiedl-am-See, Austria, April 1981*, Strasbourg: Council of Europe, p. 43.

26 Eraut, Michael (1989), *Report for the 16th session of the Standing Conference of European Ministers of Education, Istanbul, October 1989: The Information Society – A Challenge for Education Policies? Policy options and implementation strategies*, Strasbourg: Council of Europe, p. 49.

27 Zöllner, 'Social education for teenagers', pp. 32–3.

28 Roy, Alain (1989), *Final Report of the Youth Event for the 40th Anniversary of the Council of Europe, EYC, Strasbourg, 1989*, Strasbourg: Council of Europe, p. 3.

29 *Ibid.*

Selective Bibliography of Council of Europe Publications

Publications in each category are listed in order of publication using the Council of Europe's designation.

REPORTS, SUMMARIES AND PAPERS

1978

Report of the 1st European Teachers' Seminar on Europe in the Secondary School Curriculum, Donaueschingen, September 1978, by Margaret Shennan (DECS/EGT (78) 37)

Report of the Meeting of Experts on Teaching about Human Rights in Secondary Schools, Strasbourg, December 1978 (DECS/EGT (78) 45)

1979

Summary of the Case-study on the Situation in France for the Conference on Co-operation in Europe since 1945, December 1979, by Yves Pasquier (DECS/EGT (79) Misc 23)

Report on Co-operation in Europe since 1945, prepared by the Centre for European Education, Strasbourg, December 1979 (DECS/EGT (79) Misc 30)

Information Note on Co-operation in Europe since 1945 as Presented in Resources for the Teaching of History, Geography and Civics in Secondary Schools, Braunschweig, December 1979, prepared by the Commission of the European Communities (DECS/EGT (79) 72)

Report of the CDCC Conference on Co-operation in Europe since 1945, as presented in Resources for the Teaching of History, Geography and Civics in Secondary Schools, Braunschweig, FRG, December 1979 (DECS/EGT (79) 74)

Report of the 4th European Teachers' Seminar on New Trends in History Teaching in Upper Secondary Education, Donaueschingen, May 1979, by Erik Rudeng (DECS/EGT (79) 63 – E)

1980

Paper for the Symposium on Social Education for Teenagers: Aims, Issues and Problems, Solna, Sweden, September 1980, on 'Education for international understanding in a multicultural society', by François Mariet (DECS/EGT (80) 46)

Report of the 8th European Teachers' Seminar on The Teaching of Human Rights in Upper Secondary Education, Donaueschingen, May 1980, by François Mariet (DECS/EGT (80) 50)

Selection of Texts on Education for International Understanding and Teaching about Europe for the Symposium on Europe in Secondary School Curricula: Aims, Approaches and Problems, Neusiedl-am-See, April 1981 (DECS/EGT (80) 94)

1981

Report for the 11th European Teachers' Seminar on Education for International Understanding – Teaching about a Non-European Culture: The Case of Japan, Donaueschingen, May 1981, by Richard Tames (DECS/EGT (81) 2)

Report for the 13th European Teachers' Seminar on Cultural Values and Education in a Multicultural society, Donaueschingen, October 1981, on 'The training of teachers of the children of migrant workers', by Dr Jorgen S. Nielsen (DECS/EGT (81) 4)

Report for the 14th European Teachers' Seminar on Europe in the Primary School, Donaueschingen, November 1981, by A. Bruneel (DECS/EGT (81) 5)

Paper for the Symposium on Europe in Secondary School Curricula: Aims, Approaches and Problems, Neusiedl-am-See, April 1981, on 'Europe's cultural identity', by Henri Janne (DECS/EGT (81) 30)

Report of the Sectoral Meeting on The Role of the School in the Promotion of Democratic Values, Strasbourg, May 1981 (DECS/EGT (81) 48)

Paper for the Symposium on Europe in Secondary School Curricula: Aims, Approaches and Problems, Neusiedl-am-See, April 1981, on 'The role of educational exchanges and school correspondence', by James Platt (DECS/EGT (81) 52)

Report for the Symposium on The Secondary School and the Mass Media, Grenoble, France, June–July 1981, by Pierre Corset (DECS/EGT (81) 81)

Report of the Case Study on the Tropenmuseum Junior, 1982, by A. F. Gailly (DECS/EGT (81) 104)

1982

Report of the CDCC Symposium on Europe in Secondary School Curricula: Aims, Approaches and Problems, Neusiedl-am-See, Austria, April 1981, by David Peacock (ISBN 1982 – 92-871-0025-X)

Report of the CDCC Symposium on Social Education for Teenagers: Aims, Issues and Problems, Solna, Sweden, September 1980, by Hugh Starkey (ISBN 1982 – 92-871-0040-3, reprinted 1984 as DECS/EGT (84) 31)

Reflections and Observations on the CDCC Project No. 1 Preparation for Life, by R. C. R. Blackledge, 1982 (DECS/EGT (82) 13)

Report of the European Teachers' Seminar on The Role of the School in the Promotion of Democratic Values, Donaueschingen, June 1982 (DECS/EGT (82) 16)

Final Meeting and Conclusions of the Special Project: Southern Europe, CDCC Project No. 1 Preparation for Life, Treviso, Italy, February 1982 (DECS/EGT (82) 34)

Report of the European Teachers' Seminar on Development and Conflict in the Global Setting, Lahti, Finland, July 1981 (DECS/EGT (82) 67)

1983

General Report on Migrant Culture in a Changing Society: Multicultural Europe by the Year 2000, by Micheline Rey, 1983 (DECS/EGT (83) 10)

Compendium of Information on Intercultural Education Schemes in Europe, Strasbourg, 1983 (DECS/EGT (83) 62)

Report of the European Teachers' Seminar on Europe in Primary School, Gazzada (Varese), Italy, May 1983 (DECS/EGT (83) 87)

1984

Report of the 22nd European Teachers' Seminar on Teaching about China in Secondary Schools in Western Europe, Donaueschingen, November 1983, by Graham Thomas (DECS/EGT (84) 2)

Report of the CDCC Symposium on Human Rights Education in Schools in Western Europe, Vienna, May 1983, by Hugh Starkey (DECS/EGT (84) 25)

Report of the European Teachers' Seminar on Teaching about the USA in Secondary Schools in Western Europe, Donaueschingen, October 1982, by Roy Williams, 1984 (DECS/EGT (84) 39)

Report of the European Teachers' Seminar on Teaching about Canada in Secondary Schools in

Western Europe, Donaueschingen, October 1984, by Maria Emilia Galvao, 1985 (DECS/ EGT (84) 43)

Paper for the Conference on Teaching and Learning about Each Other: The USA and Western Europe, Washington DC, November 1984, on 'Reflections on European perspectives on teaching about the United States', by J. F. Fitz-Gibbon (DECS/EGT (84) Misc. 82)

1985

Report of the European Teachers' Seminar on Teaching about Africa South of the Sahara, Lahti, Finland, August 1984, by Elizabeth Gunner, 1985 (DECS/EGT (85) 15)

Report of the European Teachers' Seminar on Contemporary Spanish-American Literature, Madrid, September–October 1985 (DECS/EGT (85) 47)

Report of the 30th European Teachers' Seminar on Europe in Primary Schools, Donaueschingen, November 1985, by Klaudia Trybus, 1986 (DECS/EGT (85) 48)

Conference Report of the Conference of American and European Educators on Teaching and Learning about Each Other: The USA and Western Europe, Washington DC, USA, November 1984 (DECS/EGT (85) 57)

Report of the European Workshop for History Teachers on Portuguese Expansion in the 15th and 16th centuries and the World Encounters of Cultures, Evora, Portugal, July 1984 (DECS/ EGT (85) 81)

1986

Final Report of the Organizing Committee of European Music Year 1985, Strasbourg, 1986

Report of the Study Session of Young People for Democratic Action in Europe (Jeunes pour une action démocratique en Europe – JADE) on Training for Europe, EYC, Strasbourg, 1986 (CEJ/S (86) 13)

Report of the European Teachers' Seminar on Contemporary Spanish-American Literature, Madrid, September–October 1985 (DECS/EGT (86) 15)

Report of the European Teachers' Seminar on The Birth of Brazil: Roots of a Multicultural Society, Lisbon, Portugal, December 1985, by Arlindo Manuel Caldeira (DECS/EGT (86) 31)

Discussion paper for the Symposium at Haikko Congress Centre, near Porvoo, Finland, September 1986, on 'The world in the European classroom', prepared by Michael Williams (DECS/EGT (86) 38)

Memorandum for the Symposium on The World in the European Classroom, Haikko Congress Centre, near Porvoo, Finland, September 1986, on 'The CDCC's work on education for life in an interdependent world', prepared by the Directorate of Education, Culture and Sport (DECS/EGT (86) 41)

Report on Against Bias and Prejudice: The Council of Europe's Work on History Teaching and History Textbooks, Strasbourg 1986 (DECS/EGT (86) 42)

Report of the European Teachers' Seminar on Human Rights Education and the Teaching of Social, Civic and Political Education, Donaueschingen, November 1986 (DECS/EGT (86) 74)

1987

Final Report of the Project Group (Activities 1982–87) on Project No. 12: Learning and Teaching Modern Languages for Communication, by Denis Girard and John Trim, 1987 (GC-GP 12 (87) 11)

Report of the European Teachers' Course on Teaching about European Co-operation and Integration in Upper Secondary Schools, Ebeltoft, Denmark, March 1987, by Margaret Shennan (DECS/EGT (87) 31)

Conclusions and Recommendations of the Symposium on The World in the European Classroom, Haikko Congress Centre, Porvoo, Finland, September 1986 (DECS/EGT (87) 58)

Report of the European Teachers' Seminar on Human Rights Education in a Global Perspective, Are, Sweden, August 1987, by Sanchia Pearse, 1988 (DECS/EGT (87) 59)

Final Report of The First European Youth Theatre Encounter, Stratford-upon-Avon, UK, July–August 1987, by Hugh Lovegrove (CDCC (87) 65)

Report for the 15th session of the Standing Conference of the European Ministers of Education, Helsinki, Finland, May 1987, on New Challenges for Teachers and their Education, by U. P. Lundgren (M-ED-15-5)

1988

Report of the European Teachers' Seminar on Bullying in Schools, Stavanger, Norway, August 1987 (DECS/EGT (88) 5)

Report of the Secretary General, M. Marcelino Oreja, to the Parliamentary Assembly on Problems of Education and Training in Europe, May 1988 (Doc. 5864)

Report of the Colloquy of the European Union of Jewish Students (EUJS) on 50 Years After . . . , January 1988 (CEJ/S (88) 1)

Report of the Study Session of the European Committee for Young Farmers' and 4H Clubs on Europe's Countryside for the Year 2000, March 1988 (CEJ/S (88) 2)

Report of the 39th European Teachers' Seminar on Teaching about the French Revolution in

Secondary Schools in Europe, Donaueschingen, by Stephane Audoin-Rouzeau, May 1988 (DECS/EGT (88) 30-E)

Final Report of the Seminar and Working Materials of the Youth Peace Seminar: Helsinki and Beyond, EYC, Strasbourg, June 1988 (YPS (88) 3)

Summary Report of the Round Table on The Contribution of Young People to Furthering East–West Cooperation in Europe, Strasbourg, October 1988 (AS/Cult/JS (40) 5 rev.)

1989

Report of the Colloquy on Computerised School Links, on Using the New Technologies to Create Links between Schools throughout the World, Crossmead Conference Centre, Exeter, Devon, UK, October 1988, by J. P. Carpenter (CDCC (89) 10)

Secretariat Memorandum on Proposals for a New CDCC Programme on History, prepared by the Directorate of Education, Culture and Sport (CDCC (89) 17)

Information Document on Geographical Information and Documentation on European Countries, prepared by the Directorate of Education, Culture and Sport, Strasbourg, 1989 (CDCC (89) 26)

Report of the Study Session of European Federation of Intercultural Learning (EFIL) on Understanding and Working with European Systems, EYC, 1989 (CEJ/S (89) 4)

Final Report of the Youth Event for the 40th Anniversary of the Council of Europe, EYC, Strasbourg, 1989, by Alain Roy (CEJ/Youth Event (89) 7 rev.)

Secretary General's Memorandum on European Cultural Routes, prepared by the Directorate of Education, Culture and Sport, 1989 (ICE (89) 1)

Report for the Colloquy of Directors of Educational Research Institutions of Socialisation and Human Rights Education, Ericeira, Portugal, October 1989: The European Studies (Ireland and Great Britain) Project, by Dr Roger Austin, Director of the project (DECS/Rech (89) 18)

Report for the 16th session of the Standing Conference of European Ministers of Education, Istanbul, October 1989: The Information Society, Schools and the Media, by Professor Francis Balle (M ED-16-4). Reprinted in Eraut, M. (ed.) (1991), *Education and the Information Society,* London: Cassell, pp. 79–114.

Report for the 16th session of the Standing Conference of European Ministers of Education, Istanbul, October 1989: The Information Society and Education: Synthesis of the National Reports, by Professor Gilbert de Landsheere (M ED-16-5). Reprinted in Eraut, M. (ed.) (1991), *Education and the Information Society,* London: Cassell, pp. 115–63.

Report for the 16th session of the Standing Conference of European Ministers of Education, Istanbul, October 1989: The Information Society – A Challenge for Education Policies? Policy Options and Implementation Stategies, by Professor Michael Eraut (M ED-16-6).

Reprinted in Eraut, M. (ed.) (1991), *Education and the Information Society*, London: Cassell, pp. 164–231.

National Reports of the 16th session of the Standing Conference of European Ministers of Education, Istanbul, October 1989 on The Information Society – A Challenge for Education Policies? (MED-16-7)

1990

Report of the Symposium on Geographical Information and Documentation on European Countries, Utrecht, September 1989, by Professor Norman Graves (not yet published)

General Report of the Symposium on Museums and the European Heritage: Treasures or Tools? Salzburg, December 1990, by Kenneth Hudson (DECS/EGT (90) 41; CDCC (90) 22)

Report of the Educational Research Workshop on History and Social Studies – Methodologies of Textbook Analysis, Braunschweig, September 1990, by John Slater (DECS/Rech (90) 59)

Papers relating to the CDCC/EC Conference on International Secondary Education, Namur, Belgium, May 1990 (not yet published)

STUDIES AND PAMPHLETS

Wake, R. A., Marbeau, V., and Peterson, A. D. C., *Innovation in Secondary Education in Europe*, Strasbourg, 1979

O'Connor, Edmund, *World Studies in the European Classroom*, Strasbourg, 1980 (incorporating the results of the European Teachers' Seminar on World Problems in the European Classroom, Lillehammer, Norway, July–August 1979)

Schleicher, Klaus, *Preparation for Family Life*, Strasbourg, 1982 (DEC/EGT (81) 67)

Cacace, Nicola, *Employment and Occupations in Europe in the 1980s: Effects of Technical and Economic Changes on the Employment Situation*, 3rd edn, Strasbourg, 1981

Deforge, Yves, *Living Tomorrow: An Enquiry into the Preparation of Young People for Working Life in Europe*, trans. J. Barkas and N. Amphoux, 3rd edn, Strasbourg, 1981

Porcher, Louis, *The Education of the Children of Migrant Workers in Europe: Interculturalism and Teacher Training*, Strasbourg, 1981

Befring, Edvard, *Preparation for Personal Life and for Life in Society*, Strasbourg, 1982

Fuente, C., and Munoz-Repiso, M., *Preparation for Life in a Democratic Society in Five Countries in Southern Europe*, Strasbourg, 1982

Heater, Derek, *Human Rights Education in Schools: Concepts, Attitudes and Skills*, Strasbourg, 1984 (DECS/EGT (84) 26)

Lister, Ian, *Teaching and Learning about Human Rights*, Strasbourg, 1984 (DECS/EGT (84) 31)

Perotti, A., *Action to Combat Intolerance and Xenophobia*, Strasbourg, 1984 (DECS/EGT (84) 34)

Learning for Life: The Council of Europe's Work for Education, Strasbourg, 1984

Bahree, Patricia, *Asia in the European Classroom*, Strasbourg, 1986 (DECS/EGT (85) 79)

Jones, C. and Kimberley, K. (eds), *Intercultural Education: Concept, Context, Curriculum Practice*, Strasbourg, 1986

The Council of Europe: A Guide, Strasbourg, 1986

Liegeois, J. P., *Gypsies and Travellers*, Strasbourg, 1987

Masterman, L., *The Development of Media Education in Europe in the 1980s*, Strasbourg, 1988 (ISBN 92-871-1644X)

EUROFIT: Handbook for the EUROFIT Tests of Physical Fitness, Rome, 1988

TEXTS OF RESOLUTIONS AND RECOMMENDATIONS

The Committee of Ministers

Resolution (78) 41 on The teaching of human rights
Declaration on Intolerance – a threat to democracy, 14 May 1981
Recommendation No. R (82) 18 on Modern Languages
Recommendation No. R (83) 4 on The promotion of an awareness of Europe in secondary schools
Recommendation No. R (83) 13 on The role of the secondary school in preparing young people for life
Recommendation No. R (84) 18 on The training of teachers in education for intercultural understanding, notably in a context of migration
Recommendation No. R (85) 7 on Teaching and learning about human rights in schools
Resolution (85) 6 on European cultural identity

The Parliamentary Assembly

Recommendation 897/1980 on Educational visits and pupil exchanges between European countries
Resolution 747/1981 on Global prospects – human needs and the earth's resources
Recommendation 963/1983 on Cultural and educational means of reducing violence

Declaration adopted at the Conference on North/South: Europe's role, Lisbon, 9–11 April 1984 (The Lisbon Declaration)
Recommendation 1034/1986 on The improvement in Europe of mutual understanding between ethnic communities – 'Daring to live together'
Recommendation 1043/1986 on Europe's linguistic and literary heritage
Resolution 885 (1987) on The Jewish contribution to European culture
Compendium of documents of the Second Strasbourg Conference on Parliamentary Democracy, Strasbourg, September 1987
Recommendation 1069/1988 on Development education
Recommendation 1111 (1989) (1) on the European dimension in education

Others

Resolutions of the Standing Conference of the European Ministers of Education 1959–85 (M-ED-15-2)
The Third Medium-Term Plan of the Council of Europe: 1987–1991, Strasbourg, 1986

JOURNALS PUBLISHED BY THE COUNCIL OF EUROPE

A Future for our Past
Bulletin of the European Youth Centre and European Youth Foundation
Forum
Naturopa

Official Recommendations and Resolutions

The following are reproductions of the official texts.

COUNCIL OF EUROPE
COMMITTEE OF MINISTERS

———

RECOMMENDATION No. R (83) 4

OF THE COMMITTEE OF MINISTERS TO MEMBER STATES CONCERNING THE PROMOTION OF AN AWARENESS OF EUROPE IN SECONDARY SCHOOLS

(Adopted by the Committee of Ministers on 18 April 1983 at the 358th meeting of the Ministers' Deputies)

The Committee of Ministers, under the terms of Article 15.*b* of the Statute of the Council of Europe,

Having regard to the European Cultural Convention (1954) which underlines the need for education for European understanding;
Recalling its Resolution (64) 11 on "Civics and European Education";
Having regard to the findings of the Council for Cultural Co-operation's Project No. 1 on secondary education, "Preparation for life" (1978–82);

Having regard to the Council of Europe's Second Medium-Term Plan (1981–86), and in particular to:

i. Objective 10.1 – the encouragement of an awareness of the cultural identity of Europe in its diversity and the recognition of possibilities of dialogue and mutual understanding with other parts of the world;

ii. Objective 11.3 – the enhancement of the contribution of national education systems to public awareness of Europe and the stimulation of active co-operation and communication among Europeans;

Noting the Recommendation concerning education for international understanding, co-operation and peace and education relating to human rights and fundamental freedoms adopted by the General Conference of UNESCO at its 18th Session (Paris, 19 November 1974),

Recommends the governments of member states:

a. to take account, in the implementation of their policies for secondary education, of the principles set out in the Appendix of this recommendation, or to draw them to the attention of the competent bodies concerned, so that they can be considered and, where appropriate, taken into account;

b. to ensure that this recommendation is distributed as widely as possible among all persons and bodies concerned with the promotion of an awareness of Europe among pupils and teachers.

Appendix to Recommendation No. R (83) 4

Principles for the guidance of those drawing up educational programmes for the promotion of an awareness of Europe in secondary schools

1. Aims

1.1. Programmes to promote an awareness of Europe in secondary schools may have a wide variety of content which will be determined by the needs and interests of individual countries, regions and schools.

1.2. In spite of any differences of content, these programmes should encourage all young Europeans to:

i. show respect for, and solidarity with, peoples of other nations and cultures;

ii. see themselves not only as citizens of their own regions and countries, but also as citizens of Europe and of the wider world.

1.3. All young Europeans should be helped to acquire:

i. a willingness and ability to preserve and promote democracy, human rights and fundamental freedoms;

ii. the knowledge and skills needed to cope with life in an interdependent world, characterised by diversity and by constant and rapid change;

iii. an understanding of their common cultural heritage, its contribution to other civilisations, and the debt which it owes to those civilisations;

iv. an awareness of the institutions and organisations set up to promote European co-operation and a willingness to support their ideals and activities.

2. Approaches

It is possible to teach about Europe in secondary schools through separate subjects, or through interdisciplinary courses. While schools must be allowed freedom to choose those approaches which best suit their particular situations, care should be taken to:

i. build on what will have been learned about Europe during the earlier years of schooling;

ii. ensure that what is taught about Europe has an overall coherence. Fragmentation of knowledge and understanding can be avoided by careful planning and by cross-referencing (that is, co-ordination) between subjects.

3. Content

3.1. In teaching about Europe, secondary schools should seek to give pupils a full understanding of the following key concepts:

i.   democracy, human rights and fundamental freedoms;

ii. tolerance and pluralism;

iii. interdependence and co-operation;

iv. human and cultural unity and diversity;

v.   conflict and change.

3.2. These concepts can best be illustrated by themes and topics which demonstrate the need for international understanding and co-operation, such as:

i.   the prevention of war and the non-violent solution of conflict;

ii. the conservation of the European cultural heritage;

iii. the impact of migration;

iv. the preservation of ecological balance;

v.   the best use of energy and natural resources;

vi. changing needs in communications and trade;

vii. relations with the developing countries.

3.3. It is obvious that modern languages, history, geography and social studies have a vital contribution to make to the promotion of an awareness of Europe in secondary schools. But due attention should be paid to the contribution which can be made by science and technology, artistic activities, music and indeed of almost all subjects in the secondary school curriculum.

4. Methods

4.1. The diversity of school systems in member states inevitably leads to differences in classroom practice. Nevertheless, in implementing programmes designed to increase an awareness of Europe, many teachers will wish to:

i.   use methodologies which are active, investigational and discovery-based; use projects which involve personal research and interviewing; exploit local and national links with other countries;

ii. give young people opportunities for active participation, decision-making and responsibility within the school community in order to prepare them for life in a free demo-cratic society;

iii. encourage pupils to participate in extra-curricular activities with an international dimension, for example participation in the European Schools Day competition, UNESCO Clubs and the UNESCO Associated Schools Project, the establishment of European clubs in schools, school correspondence and exchanges, visits to the European institutions and events linked to town twinnings;

iv. encourage pupils to make an informed and critical interest in coverage of inter-national events by the mass media;

v. make use of primary sources and material from other countries and from inter-national organisations, both intergovernmental and non-governmental.

4.2. As European society is becoming increasingly multicultural, schools should actively involve people from other cultural backgrounds in the learning process, wherever possible. This would help pupils to develop truly tolerant attitudes and a realisation that – despite differences of colour, creed and customs – all share a basic common dignity and basic common needs.

5. Teacher training

The success of programmes to develop an awareness of Europe in secondary schools depends, to a large extent, on the knowledge, skills and attitudes of those who teach them. It is, therefore, essential to provide appropriate courses of both pre-service and in-service education, not only for practising teachers, but also for senior administrators, inspectors, advisers and school principals. Furthermore, teachers and other educators should be encour-aged to avail themselves of opportunities for studies in, and exchanges with, other European countries.

6. Monitoring and evaluation

In order to avoid duplication of effort and to make the best possible use of resources, there should be careful monitoring and evaluation of programmes to promote an awareness of Europe in secondary schools in member states. This would ascertain the extent to which:

i. the aims and objectives of the programmes are being achieved;

ii. the interests and needs of the learners are being satisfactorily met.

Such evaluation could also lead to a sharing of experiences among member states and to the identification and dissemination of good practice.

COUNCIL OF EUROPE
COMMITTEE OF MINISTERS

RECOMMENDATION No. R (82) 18

**OF THE COMMITTEE OF MINISTERS TO MEMBER STATES
CONCERNING MODERN LANGUAGES**

(Adopted by the Committee of Ministers on 24 September 1982 at the 350th meeting of the Ministers' Deputies)

The Committee of Ministers, under the terms of Article 15.*b* of the Statute of the Council of Europe,

Considering that the aim of the Council of Europe is to achieve greater unity between its members and that this aim can be pursued in particular by the adoption of common action in the cultural field;

Bearing in mind the European Cultural Convention signed in Paris on 19 December 1954;

Having regard to its Resolution (69) 2 of 25 January 1969 on an intensified modern language teaching programme for Europe;

Recalling Recommendation 814 (1977) of the Assembly concerning modern languages in Europe;

Having noted the report "Modern languages: 1978–81" drawn up by Project Group No. 4 of the Council for Cultural Co-operation;

Having noted the work of the Conference entitled "Across the threshold towards multilingual Europe – Vivre le multilinguisme européen", which was organised by the Council of Europe in Strasbourg from 23 to 26 February 1982;

Considering that the rich heritage of diverse languages and cultures in Europe is a valuable common resource to be protected and developed, and that a major educational effort is needed to convert that diversity from a barrier to communication into a source of mutual enrichment and understanding;

Considering that it is only through a better knowledge of European modern languages that it will be possible to facilitate communication and interaction among Europeans of different mother tongues in order to promote European mobility, mutual understanding and co-operation, and overcome prejudice and discrimination;

Considering that member states, when adopting or developing national policies in the field of modern language learning and teaching, may achieve greater convergence at the European level, by means of appropriate arrangements for ongoing co-operation and co-ordination of policies,

Recommends the governments of member states, in the framework of their national educational policies and systems, and national cultural development policies, to implement by all available means and within the limits of available resources, the measures set out in the appendix to the present recommendation;

Requests the governments of member states to convey this recommendation and the reference document which forms its basis,[1] through appropriate national channels, to the attention of competent public and private bodies in their countries.

1 Report "Modern languages: 1971–81".

Appendix to Recommendation No. R (82) 18

Measures to be implemented concerning the learning and teaching of modern languages

A. *General measures*

1. To ensure, as far as possible, that all sections of their populations have access to effective means of acquiring a knowledge of the languages of other member states (or of other communities within their own country) as well as the skills in the use of those languages that will enable them to satisfy their communicative needs and in particular:

1.1. to deal with the business of everyday life in another country, and to help foreigners staying in their own country to do so;

1.2. to exchange information and ideas with young people and adults who speak a different language and to communicate their thoughts and feelings to them;

1.3. to achieve a wider and deeper understanding of the way and forms of thought of other peoples and of their cultural heritage.

2. To promote, encourage and support the efforts of teachers and learners at all levels to apply in their own situation the principles of the construction of language-learning systems (as these are progressively developed within the Council of Europe "Modern languages" programme):

2.1. by basing language teaching and learning on the needs, motivations, characteristics and resources of learners;

2.2. by defining worthwhile and realistic objectives as explicitly as possible;

2.3. by developing appropriate methods and materials;

2.4. by developing suitable forms and instruments for the evaluation of learning programmes.

3. To promote research and development programmes leading to the introduction, at all educational levels, of methods and materials best suited to enabling different classes and types of student to acquire a communicative proficiency appropriate to their specific needs.

B. *Language learning in schools*

4. To encourage the teaching of at least one European language other than the national language or the vehicular language of the area concerned to pupils from the age of ten or the point at which they enter secondary education (or earlier according to national or local

situations) with adequate time allocation and in such a way as to enable them by the end of the period of compulsory schooling, within the limits set by their individual ability, to use the language effectively for communication with other speakers of that language, both in transacting the business of everyday living and in building social and personal relations, on the basis of mutual understanding of, and respect for, the cultural identity of others.

5. To make provision for the diversification of language study in schools:

5.1. by making it possible for pupils, wherever appropriate, to study more than one European or other modern language;

5.2. by ensuring the availability, according to local circumstances, of facilities for learning as wide a range of languages as possible.

6. To promote international contacts by individual pupils and classes through exchanges, study visits abroad and other means.

C. *Language learning in upper secondary school, higher education, further education and adult education*

7. To encourage educational institutions to provide facilities for the continuation of language learning by all students in upper secondary, higher and further education, as appropriate to their special fields of work and study, in order to facilitate international professional mobility and co-operation at all levels.

8. To ensure that adequate resources are available to enable students who have completed their full-time education to acquire further knowledge of languages in accordance with their professional, social and personal needs and motivations.

9. To take all the measures necessary to enable adults who have had hitherto little or no chance of learning a modern language to acquire the ability to use a modern language for communicative purposes.

D. *Language learning by migrants and their families*

10. To promote the provision of adequate facilities for migrant workers and the members of their families:

10.1. to acquire sufficient knowledge of the language of the host community for them to play an active part in the working, political and social life of that community, and in particular to enable the children of migrants to acquire a proper education and to prepare them for the transition from full-time education to work;

10.2. to develop their mother tongues both as educational and cultural instruments and in order to maintain and improve their links with their culture of origin.

11. To promote the introduction and development of appropriate initial and further training programmes for teachers of languages to migrants, leading to recognised qualifications.

12. To participate in the development of language programmes involving co-operation between authorities or other bodies representing the host community, the migrant community and the country of origin, especially with regard to the production of teaching materials, teacher training and mother tongue development.

D. *Initial and further teacher training*

13. To promote the development and introduction of methods for such initial and further training of teachers of modern languages as will enable them to develop the attitudes and acquire the knowledge, skills and techniques necessary to teach languages effectively for communicative purposes, for example by:

13.1. considering the extent to which the pattern of modern language studies in higher education provides an adequate preparation for future language teachers;

13.2. providing facilities through bilateral and multilateral agreements for all future teachers to spend a substantial period of their course of study in a country where they language they will teach is spoken as a mother tongue;

13.3. contributing to an intensified programme of in-service teacher training, including internationally organised, staffed and recruited in-service courses for language teachers, and facilitating the participation of serving teachers in such courses;

13.4. promoting stays at regular intervals by serving teachers in the countries whose languages they teach.

F. *International co-operation*

14. To promote the national and international collaboration of governmental institutions engaged in the development of methods of teaching and evaluation in the field of modern language learning and in the production and use of materials, including institutions engaged in the production and use of multi-media material.

15. To encourage by all appropriate means, taking into account their particular status, radio and television bodies to co-operate with those in other member states in the planning, production and exploitation of modern language learning programmes as well as of documentaries on life, society and culture in the countries where the language being learnt is spoken.

16. To consider means of international co-operation for monitoring the quality of language teaching materials and courses.

17. To take such steps as are necessary to complete the establishment of an effective European system of information exchange covering all aspects of language learning, teaching and research, and making full use of advanced information technology.

18. To ensure, as far as possible, that programmes which implement measures set out in the different chapters of this recommendation are notified to the Council for Cultural Co-operation, and that government-sponsored programmes contain provision wherever possible for consultation and co-operation between the agencies concerned and their counterparts in other member states.

RESOLUTION

OF THE COUNCIL AND THE MINISTERS OF EDUCATION MEETING WITHIN THE COUNCIL

on the European dimension in education
of 24 May 1988
(88/C 177/02)

THE COUNCIL AND THE MINISTERS OF EDUCATION MEETING WITHIN THE COUNCIL,

Referring to their conclusions of 27 September 1985,

Reaffirming their resolve to strengthen the European dimension in education in accordance with the 'solemn declaration on European union' of Stuttgart (June 1983), the conclusions of the European Council in Fontainebleau (June 1984) and the

'People's Europe' report adopted at the European Council in Milan (June 1985);

Considering enhanced treatment of the European dimension in education to be an element contributing to the development of the Community and achievement of the objective of creating a unified internal market by 1992;

Noting the resolution of the European Parliament adopted on 20 November 1987;

Noting the report of the Education Committee;

Stressing the link between improving the presence of the European dimension in education and all the activities undertaken as part of:

— the action programme on education (9 February 1976),

— the programme of pilot projects for the improvement of the transition from school to working life,

— the Erasmus, Comett and Youth for Europe (YES) programmes;

Emphasizing the particular importance for understanding among Europeans of the learning of languages of other Member States and of exchanges among young people,

HEREBY ADOPT THIS
RESOLUTION:

I. OBJECTIVES

The purpose of this resolution is to strengthen the European dimension in education by launching a series of concerted measures for the period 1988 to 1992; these measures should help to:

— strengthen in young people a sense of European identity and make clear to them the value of European civilization and of the foundations on which the European peoples intend to base their development today, that is in particular the safeguarding of the principles of democracy, social justice and respect

for human rights (Copenhagen declaration, April 1978),

— prepare young people to take part in the economic and social development of the Community and in making concrete progress towards European union, as stipulated in the European Single Act,

— make them aware of the advantages which the Community represents, but also of the challenges it involves, in opening up an enlarged economic and social area to them,

— improve their knowledge of the Community and its Member States in their historical, cultural, economic and social aspects and bring home to them the significance of the cooperation of the Member States of the European Community with other countries of Europe and the world.

II. ACTION

In accordance with the decision of the European Council on a People's Europe, new impulses should be given to the achievement of these objectives, involving strengthened measures both at Member state level and Community level.

A. **At the level of the Member States**

Within the limits of their own specific educational policies and structures, the Member States will make every effort to implement the following measures:

*Incorporation of the European
dimension in educational systems*

1. To set out in a document their current policies for incorporation of the European dimension in education and make this available to schools and other educational institutions;

2. To encourage meaningful initiatives in all sectors of education aimed at strengthening the European dimension in education.

School programmes and teaching

3. To include the European dimension explicitly in their school curricula in all appropriate disciplines, for example, literature, languages, history, geography, social sciences, economics and the arts.

Teaching material

4. To make arrangements so that teaching material takes account of the common objective of promoting the European dimension.

Teacher training

5. To give greater emphasis to the European dimension in teachers' initial and in-service training. The following can contribute to achieving this objective:

— making suitable teaching material available;

— access to documentation on the Community and its policies;

— provision of basic information on the educational systems of the other Member States;

— cooperation with teacher training institutions in other Member States, particularly by developing joint programmes providing for student and teacher mobility,

— making provision in the framework of in-service training for specific activities to enhance serving teachers' awareness of the European dimension in education and give them the opportunity of keeping up to date with Community developments,

— opening up, to some teachers from other Member States, certain in-service training activities, which would constitute the practical expression of belonging to Europe and a significant means of favouring the integration process.

Promotion of measures to boost contacts between pupils and teachers from different countries

6. To encourage contacts and meetings across borders between pupils and teachers from different Member States at all levels in order to give them direct experience of European integration and the realities of life in other European countries;

to use these contacts and meetings both for improving linguistic proficiency and for gaining knowledge and experience on cultural, scientific and technical matters; in this way the largest possible number of young people and teachers should be covered by these initiatives;

to encourage parents and parents' organizations to participate in organizing contacts, exchanges and visits;

to provide information and advice to schools, teachers and pupils interested in contacts, exchanges and visits abroad and to support them in the implementation of contacts and exchanges;

to examine the conditions for longer-term stays abroad by pupils and to promote such stays abroad.

Complementary measures

7. To give a new stimulus in the perspective of 1992 to the strengthening of the image of Europe in education, in the sense of the People's Europe report, by organizing particular events: in this connection the following would appear appropriate:

— colloquia and seminars on effective ways of introducing the European dimension in education and on the use and preparation of teaching material adapted to the different levels of teaching,

— the promotion of school initiatives and extra-curricular activities such as school twinning and the formation of 'European clubs', opening up new paths for the strengthening of the European dimension,

— the participation of schools in activities organized as part of the Europe Day (9 May),

— the participation of schools in the European schools' competition and encouragement of cooperation between competitions in the linguistic, artistic, scientific or technical fields organized in individual Member States,

— increased cooperation between the Member States in the area of school sports.

B. **At the level of the European Community**

In order to back up the action of the Member States and achieve effective collaboration in this field, the Commission, assisted by the working party mentioned in paragraph 19 below, is invited:

Information exchange

8. — To promote an exchange of information on concepts and measures in the different Member States, thereby ensuring that the results of the experience acquired are known in all Member States.

Teaching material

9. — To prepare basic documentation on the Community (its institutions, aims and current tasks) for schools and teaching staff,

— to facilitate the exchange, by subjects or groups of subjects, of information on teaching material aimed at strengthening the European dimension in teaching,

— to carry out comparative analysis of the substance and new forms of treatment of teaching material,

— to make authors and publishers of teaching material more aware of the need to include the European dimension in their production.

Teacher training

10. To use the programme of study visits for education specialists (Arion programme) for the aim of introducing the European dimension in education.

11. To use the possibilities offered by the Erasmus programme for providing students training to be teachers with experience of a foreign country during their training and for intensifying cooperation between training institutions and between trainers.

12. To support cooperation by institutions of initial and further training for teachers of several Member States in the development of teaching material promoting the European dimension in education.

13. To promote each year, in the period 1989 to 1992, the organization of a European Summer University for trainers in order to enable them to exchange the experience acquired and to identify new ways of improving the introduction of the European dimension in teacher training.

Specific additional measure

14. To encourage cooperation and exchange of views among the national bodies responsible for the encouragement of exchanges of pupils and teachers.

15. To promote the participation of non-governmental organizations in the introduction of the European dimension in education.

16. To examine the possibilities for reinforcing the European dimension in education by using audio-visual means at European level.

17. To foster cooperation between educational research institutes and centres in the various Member States working towards the introduction of the Euro-

pean dimension in education, taking into account the potential contribution of the European University Institute (Florence), the College of Europe (Bruges), the European Institute of Public Administration (Maastricht) and the European schools.

18. To examine how school sport can be better used for European contact and mutual understanding and on what conditions the establishment of European school games would be possible.

Working party

19. In the implementation of these tasks and to achieve effective collaboration in this field, the Commission will be assisted by a working party composed of representatives of the Member States with coordinating responsibilities in European dimension questions,

appointed by the Commission on the proposal of the Member State concerned.

III. REPORT ON MEASURES UNDERTAKEN

They invite the Education Committee to submit an initial report by 30 June 1991 on the development of measures undertaken at the level of the Member States and the Community to reinforce the European dimension in teaching.

IV. FINANCE

Community finance for the measures referred to in point II.B and the amount thereof are to be decided on in accordance with the Community's rules and procedures.

European Culture in the Opinion of European Writers

What picture comes to mind with these three words: 'European cultural identity'?

Alberto Moravia (Italy):

A reversible fabric, one side variegated – European particularism – the other a single colour, rich and deep: that's the unique European cultural identity which is to be found in every book and painting.

Gyorgy Konrad (Hungary):

It is an expansion of national consciousness, a transcending of the nation-state. It is identifiable in the surrounding context, by making comparisons, establishing similarities with the rest of the world. I believe there are concentric circles: the regions, countries and continents. European culture is a stage on the way to global awareness.

Vasco Brace Moura (Portugal):

I detect an historical image, both mythical and actual and relevant. An historical image because, although difficult to define, European identity is a continental, historical constant. A mythical image because it originates in distant Greek and Latin Antiquity, possessing a motive force to propel Europeans forward in time: and in the minds of contemporary Europeans today, this is tantamount to something of a myth. Finally, the image is relevant because in view of the two superpowers threatening to crush her, Europe must find ways of reinforcing her consciousness of identity.

Pierre Mertens (Belgium):

'Identity' is the most problematic of the three words. It assumes that one brings to quite simple concepts a complex and confused reality. Effectively in terms of identity, the European is an alien, a hybrid of history. What about the word 'culture'? It is on the agenda because of the publication of a number of essays which have appeared in France and elsewhere on the decline of intellectual thought, the treason of scholars. This is not a new debate because Raymond Aron and Paul Valéry tackled it in almost the same terms. I should add that one can't have a European debate worthy of the name if the problem of Central Europe – wrongly described as Eastern Europe – is ducked. I only feel myself to be truly European if I can count as brothers those people who live on the other side of the Iron Curtain, from whom we are separated: 'the kidnapped West', to use Milan Kundera's phrase. That's why to be a European today means we have to put up with a bad conscience.

Cees Nooteboom (Netherlands):

As far as I'm concerned, European cultural identity is a normal state of affairs. I feel myself wholly European. I speak five languages, I've travelled throughout Europe. This identity has been tattooed on me, as it were, as it has on many Dutch people. We are made to learn foreign languages and so we feel at home anywhere. ·

What is the future for European culture?

Alberto Moravia:

Extremely good! You need only fifteen or twenty truly creative people for an epoch-making period. Actually, at the moment we are benefiting from a very high general level of culture, though the truly creative mind is rather rare. We need individuals to emerge who are capable of producing new syntheses and new ideas. That's where the future of Europe lies, not with military force.

Gyorgy Konrad:

The future of European culture is to remain the workshop of paradoxical ideas, to bring together all spiritual families in a dialectical dialogue, to take particular methodological care in separating judgements from description. All that revolved around individual conscience and freedom.

Vasco Braca Moura:

The future of European culture is concerned with the possibility of renewal, dialogue, contact with other cultures of the world. Europe will have no future if she does not remain open to all those influences which she herself has sown in other parts of the globe. European culture cannot be solely concerned with the question of its own prestige.

Pierre Mertens:

What's the future of European culture? It will always be towards greater complexity, more contradiction and equivocation, and just as well. We ought to rejoice in that. If European identity were to be made clear all at once, if it were to become completely predictable, the price paid would be one of extraordinary impoverishment.

Cees Nooteboom:

I don't believe in massive acculturation, and I don't believe it will happen very quickly. When France becomes too centralized, people resist. The same thing will happen in Europe. People are inclined to look for individuality. They are stubborn, and it is right that what is truly distinctive should not be lost. That is why I don't believe in the threat of the Coca-Cola civilization. There will always be Coca-Cola but people will go on eating pickled pork from the Auvergne.

Source: Translated from an article by Eve Livet, *Le Monde de l'Éducation*, September 1988

National and International Agencies

NATIONAL AGENCIES

Austria
Bundesministerium für Unterricht, Kunst und Sport,
Abt. I/13a, Minoritenplatz 5. – Postfach 65,
1014 Wien

Belgium
Ministère de l'Education nationale,
Direction générale de l'Organisation des Études,
Bibliothèque centrale,
27 rue de Louvain,
1000 Bruxelles

Seminarie en Laboratorium voor Didactiek,
Pasteurlaan 2,
9000 Gent

Cyprus
Pedagogical Institute,
P.O. Box 512,
Nicosia

Czechoslovakia
Slovak Educational Library and Institute of Educational Information,
Mlynská dolina,
842 44 Bratislava

Denmark
Danmarks Pædagogiske Bibliotek,
Lersø Parkallé 101,
2100 København ø

Finland
Institute for Educational Research, University of Jyväskylä,
Seminaarinkatu 15,
40100 Jyväskylä 10

France
INIST – Sciences humaines et sociales,
54 Boulevard Raspail,
75270 Paris Cedex 06

Institut National de Recherche Pédagogique,
29 rue d'Ulm,
75230 Paris Cedex 05

Federal Republic of Germany
Sekretariat der Ständigen Konferenz der Kultusminister der Länder,
1 Nassestrasse 8,
5300 Bonn 1

in co-operation with
Informationszentrum Sozialwissenschaften,
Lennéstrasse 30,
5300 Bonn 1

Greece
Pedagogical Institute,
Greek National Unit for EUDISED,
396 Messogion Street,
153 41 Ag. Paraskevi,
Athens

Hungary
National Institute of Education,
Gorkij-fasor 17–21,
1071 Budapest

Ireland
Educational Research Centre,

St Patrick's College,
Drumcondra,
Dublin 9

Italy
Biblioteca di Documentazione pedagogica,
Via M. Buonarroti 10,
501 22 Firenze

Luxembourg
Ministère de l'Éducation Nationale et de la
Jeunesse,
2926 Luxembourg

Netherlands
Ministerie van Onderwijs en Wetenschappen,
Postbus 25000,
2700 LZ Zoetermeer

Institute for Educational Research in the
Netherlands (SVO),
Sweelinckplein 14,
2517 GK Den Haag

Norway
Norsk Pedagogisk Studiesamling,
P.O. Box 474 Sentrum,
0105 Oslo 1

Portugal
Instituto Nacional de Investigação Cientifica,
Centre de Documentação Cientifica e
Técnica,
Av. Prof. Gama Pinto 2,
1699 Lisboa Codex

Spain
Centro Nacional de Investigación y
Documentación Educavita (CIDE),

Ministerio de Educación y Ciencia,
Ciudad Universitaria s/n,
28040 Madrid

Sweden
Statens Psykologisk-Pedagogiska Bibliotek,
Box 50063,
104 05 Stockholm

Switzerland
Schweizerische Koordinationsstelle für
Bildungsforschung/Centre Suisse de
coordination pour la recherche en matière
d'éducation,
Francke-Gut, Entfelderstrasse 61,
5000 Aarau

Turkey
TÜBITAK,
Atutürk Bulvari 221,
Kavaklidere-Ankara

United Kingdom
National Foundation for Educational
Research in England and Wales,
The Mere, Upton Park,
Slough SL1 2DQ

Northern Ireland Council for Educational
Research,
The Queen's University of Belfast,
52 Malone Road,
Belfast BT9 5BS

Yugoslavia
Institute for Development of Education in the
SR of Serbia,
Kneza Miloša 101/III,
11000 Beograd

SUPRANATIONAL AND INTERGOVERNMENTAL ORGANIZATIONS

The Commission of the European
Communities,
President: Mr Jacques Delors,
200 rue de la Loi,
B-1049 Brussels,
Belgium

The Council of Europe,
Secretary General: Ms Catherine Lalumiere,
BP 431 R6,
F-67006 Strasbourg Cedex,
France

The European Free Trade Association
(EFTA),
Secretary General: Mr George Reisch,
9–11, rue de Varembé,
Switzerland

The Nordic Council of Ministers,
Secretary General: Mr Fridtjov Clemet,
18, Store Strandstraede,
DK-1255 Copenhagen K,
Denmark

The Organisation for Economic Co-operation
and Development (OECD),
Secretary General: Mr Jean-Claude Paye,
2, rue André-Pascal,
F-75775 Paris Cedex 16,
France

The United Nations Educational, Scientific
and Cultural Organization (UNESCO),
Director General: Mr Federico Mayor,
7, place de Fontenoy,
F-75700 Paris,
France

EUROPEAN AND INTERNATIONAL ASSOCIATIONS OF TEACHERS AND TEACHER TRAINERS

The Association for Teacher Education in
Europe (ATEE),
Secretary General: Mr Yves Beernaert,
51, rue de la Concorde,
B-1050 Brussels,
Belgium

The European Association of Teachers
(EAT),
Secretary General: Mr Guus Wijngaards,
Koningsholster 64,
NL-6573 VV Beek-Ubbergen,
The Netherlands

The European Secondary Heads Association
(ESHA),
Secretary General: Mr Luc Kenter,
p/a Ambtenarencentrum,
Laan van Meerdervoort 48,
NL-2517 AM The Hague,
The Netherlands

The European Trade Union Committee on
Education (ETUCE),
Secretary General: Ms Luce Pépin,
33, rue de Trèves,
B-1040 Brussels,
Belgium

The International Federation of Free Teachers'
Unions (IFFTU),
Secretary General: Mr Fred van Leeuwen,
NZ Voorburgwal 120–126,
NL-1012 SH Amsterdam,
The Netherlands

The International Federation of Teachers'
Associations (IFTA),
Secretary General: Mr Jean-Bernard Gicquel,
3, rue de la Rochefoucauld,
F-75009 Paris,
France

The World Confederation of Organisations of
the Teaching Profession (WCOTP),
Secretary General: Mr Robert Harris,
5, avenue du Moulin,
CH-1110 Morges,
Switzerland

The World Confederation of Teachers
(WCT),
Secretary General: Mr Roger Denis,
33, rue de Trèves,
B-1040 Brussels,
Belgium

The World Organisation for Early Childhood
Education (OMEP),
World President: Ms Eva Balke,
Lille Frøens vei 10,
N-0369 Oslo 3,
Norway

The World Union of Catholic Teachers
(UMEC),
General Secretariat,
Piazza San Calisto 16,
I-00153 Rome,
Italy

EUROPEAN AND INTERNATIONAL EDUCATIONAL NON-GOVERNMENTAL ORGANIZATIONS, CENTRES AND NETWORKS

Children's International Summer Villages,
Secretary General: Mr Joseph Banks,
MEA House,
Ellison Place,
Newcastle upon Tyne NE1 8XS,
United Kingdom

The Consortium of Institutions for
Development and Research in Education in
Europe (CIDREE),
Secretary General: Mr Johan van Bruggen,
National Institute for Curriculum
Development,
PO Box 2041,
NL-7500 CA Enschede,
The Netherlands

The Council of European National Youth
Committees (CENYC),
Secretary General: Mr Bengt Persson,
8, avenue des Courses,
B-1050 Brussels,
Belgium

The European Association for Schools for
Co-operative Projects (EURELEM 2000),
c/o OCCE,
101bis, rue du Ranelagh,
F-75016 Paris,
France

The European Association for Special
Education (EASE),
President: Mr Klaus Wenz,
Reutlinger Strasse 31,
D-7000 Stuttgart 70,
Germany

The European Bureau of Adult Education,
Secretary General: Mr Walter Bax,
PO Box 367,
NL-3800 AJ Amersfoort,
The Netherlands

The European Council of National
Associations of Independent Schools
(ECNAIS),
Secretary General: Mr K. P. Ahlmann

Olesen,
FGF,
Langes Gaard 12, 2. tv.,
DK-4200 Slagelse,
Denmark

The European Committee for Catholic
Education,
Secretary General: Mr Raf de Zutter,
42, rue de l'Industrie,
B-1040 Brussels,
Belgium

The European Cultural Centre,
Secretary General: Mr Gérard de Puymege,
Villa Moynier,
122, rue de Lausanne,
CH-1211 Geneva 21,
Switzerland

The European Cultural Foundation,
Secretary General: Mr Raymond Georis,
5, Jan van Goyenkade,
NL-1075 HN Amsterdam,
The Netherlands

The European Curriculum Network,
c/o CEVNO,
8, Nassauplein,
NL-1815 GM Alkmaar,
The Netherlands

The European Educational Publishers' Group
(EEPG),
Contact persons: Mr Douwe van Foeken and
Ms Barbro Larsson,
Meulenhoff Educatief,
507 Herengracht,
NL-1017 BV Amsterdam,
The Netherlands

The European Federation for the Education of
the Children of Occupational Travellers
(EFECOT),
Secretary General: Mr Ludo Knaepkens,
42/10, rue de l'Industrie,
B-1040 Brussels,
Belgium

The European Federation for Intercultural
Learning (EFIL),
Secretary General: Ms Hilary Maher,
36, rue de la Montagne,
B-1000 Brussels,
Belgium

The European Forum for Educational
Administration (EFEA),
President: Mr Nils Stego,
PO Box 249,
S-581 02 Linköping,
Sweden

The European Movement,
Secretary General: Mr J. H. C. Molenaar,
98, rue du Trône/Bte 8,
B-1050 Brussels,
Belgium

The European Museum of the Year Award,
Director: Mr Kenneth Hudson,
18 Lansdown Crescent,
Bath BA1 5EX,
United Kingdom

The European Parents' Association (EPA),
c/o BEJCE,
2–3, place du Luxembourg,
B-1040 Brussels,
Belgium

The European Standing Conference of
Geography Teachers' Associations,
Secretary General: Mr Jean-Pierre
Vandenbosch,
19, rue des Amaryllis,
B-1080 Brussels,
Belgium

The Experiment in International Living,
Secretary General: Mr Gilbert Guillemoto,
89, rue de Turbigo,
F-75003 Paris,
France

The Foundation for European Languages and
Educational Centres (EUROCENTRES),
Director General: Mr Rolf Schärer,
247, Seestrasse,
CH-8038 Zürich,
Switzerland

The Georg Eckert Institute for International
Textbook Research,
Director: Mr Ernst Hinrichs,
Celler Strasse 3,
D-3300 Braunschweig,
Germany

The Institute for European Teacher
Education,
Director: Mr Günter Renner,
Europäische Akademie,
46–48, Bismarckallee,
D-1000 Berlin 33,
Germany

The Intereuropean Commission on Church
and School (ICCS),
President: Mr Alan Brown,
The National Society's RE Centre,
23 Kensington Square,
London W8 5HN,
United Kingdom

The International Association for Educational
and Vocational Guidance (IAEVG),
Secretary General: Ms Kathleen Hall,
Job Market,
Gloucester House,
57 Chichester Street,
Belfast BT1 4RA,
United Kingdom

The International Association for the
Evaluation of Educational Achievement
(IEA),
Executive Director: Mr William Loxley,
c/o SVO,
14, Sweelinckplein,
NL-2517 GK The Hague,
The Netherlands

The International Association for Intercultural
Education (IAIE),
Secretary General: Mr Pieter Batelaan,
c/o APbO Pieter Batelaan,
Sumatralaan 37,
NL-1217 GP Hilversum,
The Netherlands

The International Association of Universities
(IAU),
Secretary General: Mr Franz Eberhard,
1, rue Miollis,
F-75732 Paris 15,
France

The International Baccalaureate Organisation,
Director General: Mr Roger Peel,
15, route des Morillons,
CH-1218 Grand Saconnex/Geneva,
Switzerland

The International Community Education
Association (ICEA),
Secretary General: Mr Alan Blackhurst,
Lyng Hall,
Blackberry Lane,
Coventry CV2 3JS,
United Kingdom

The International Confederation of Parents,
President: Mr Jean-Marie Schleret,
15, rue Winston Churchill,
F-54000 Nancy,
France

The International Education Centre (IUC),
Director: Mr Ingolf Knudsen,
45 Vestergade,
Postbox 150,
DK-5700 Svendborg,
Denmark

The International Federation of Europe
Houses (FIME),
President: Mr Arno Krause,
Bahnhofstrasse 47–49,
Postfach 311,
D-6600 Saarbrücken 3,
Germany

The International Federation for School
Correspondence and Exchange Organisations
(FIOCES),
c/o 29 rue d'Ulm,
F-75230 Paris Cedex 05,
France

The International League for Child and Adult
Education,
Secretary General: Mr François Coursin,
3, rue Recamier,
F-75341 Paris Cedex 07,
France

The International Organisation for the
Development of the Freedom of Education
(OIDEL),
Director General: Mr Alfred Fernandez,

10 rue Richemont,
CH-1202 Geneva,
Switzerland

The International Round Table for the
Advancement of Counselling (IRTAC),
President: Mr H. Z. Hoxter,
7 Merlins Eyot,
11 Old Church Street,
London SW3 5DL,
United Kingdom

The International Society for Business
Education,
Secretary General: Mr Erik Lange,
122A 1v, Hundernpvej,
DK-Odense M,
Denmark

The International Society for History
Didactics,
Director: Mr W. Fürnrohr,
160 Regensbergerstrasse,
D-8500 Nuremberg,
Germany

The International Society for Intercultural
Education, Training and Research (SIETAR),
1505 Twenty-Second Street NW,
Washington, DC 20037,
USA

Key to Europe,
President: Mr Henk Dekker,
11, rue de Laubespin,
B-1020 Brussels,
Belgium

The Organising Bureau of European School
Student Unions (OBESSU),
Secretary General: Mr Mathias Kälvemark,
c/o NGS,
Postboks 6770,
St Olavsplads,
N-0130 Oslo 1,
Norway

School Links International,
Contact person: Mr Ray Harris,
International Curriculum Linking Unit,
Bath Teachers' Centre,
Lymore Avenue,
Bath BA2 1AY,
United Kingdom

Secretariat of European Association in Higher
Education (HEURAS),
Secretary General: Mr Yves Beernaert,
51, rue de la Concorde,
B-1050 Brussels,
Belgium

Standing Conference of Rectors, Presidents
and Vice-Chancellors of the European
Universities (CRE),
Secretary General: Mr Andris Barblan,
10, rue du Conseil Général,
CH-1211 Geneva 4,
Switzerland

World Association for the School as an
Instrument of Peace (EIP),
Secretary General: Ms Monique Prindezis,

5, rue du Simplon,
CH-1207 Geneva,
Switzerland

World Federation of Modern Language
Associations (FIPLV),
President: Mr Edward Batley,
Department of European Languages,
Goldsmiths' College,
University of London,
New Cross,
London SE14 6NW,
United Kingdom

NB. The above list is not exhaustive. The
number of non-governmental organizations,
centres and networks involved in education is
growing rapidly.

Organizations with Resources for Teaching about Europe

BRITISH BROADCASTING CORPORATION

A large amount of material is available from the BBC Schools Broadcasting Service. Annual Programmes and subject leaflets can be obtained from: Education Information, Villiers House, The Broadway, Ealing, London W5 2PA. Tel: 081-991 8031

COUNCIL OF EUROPE

The Council of Europe produces a wealth of information for teachers. *Forum* is published quarterly in English, French, German and Italian and features European issues of current concern. For details of publications on:

i.   primary education
ii. secondary education
iii. immigrants/ethnic minorities education
iv. teacher training

please write to School Education Division, Council of Europe, BP 431/R6, F-67006 Strasbourg Cedex.

For *Forum* and other general information please write to the Directorate of Press and Information at the same address.

Newsletter/Faits Nouveaux. Five issues are published annually by the Council of Europe's Documentation Centre for Education in Europe. The periodical is designed to meet the needs of those who are interested in comparative education by giving information on educational developments in member states of the Council for Cultural Co-operation. Articles are in either English or French. Requests for specimen copies should be addressed to Council of Europe, BP 431/ R6, F-67006 Strasbourg Cedex.

The EUDISED database gives information in abstract form on recently completed and ongoing educational research projects in over 20 European countries. The database is available online (for additional information about online access contact IRS DIALTECH, Department of Trade and Industry, Ashdown House, 123 Victoria Street, London SW1E 6RB) and in printed form (*EUDISED R & D Bulletin*, distributed by Saur Verlag, Munich). For EUDISED working documents contact Council of Europe, see above.

DEPARTMENT OF TRADE AND INDUSTRY

The DTI has produced a booklet, *Why You Need to Know More about the Single Market*. This can be obtained, together with further information, by writing to Kingsgate House, 66–74 Victoria Street, London SW1E 6SW.

COMMISSION OF THE EUROPEAN COMMUNITIES

A free publications list is available from the Commission of the European Communities, 8 Storey's Gate, London SW1P 3AT. Tel: 071-222 8122.

EUROPEAN COMMUNITY

The EC publishes a variety of information, brochures and magazines concerned with education. The main information outlet for developments in social affairs at European level is *Social Europe*. Contact address: Official Publications Office of the EC, L-2985 Luxembourg.

EUROPEAN DEMOCRATIC GROUP

A free publications list is available from this

organization: 2 Queen Anne's Gate, London SW1H 9AA. Tel: 071-222 1720.

EUROPEAN CULTURAL FOUNDATION

The Foundation produces a free newsletter twice a year, offering a comprehensive picture of its central and network activities. A *Joint List of Publications* from members of the network is produced every two years and is obtainable from: ECF, Jan van Goyenkade 5, NL-1075 HN Amsterdam, Netherlands. Other publications include an information brochure and annual report.

COUNCIL OF EUROPEAN MUNICIPALITIES AND REGIONS AND INTERNATIONAL UNION OF AUTHORITIES, BRITISH SECTIONS

35 Great Smith Street, London SW1P 3BJ. Tel: 071-222 1636

European Information Service is a useful document produced by this body, and obtainable from the above address. *Bulletin No. 90* includes information on agriculture, conservation, protection, education, employment, environment, health, safety, housing and industry.

TRINITY AND ALL SAINTS' COLLEGE, LEEDS

Brownberrie Lane, Horsforth, Leeds LS18 5HD. Tel: (0532) 584341

Publishes *The European Dimension in Initial Teacher Training Courses in the UK: A Survey of Recommendations*.

EUROPEAN PARLIAMENT INFORMATION OFFICE

2 Queen Anne's Gate, London SW1H 9AA. Tel: 071-222 0411

Has a selection of free publications, mainly for schools above primary level, in which the structure, work and organization of the European Parliament are expressed simply and colourfully.

HMSO

Publications Centre, 51 Nine Elms Lane, London SW8 5DR (Tel: 071-873 8350) and Bookshop, 49 High Holborn, London WC1V 6HB (counter service only) are the agents for the UN, WHO, FAO, OECD and UNESCO.

INDEPENDENT BROADCASTING AUTHORITY

The IBA, as a full member of the European Broadcasting Union, has encouraged a European dimension throughout its networks by developing various forms of co-production as well as origination, acquisition and exchange of programmes dealing with European affairs and the teaching and learning of European languages. It also participates in European seminars and conferences on a range of relevant cultural, legal, educational, social and technical issues. Some of these proceedings are made available to the public in the form of reports, bulletins and occasional articles. On the programming side, there are many series on ITV and ILR which deal with European matters. Some are designated educational programmes which may be recorded free of charge. Others are broadcast as part of general output and are subject to other licensing conditions. Most are accompanied by back-up materials, often at cost price. For information on programmes and materials dealing with Europe and European affairs: Education Officer (Liaison), IBA, 70 Brompton Road, London SW3 1EY (Tel: 071-584 7011).

STANDING CONFERENCE ON EDUCATION FOR INTERNATIONAL UNDERSTANDING

Publishes an *International Newsletter* available from the Hon. Secretary, R. Morgan, Centre for International Studies, Polytechnic of the South West, Faculty of Education, Exmouth, Devon EX8 2AT. Tel: (0395) 264902.

MILIEU. Special Edition for European Year of the Environment 1987 draws together a selection of articles published over the previous seven years. It contains material on both the theory and practice of environmental education in a variety of contexts: schools, ecology centres and work camps. Special consideration is given to the relevance of environmental education in disadvantaged areas such as the inner city or neglected rural towns and villages. Information is available from the CDVEC Curriculum Development Unit, Trinity College, 28 Westland Row, Dublin 2, Ireland (Tel: Dublin 602433/602557).

New European is a quarterly journal in which many of Europe's leading and most original figures give their views on Europe's future and the underlying trends behind events. Its 'Europe of Many Circles' provides a unique model for co-operation in Europe, particularly in the light of developments in the European Community and the changes taking place in Eastern Europe.

THE WILLIAM AND MARY TERCENTENARY TRUST LTD
c/o AGB Research plc, 76 Shoe Lane, London EC4 3JB. Tel: 071-583 8888
Publishes a *Newsletter* giving full details of events organized by this body.

THE HANSARD SOCIETY FOR PARLIAMENTARY GOVERNMENT
16 Gower Street, London WC1E 6DP. Tel: 071-323 1131
Seeks to strengthen parliamentary democracy by encouraging international participation and study in its institutions.

OFFICE COMMUN DE FORMATION EUROPÉENNE POUR LA JEUNESSE
Publishes *20 Centuries of Europe in Your Hands* in two volumes: a teachers' book and a book aimed at students aged 12–15. Information from The Editor in Charge, Ivanka Zonta, rue de Boussoit 15, 7040 Mons-Havre, Belgium.

YOUTH EXCHANGE CENTRE
Seymour Mews House, Seymour Mews, London W1H 9PE. Tel: 071-486 5101
Publishes *Youth Exchange News*.

YOUTH FORUM OF THE EUROPEAN COMMUNITIES
112 rue Joseph II, B-1040 Brussels (Tel: (32 2) 230 64 90)
Produces *Youth Opinion* (a quarterly publication). The Youth Forum is the political platform of national and international youth organizations in Europe. A monthly bulletin on EC affairs is also published.

ORGANIZATIONS CONCERNED WITH AN AWARENESS OF EUROPE IN THE UK

Many of the following organizations and institutions run conferences and meetings relevant to this work and should be contacted direct for details of current and future programmes.

UK CENTRE FOR EUROPEAN EDUCATION (UK CEE)
Central Bureau for Educational Visits and Exchanges, Seymour Mews House, Seymour Mews, London W1H 9PE. Tel: 071-486 5101

ASSISTANT MASTERS AND MISTRESSES ASSOCIATION
7 Northumberland Street, London WC2N 5DA. Tel: 071-930 6441

AMMA is actively involved in promoting the European dimension in education and is represented on the UK CEE Advisory Committee.

ASSOCIATION FOR LANGUAGE LEARNING
16 Regent Place, Rugby CV23 2PN. Tel: (0788) 546443

The Association for Language Learning (ALL) was fully constituted on 1 January 1990 with the amalgamation of the Joint Council of Language Associations, the Association of Dutch Language Teachers, the Association of Teachers of German, the Association of Teachers of Italian, the Association of Teachers of Russian, the Association of Teachers of Spanish and Portuguese, and the Modern Language Association. ALL provides support and help for those involved in language teaching and learning in all sectors of education and languages.

ASSOCIATION OF COUNTY COUNCILS
Education Department, Eaton House, 66a Eaton Square, London SW1 9BH

The ACC is a member of the UK CEE National Conference.

ASSOCIATION OF DIRECTORS OF EDUCATION IN SCOTLAND
Mr J. Dobie, Assistant Director of Education,

Lothian Region Department of Education, 40 Torphichen Street, Edinburgh EH3 8JJ. Tel: 031-229 9166

ASSOCIATION OF EDUCATIONAL ADVISERS IN SCOTLAND
Mr J. R. Carson, Education Offices, 129 Bath Street, Glasgow G2 2SY. Tel: 041-204 2900

ASSOCIATION OF EUROPEAN DOCUMENTATION CENTRE LIBRARIANS
Mr I. Thomson, Secretary, Association of EDC Librarians, The Arts and Social Studies Library, UWCC, PO Box 430, Cardiff CF1 3XT. Tel: (0222) 874262

ASSOCIATION OF LECTURERS IN COLLEGES OF EDUCATION IN SCOTLAND
Mr I. MacPherson, National Secretary – ALCES, Dundee College of Education, Gardyne Road, Dundee DD5 1NY. Tel: (0382) 453433

ASSOCIATION OF METROPOLITAN AUTHORITIES
Mr A. Gronow, Secretary – AMA, 35 Great Smith Street, Westminster, London SW1P 3BJ. Tel: 071-222 8100

ASSOCIATION OF NORTHERN IRELAND EDUCATION AND LIBRARY BOARDS
182 Galgorm Road, Ballymena, Co. Antrim, Northern Ireland BT42 1HN. Tel: (0266) 3333

ASSOCIATION OF POLYTECHNIC TEACHERS
Caxton Chambers, 81 Albert Road, Southsea, Hampshire PO5 2SG. Tel: (0705) 818625

ASSOCIATION OF UNIVERSITY TEACHERS
United House, 1 Pembridge Road, London W11 3JY. Tel: 071-221 4370

BIRMINGHAM POLYTECHNIC
West Midlands Centre for European Education, Birmingham Polytechnic, Faculty of Education, Westbourne Road, Edgbaston, Birmingham B15 3TN. Tel: 021-331 6139/6100

An active European Education Centre. Contact Prof D.E. Hellawell or Mr I. Porter.

BRITISH BROADCASTING CORPORATION
BBC School Television, Villiers House, Room 606, The Broadway, Ealing, London W5 2PA. Tel: 081-743 8000

BRITISH COMPARATIVE AND INTERNATIONAL EDUCATION SOCIETY
Though worldwide in scope the Society has a lively interest in European (west and east) and overseas countries especially those with a close European connection. It has concerned itself with problems of curricula (including bilingualism), of adult/community education, teacher education and school organization.

Chairman: Mr T. Corner, Dept of Education, University of Glasgow, 4 University Gardens, Glagow G12 8QQ

BRITISH COUNCIL
Education Department, British Council, 10 Spring Gardens, London SW1A 2BN. Tel: 071-930 8466

CEDEFOP
The European Centre for the Development of Vocational Training, Bundesallee 22, D-1000 Berlin 15. Tel: 030 88 41 20

The Centre was established by Regulation (EEC) No. 337/75 of the Council of the European Communities. *CEDEFOP News*, the information letter published every three months, presents a panorama of vocational training news from EC Member States. *Vocational Training*, its specialized journal, is published in nine languages three times a year. It is a source of reference for all those involved in vocational training (decision-makers, programme planners, administrators).

CENTRAL BUREAU FOR EDUCATIONAL VISITS AND EXCHANGES
Seymour Mews House, Seymour Mews, London W1H 9PE. Tel: 071-486 5101
3 Bruntsfield Crescent, Edinburgh EH10 4HD. Tel: 031-447 8024

16 Malone Road, Belfast BT9 5BN. Tel: (0232) 664418/9

The Central Bureau is the national office responsible for the provision of information and advice on all forms of educational visits and exchanges; the development and administration of a wide range of curriculum related pre-service and in-service exchange programmes; the linking of educational establishments and local education authorities with counterparts abroad; and the organization of meetings and conferences related to professional international experience. Its information and advisory services extend throughout the educational field.

CENTRE FOR INFORMATION ON LANGUAGE TEACHING AND RESEARCH (CILT)

Regent's College, Inner Circle, Regent's Park, London NW1 4NS. Tel: 071-486 8221

CILT is a national information centre on the learning and teaching of languages. It runs an enquiry service on all aspects of language teaching and learning, including research, has an extensive library collection freely accessible to visitors, and publishes a wide variety of titles on both the theoretical and practical aspects of language, learning and teaching.

CENTRE FOR INTERNATIONAL STUDIES

Faculty of Education Campus, Polytechnic of the South West, Exmouth, Devon EX8 2AT. Tel: (0395) 264902

COUNCIL FOR EDUCATION IN WORLD CITIZENSHIP

Seymour Mews House, Seymour Mews, London W1H 9PE. Tel: 081-908 2588/0457

COUNCIL OF SUBJECT TEACHING ASSOCIATIONS

Mr A. R. Hall, 15 Courthill Terrace, Love Lane, Rochester, Kent ME1 1TN. Tel: (0634) 826357

DEPARTMENT OF EDUCATION, NORTHERN IRELAND

Mr R. Jordon, Department of Education for Northern Ireland, Rathgael House, Baloo

Road, Bangor, Co. Down, Northern Ireland BT19 2PR. Tel: (0247) 270077

DEPARTMENT OF EDUCATION AND SCIENCE, LONDON

International Relations Division, DES, Grove House, 2–8 Orange Street, London WC2H 7WE. Tel: 071-321 0433

THE ECONOMICS ASSOCIATION

Maxwelton House, 41/43 Boltro Road, Haywards Heath, West Sussex RH16 1BJ. Tel: (0444) 55084

EDUCATIONAL INSTITUTE OF SCOTLAND

46 Moray Place, Edinburgh EH3 6BH. Tel: 031-225 6244

ESSEX EUROPEAN RESOURCE CENTRE

Mr S. Haines, Colchester Institute, Marine Parade, Clacton on Sea, Essex CO15 6JQ. Tel: (0255) 422324

EUROPEAN ASSOCIATION OF TEACHERS

Hon Secretary, 20 Brookfield, Highgate West Hill, London N6 6AS. Tel: 081-340 9136

EUROPEAN CENTRE FOR TRADITIONAL AND REGIONAL CULTURES

Parade Street, Llangollen, Clwyd, Wales LL20 8RB. Tel: (0898) 861514

An institution dedicated to the research and promotion of all aspects of European regional traditions and cultures as well as the dissemination of information related to its research projects.

EUROPEAN CULTURAL FOUNDATION (UK COMMITTEE)

Mr M. Cullis, County End, Bushey Heath, Herts. WD2 1NY. Tel: 081-950 1057

EUROPEAN MOVEMENT

Mr P. Luff, The European Movement, Europe House, 1 Whitehall Place, London SW1A 2HA. Tel: 071-839 6622

THE EUROPEAN WORKING
COMMITTEE ON ECONOMICS
EDUCATION
The Economics Association, Maxwelton
House, 41/43 Boltro Road, Haywards Heath,
West Sussex. Tel: (0444) 455084

EURYDICE
Rue Archimède 17 (bte 17), B-1040 Brussels.
Tel: 02 230 03 98/230 03 82

FESTIVAL OF LANGUAGES AND
YOUNG LINGUISTS AWARDS
c/o ALL, 16 Regent Place, Rugby CV23
2PN. Tel: (0788) 546443

GENERAL STUDIES ASSOCIATION
6 New Row, Wass, West Yorkshire YO6
4BG. Tel: (0347) 6388

THE GEOGRAPHICAL ASSOCIATION
343 Fulwood Road, Sheffield S10 3BP. Tel:
(0742) 670666

HEADMASTERS CONFERENCE
1 Russell House, Bepton Road, Midhurst,
West Sussex GU29 9NS. Tel: (0730) 815635

THE HISTORICAL ASSOCIATION
Secretary, 59a Kennington Park Road,
London SE11 4JH. Tel: 071-735 3901

HUMBERSIDE COUNTY COUNCIL
Mr J. Kear, Education Department, County
Hall, Beverley, North Humberside HU17
9BA. Tel: (0482) 867131

Active in the field of European awareness.

INDEPENDENT BROADCASTING
AUTHORITY
IBA Education Department, 70 Brompton
Road, London SW3 1EY. Tel: 071-584 7011

INSTITUTE OF LINGUISTS
Mangold House, 24a Highbury Grove,
London N5 2EA. Tel: 071-359 7445

INTERNATIONAL BACCALAUREATE
OFFICE
University of London Institute of Education,
18 Woburn Square, London WC1H 0NS.
Tel: 071-637 1682/1861

KENT, UNIVERSITY OF,
CANTERBURY
Dr C. H. Church, Eliot College, University
of Kent, Canterbury, Kent CT2 7NS. Tel:
(0227) 66822 ext 586 or 7470

LANCASHIRE COUNTY COUNCIL
Curriculum and Professional Centre, 103
Preston New Road, Blackburn, Lancashire
BB2 6BJ. Tel: (0254) 60877/55443

LANCASTER, UNIVERSITY OF,
EUROPEAN DOCUMENTATION
CENTRE
Lancaster LA1 4YW

LEICESTERSHIRE & EUROPE
RESOURCES CENTRE
Forest Lodge Education Centre, Charnor
Road, Leicester LE3 6LH. Tel: (0533) 874571

LEICESTERSHIRE DEPARTMENT OF
EDUCATION
County Hall, Glenfield, Leicester LE3 8RF.
Tel: (0533) 871313

MANCHESTER, UNIVERSITY OF,
DEPARTMENT OF EDUCATION
Centre for Curriculum Policy, University of
Manchester, Department of Education,
Oxford Road, Manchester M13 9PL. Tel:
061-275 2000

NATIONAL ASSOCIATION FOR
ENVIRONMENTAL EDUCATION
West Midlands College of Higher Education,
Gorway, Walsall WS1 3BD. Tel: (0922) 31200

NATIONAL ASSOCIATION OF HEAD
TEACHERS
Holly House, 6 Paddockhall Road, Haywards
Heath, West Sussex RH16 1RG. Tel: (0444)
416381

NATIONAL ASSOCIATION OF
INSPECTORS AND EDUCATIONAL
ADVISERS
Mr M. J. Gifford, The Old Grammar School,
Broadway, Letchworth SG6 3PP. Tel: (0462)
677030

NATIONAL ASSOCIATION OF
LANGUAGE ADVISERS
Mr R. Bailess, 14a/6 North Street, Guildford,
Surrey GU1 4AF. Tel: (0483) 572881

NATIONAL ASSOCIATION OF
SCHOOLMASTERS/UNION OF
WOMEN TEACHERS
Hillscourt, Rose Hill, Rednal, Birmingham
B45 8RS. Tel: 021-453 6150

NATIONAL ASSOCIATION OF THE
TEACHERS IN WALES
Prif Swyddfa UCAC, Pen Roc, Rhodfa'r
Mor, Aberystwyth, Dyfed SY23 2AZ. Tel:
(0970) 615577

NATIONAL CONFEDERATION OF
PARENT–TEACHER ASSOCIATIONS
2 Ebbsfleet Industrial Estate, Stonebridge
Road, Northfleet, Gravesend, Kent DA11
9DS. Tel: (0474) 560618

Supports and represents 7,000 member
home–school associations in England and
Wales. It promotes partnership between home
and school, encourages parents to give help
and support to their children, and ensures that
parents have a say in national policy-making.
NCPTA is a member of the European
Parents' Association.

NATIONAL CURRICULUM COUNCIL
15–17 New Street, York YO1 2XA. Tel:
(0904) 627799

NATIONAL FOUNDATION FOR
EDUCATIONAL RESEARCH (NFER)
EURYDICE, The Mere, Upton Park,
Slough, Berkshire SL1 2DQ. Tel: (0753)
74123

NATIONAL UNION OF STUDENTS
Research and Policy Department, 461
Holloway Road, London N7 6LJ. Tel: 071-
272 8900

NATIONAL UNION OF TEACHERS
Douglas McAvoy, General Secretary,
Hamilton House, Mabledon Place, London
WC1H 9BD. Tel: 071-388 6191

NORTH EAST CENTRE FOR
EDUCATION ABOUT EUROPE
University of Durham School of Education,
Leazes Road, Durham DH1 1TA. Tel: 091-
374 3497/3498

NORTH EAST LONDON
POLYTECHNIC
School of Education and Humanities, North
East London Polytechnic, Longbridge Road,
Dagenham, Essex RM8 2AS. Tel: 081-590
7722

NORTHERN COLLEGE OF
EDUCATION
Department of Education, Northern College
of Education, Hilton Place, Aberdeen AB9
1FA. Tel: (0224) 482341

NOTTINGHAM POLYTECHNIC
Centre for European Education, Clifton Hall,
Clifton Village, Nottingham NG11 8NJ. Tel:
(0602) 418418

Newly established centre especially active in
the primary field.

NOTTINGHAM, UNIVERSITY OF
School of Education, University of
Nottingham, University Park, Nottingham
NG7 2R. Tel: (0602) 56101

OXFORDSHIRE COUNTY COUNCIL
Education Department, Macclesfield House,
New Road, Oxford OX1 1NA. Tel: (0865)
792422

PROFESSIONAL ASSOCIATION OF
TEACHERS
99 Friar Gate, Derby DE1 1EZ. Tel: (0332)
372337

READING, UNIVERSITY OF, FACULTY
OF EDUCATION
Faculty of Education and Community
Studies, University of Reading, 22 London
Road, Reading RG1 5AQ. Tel: (0734) 85234

SCHOOL EXAMINATIONS AND
ASSESSMENT COUNCIL
Newcombe House, 45 Notting Hill Gate,
London W11 3JB. Tel: 071-229 1234

SCOTTISH ASSOCIATION OF
GEOGRAPHY TEACHERS
Geography Department, Jordanhill College of
Education, 76 Southbrae Drive, Glasgow G13
1PP. Tel: 041-950 3399

SCOTTISH ASSOCIATION OF
TEACHERS OF HISTORY
Perth High School, Oakbank Road, Perth.
Tel: (0738) 28271

SCOTTISH EDUCATION
DEPARTMENT
Room 3/112a, New St Andrew's House,
Edinburgh EH1 3SY. Tel: 031-556 8400

SCOTTISH EXAMINATION BOARD
Ironmills Road, Dalkeith, Midlothian EH22
1LE. Tel: 031-663 6601

SCOTTISH SECONDARY TEACHERS'
ASSOCIATION
15 Dundas Street, Edinburgh EH3 6QG. Tel:
031-556 5919

SCOTTISH VOCATIONAL
EDUCATION COUNCIL
Hanover House, 24 Douglas Street, Glasgow
C2 7NQ. Tel: 041-248 7900

SECONDARY HEADS ASSOCIATION
130 Regent Road, Leicester LE1 7PG. Tel:
(0533) 471797

SHEFFIELD CITY POLYTECHNIC
Faculty of Education, Collegiate Crescent,
Parkholme, Sheffield S10 2BP. Tel: (0742)
369941

SOCIETY OF EDUCATION OFFICERS
21–27 Lambs Conduit Street, London WC1N
3NJ. Tel: 071-831 1973

SOUTHAMPTON UNIVERSITY
Centre for International Studies in Education,
Faculty of Educational Studies, The
University, Southampton SO9 5NH. Tel:
(0703) 559122

SOUTH WEST CONSORTIUM FOR
EDUCATIONAL TRAVEL AND
EXCHANGE
Education Department, County Hall, Exeter
EX2 4QG. Tel: (0392) 77977

TRINITY & ALL SAINTS' COLLEGE,
LEEDS
Brownberrie Lane, Horsforth, Leeds LS18
5HD. Tel: (0532) 584341

UNIVERSITIES COUNCIL FOR THE
EDUCATION OF TEACHERS
58 Gordon Square, London WC1H 0NT. Tel:
071-580 8060

UNIVERSITY ASSOCIATION FOR
CONTEMPORARY EUROPEAN
STUDIES
King's College London, Strand, London
WC2R 2LS. Tel: 071-240 0206

UNIVERSITY OF READING
Graduate School of European and
International Studies, Whiteknights Park,
Reading RG6 2AA. Tel: (0743) 318378

WELSH JOINT EDUCATION
COMMITTEE
Arlbee House, 4th Floor, Greyfriars Road,
Cardiff CF1 3AE. Tel: (0222) 561231

WELSH OFFICE EDUCATION
DEPARTMENT
New Crown Buildings, Cathays Park,
Cardiff CF1 3NQ. Tel: (0222) 825111

WELSH SECONDARY SCHOOLS
ASSOCIATION
Croescyceiliog Comprehensive School,
Woodland Road, Cwmbran, Gwent NP44
2YB. Tel: (06333) 2698

WEST MIDLANDS CENTRE FOR
EUROPEAN EDUCATION
Birmingham Polytechnic, Faculty of
Education, Westbourne Road, Birmingham
B15 3TN. Tel: 021-331 6139/6100

WORCESTER COLLEGE OF HIGHER
EDUCATION
Henwick Grove, Oldbury Road, Worcester
WR2 6AJ. Tel: (0905) 748080

Offers degree-level courses in geography
which contain major elements of European
dimension.

YOUTH EXCHANGE CENTRE
Seymour Mews House, Seymour Mews,
London W1H 9PE. Tel: 071-486 5101.

Concerned with youth exchanges that do not
form part of the stated curriculum of an
educational establishment but rather are part
of the social and cultural development of
young people. The YEC is responsible for

grant aid, information and counselling and
training services to youth groups involved in
international exchanges.

THE YOUTH FORUM OF THE
EUROPEAN COMMUNITIES
10 rue Joseph II, 112, B-1040 Brussels. Tel:
322-230 64 90

EMBASSIES AND INSTITUTES

*The following embassies and institutes provide free
resource material for the use of teachers and
students.*

AUSTRIA
18 Belgrave Mews West, London SW1X
8HU. Tel: 071-235 3731

Austrian Institute (Austrian Embassy Cultural
Affairs Section), 28 Rutland Gate, London
SW7 1PG. Tel: 071-584 8654

BELGIUM
103 Eaton Square, London SW1W 9AB. Tel:
071-235 5422

BULGARIA
186–8 Queen's Gate, London SW7 5HL. Tel:
071-584 9400

CZECHOSLOVAKIA
25 Kensington Palace Gardens, London W8
4QY. Tel: 071-229 1255

DENMARK
55 Sloane Street, London SW1X 9SR. Tel:
071-235 1255

FINLAND
38 Chesham Place, London SW1X 8HW. Tel:
071-235 9531

FRANCE
58 Knightsbridge, London SW1X 7JT. Tel:
071-235 8080

FEDERAL REPUBLIC OF GERMANY
23 Belgrave Square, London SW1X 8PZ. Tel:
071-235 5033

The Goethe Institute, 50 Princes Gate,
London SW7 2PH. Tel: 071-581 3344/7

GREECE
1a Holland Park, London W11 3TP. Tel: 071-
727 8040

HUNGARY
16 Lowndes Close, London SW1X 8BZ. Tel:
071-235 8630

ICELAND
1 Eaton Terrace, London SW1W 8EY. Tel:
071-730 5131/2

IRELAND
17 Grosvenor Place, London SW1X 7HR.
Tel: 071-235 2171

ITALY
The Italian Cultural Institute, 39 Belgrave
Square, London SW1X 8NX. Tel: 071-235
1461

LUXEMBOURG
27 Wilton Crescent, London SW1X 8SD. Tel:
071-235 6961

NETHERLANDS
38 Hyde Park Gate, London SW7 5DP. Tel:
071-584 5040

NORWAY
25 Belgrave Square, London SW1X 8QD.
Tel: 071-235 7151

POLAND
Polish Cultural Institute, 34 Portland Place,
London W1N. Tel: 071-636 6032

PORTUGAL
11 Belgrave Square, London SW1X 8PP. Tel: 071-235 5331

ROMANIA
4 Palace Green, London W8 4QD. Tel: 071-937 9666

SPAIN
24 Belgrave Square, London SW1X 8QA. Tel: 071-235 5555

The Spanish Institute
102 Eaton Square, London SW1W 9AN. Tel: 071-235 1485

SPAIN/PORTUGAL/LATIN AMERICA
The Hispanic and Luso Brazilian Council, Canning House, 2 Belgrave Square, London SW1X 8PJ. Tel: 071-235 2303/7

SWEDEN
1 Montagu Place, London W1H 2AL. Tel: 071-724 2101

SWITZERLAND
16–18 Montagu Place, London W1H 2BQ. Tel: 071-723 0701

USSR
13 Kensington Palace Gardens, London W8 4QX. Tel: 071-229 6412

YUGOSLAVIA
5 Lexham Gardens, London W8 5JU. Tel: 071-370 6105

Name Index

Subject Index

Abortion 14, 132, 134, 145
Activity holidays 166–8
Activity-based learning 34, 64, 154, 166, 181, 208–9
Adolescence 19, 128–30, 132, 136–7, 175, 210, 215
Adolf Grimme Institut 111
Adulthood 128, 130, 153, 167, 215
Aesthetic Education 89–90, 96–9, 132, 207
Afghanistan 7, 175
Africa xviii, 4, 13, 177, 185–6, 188–90, 216
    North Africa 82, 175
    South Africa 188
Agriculture 7, 65, 69, 186, 198
Aigues Mortes (France) 89
Albania 102
Ålborg (Denmark) 160–1
Alchemy 86
Algeria 139
Almere (Netherlands) 160–1
Alps, the 68
Alsace xvii, 6, 49, 108–9
Alternative tourism 167, 198
Alto Adige (Italy) 157: see also South Tyrol
Ambérieu (France) 159
America 44
    American continents 52, 216
    Latin America xviii, 177, 188–90
    North America 25–6, 82, 95, 177, 180–1
    see also United States of America
American Studies 177, 179, 181, 183
Amnesty International 141
Amsterdam (Netherlands) 138
Anatolian civilization 91
Andalusia 108
Anglo-Saxons 80, 82, 181

Antibes (France) 160
Anti-Semitism 83, 137
Arabic language 103
Arabs 50
Archaeology 93, 117, 156
    industrial 70, 74, 90, 93
Architecture 74, 76, 80, 87, 89, 93
    vernacular 89, 93–4
Arctic Circle 25
Arctic Ocean 23
Arctic region 26
Ardennes 68
Area Studies 176–7, 185
Arezzo (Italy) 157
Armenia 11
Art Education 208
    teachers 90–1
Artificial intelligence: see New information and communication technology
Arts, the 53, 83, 87–91, 94, 96, 138, 153, 164, 167, 176–7, 184, 186, 205–6
    Creative Arts 21, 29, 87, 90, 96, 132
Arts and Crafts movement 92
Asia xviii, 23, 139, 177, 181–4, 216
    Asia Minor 25, 184
    Central 8, 14, 23, 185
    South-East 174, 182–3
Assessment procedures 29, 55, 97, 140, 209
Assimilation, concept and policy of 137
Associated Schools Project (ASPRO) 141, 163, 172, 214
Association for Language Learning (ALL) 113
Association for Teacher Education in Europe (ATEE) xiv, 113, 139, 164
Association of Socialist Teachers (AST) 30
Astrology 86

40702 EUROPE - £12.99

40702 EUROPE - £12.99